How to Fix Copyright

How to Fix Copyright

William Patry

OXFORD
UNIVERSITY PRESS

OXFORD
UNIVERSITY PRESS

Oxford University Press, Inc., publishes works that further
Oxford University's objective of excellence
in research, scholarship, and education.

Oxford   New York
Auckland   Cape Town   Dar es Salaam   Hong Kong   Karachi
Kuala Lumpur   Madrid   Melbourne   Mexico City   Nairobi
New Delhi   Shanghai   Taipei   Toronto

With offices in
Argentina   Austria   Brazil   Chile   Czech Republic   France   Greece
Guatemala   Hungary   Italy   Japan   Poland   Portugal   Singapore
South Korea   Switzerland   Thailand   Turkey   Ukraine   Vietnam

Published by Oxford University Press, Inc.
198 Madison Avenue, New York, NY 10016

www.oup.com

Library of Congress Cataloging-in-Publication Data
Patry, William F.
How to fix copyright / William Patry.
    p. cm.
Includes bibliographical references and index.
ISBN 978-0-19-976009-1 (hardcover : alk. paper)
1. Copyright.   I. Title.
K1420.5.P3757   2011
346.04'82—dc22   2011016431

9 8 7 6 5 4 3 2 1

Printed in the United States of America
on acid-free paper

For Margalit and Yonah

יְשִׂמְךָ אֱלֹהִים כְּאֶפְרַיִם וְכִמְנַשֶּׁה:

יְשִׂמֵךְ אֱלֹהִים כְּשָׂרָה. רִבְקָה. רָחֵל וְלֵאָה:

יְבָרֶכְךָ יְיָ וְיִשְׁמְרֶךָ:

יָאֵר יְיָ פָּנָיו אֵלֶיךָ וִיחֻנֶּךָּ:

יִשָּׂא יְיָ פָּנָיו אֵלֶיךָ וְיָשֵׂם לְךָ שָׁלוֹם:

Contents

Acknowledgments   ix

Disclaimer   xi

Introduction Unlearning Copyright   1

1 Why We Need to Fix Our Copyright Laws   7

2 Replacing a Faith-Based Approach to Copyright with an
   Evidence-Based Approach   49

3 What Are Copyright Laws Supposed to Do?   75

4 The Public Interest   131

5 Law Is Not the Solution to Business Problems   141

6 Does Deterrence Work?   163

7 Abandoning Exclusivity and Getting Paid Instead   177

8 The Length of Copyright Is Damaging
  Our Cultural Heritage   189

9 Reimposing Some Formalities   203

10 The Moral Panic over Fair Use   211

11 "The Answer to the Machine Is in the Machine"
   Is a Really Bad Metaphor   231

12 Effective Global Copyright Laws   245

Notes   263
Index   319

Acknowledgments

I thank Niko Pfund, Oxford University Press's president, and publisher of academic and trade books, as well as David McBride, my editor at OUP, for their insights and time spent tightening up an unwieldy manuscript. The title is Niko's. Both Niko and David are real book people, and are a joy to work with. In alphabetical order: Nick Ashton-Hart helped me see things better from the individual creator's perspective, and also tightened things up. Professor James Boyle saved me from hyperbole that weakened my argument. Professors Daniel Gervais and Stef von Gompel gave me excellent comments from an international perspective. George Lakoff read various versions of the manuscript and greatly helped me focus my analysis. Tom Olson looked at the whole manuscript and caught many errors. Will Page's challenges to broad-brushed conclusions saved me much embarrassment. Professor Randall Picker of the University of Chicago Law School and his Winter 2010 technology policy class read the manuscript, and put me through the wringer. Irwin Stelzer carefully read the manuscript numerous times and gave me invaluable, detailed comments. Hannu Wagner provided important insights into the relationship between international and domestic copyright laws. All errors are mine.

Juliana Cunha took the photograph for the book jacket, which is a take-off on pictures of multi-instrumentalist Rahsaan Roland Kirk. Lisa Force designed the cover. I did the index, which contains some humor. Thanks also to Amy Whitmer, my long-suffering production editor, who made sure the book actually came out.

Disclaimer

Although I serve as Senior Copyright Counsel to Google Inc.,
the views in this book are entirely mine, and should not be
attributed to Google. The book is not Google's book, nor did
I write it as a Google employee or to advance Google's interests,
as much as I identify with and value those interests. Instead,
I wrote the book on my own initiative to make personal observations—observations that come from being a full-time copyright lawyer for thirty years, twenty-five of which occurred
before I joined Google. I did send the manuscript to about twenty
people within Google (and to some people twice), but as with
my *Moral Panics and the Copyright Wars* book, not a single Google
employee gave me any comments on it. I would have loved such
comments, not to ensure that the book somehow aligns with
Google's interests, but because my colleagues are really smart,
insightful people. In short, Google does not endorse this book,
does not share the views expressed in this book (and may even
strongly object to some passages), so please don't preface any discussion of this book with: "Google's Senior Copyright Counsel
said," or any other variant. It's my book alone.

Introduction: Unlearning Copyright

My late mother, *zikhronah livrakha*, taught me that I have a religious duty to learn every day. This is *Torah lishma*, learning for learning's sake. In fulfilling this duty, I have discovered that for me the most important type of learning is not learning new things (as fun as that is), but rather unlearning things I thought I knew but didn't.[1] Unlearning requires reexamining beliefs we hold dear, and on occasion admitting we were wrong.

Socrates thought the unexamined life not worth living.[2] Self-examination occurs only if we rigorously inquire into our habits, including habits of mind. Among the habits of mind this book examines are the fundamental beliefs that copyright laws directly cause people to create works they wouldn't otherwise create, directly put substantial money in authors' pockets; that culture depends on copyright; and, more recently, that copyright law is a key driver of competitiveness and of the knowledge economy.

Do copyright laws cause these wonderful things to come true in real life and not just in our beliefs? Simply believing things will happen isn't enough. If we want wonderful things to come true (and who doesn't?) we must do more than believe that they will; we must ensure they do. Ensuring they do requires, at a minimum, that copyright laws are consistent with prevailing markets and technologies. Laws must be consistent with prevailing markets and technologies because technologies play a large (although not exclusive) role in creating consumer demand; markets then satisfy that demand. Without consumer demand for your book or musical work, owning a copyright is meaningless. Laws cannot create consumer demand, but they can greatly interfere with the ability of market actors to satisfy that demand. Hence, the need for law to be consistent with prevailing markets and technologies.

My conclusion is that market forces and technology have moved well beyond our current laws and are now in conflict with them. Copyright laws arose out of eighteenth-century markets and technologies, the most important characteristic of which was artificial scarcity. Artificial scarcity was created by a small number of gatekeepers, by relatively high barriers to entry, and by analog limitations on unauthorized copying. Artificial scarcity was important because it created monopoly value: not profits earned above costs of production, but rather profits disconnected to costs. Those profits were dependent on the creation and legal enforcement of artificial scarcity through copyright laws. This is the environment in which copyright, at least Anglo-American copyright, arose.

But markets and technologies change, in a symbiotic way. New technologies create new demand, requiring new business models: Even artificial scarcity is worthless if no one wants your product in the first place. New markets are an economic fact of life, and sometimes unpleasantly so when they cause unemployment in legacy businesses. Buggy whip makers, however, could no more claim a right to a continued market after the Model T car eliminated the demand for horse-drawn carriages than musicians who accompanied silent movies had a right to be paid after the talkies made their performances unnecessary. No copyright law can preserve markets that have been passed by.

The new markets created by the Internet and digital tools are the greatest ever: Barriers to entry are low, costs of production and distribution are low, the reach is global, and large sums of money may be made off of a multitude of small transactions. This contrasts dramatically with the world of analog artificial scarcity, which based sales on a small number of expensive transactions, a situation that favored gatekeepers over individuals. The democratization of creation has arrived thanks to digital abundance replacing analog artificial scarcity. Policymakers should be encouraging further development in this area, but far too often, after the obligatory, flowery rhetoric praising new markets and technologies is made, policymakers' actions go in the opposite direction: Ill-thought-out laws are passed with the type of righteous fervor usually reserved for evangelical prophets proclaiming the end of the world.

Why this schizophrenia among the world's policymakers? The answer is simple: the Internet and other digital technologies have undermined the central premise around which copyright markets have historically been built: artificial scarcity. The central purpose of copyright has been to enable copyright owners to control markets, and in controlling them to make monopoly profits by selling fewer works for more money. Artificial scarcity also included markets being segmented geographically (Hollywood movies are released first in the United States, and then on a schedule in foreign countries), over time (first movie theatres, then home videos, then television, then airplanes), and by format (consumers have to buy separate copies of musical works for each type of device they want to listen to the works on, and where they want to listen to them). Copyright and analog technological constraints made possible such balkanized markets and wasteful, duplicative purchases by consumers. Copyright = control = monopoly profits has been the central economic equation and therefore the focal point of copyright owners. Unauthorized copying has always been a rhetorical bogey-man employed for the purpose of ensuring continued artificial scarcity over *lawful* copies.

We are now in the very different world of digital abundance, where the copyright industries face global expectations of instant access to everything, where everyone is both a creator and a user, and where having works streamed to you rather than owning physical copies is the dominant trend. To be effective, our copyright laws must be based on the world of digital abundance. Our copyright laws are, alas, still firmly rooted in the world of physical, artificial scarcity. To date, copyright owners' efforts have been devoted to either preserving analog-based laws or to constructing a mutant, Minotaur-like hybrid where analog artificial scarcity is grafted onto digital abundance (e.g., digital lock provisions). While this is a classic response of incumbents— fight the new and when you can't defeat it, remake it so that it is a tame, safe version of the old—that tactic won't work anymore. Technological control, the essential element of gatekeepers' markets since the inception of copyright laws, is no longer possible. As a direct result of the failure of policymakers to make new laws consistent with the technologies and markets of the new world of digital abundance, our old laws are inhibiting rather than encouraging creativity. The May 2011 independent review by Professor Hargreaves for the British government made this point directly:

Could it be true that laws designed more than three centuries ago with the express purpose of creating economic incentives for innovation by protecting creators' rights are today obstructing innovation and economic growth? The short answer is yes.[3]

The unfortunate descent of copyright law from a lofty vehicle to protect healthy business models into a rearguard business model of its own doesn't mean copyright laws aren't necessary (they are, in some form) or that they don't benefit some authors (they do, but not as many as they should). If we are honest, we will recognize that our current copyright laws too often harm authors and the public. This book is about how to make our copyright laws work better. I believe in the goals of copyright laws, and I believe in them so much I want them to be actually achieved.

I want to explain why there is no concluding chapter with a list of recommendations. Some will regard this as odd for a book whose title is *How to Fix Copyright*. There are numerous specific recommendations on how to fix copyright in the book in every chapter. The book doesn't lack for recommendations. So why didn't I go through each chapter, extract the recommendations, and assemble them in a punchy final chapter? That's what my publisher wanted me to do. My opinion, though, is that lists of recommendations cannot serve as a basis for the necessary self-examination because lists are divorced from the context that explains why the changes are necessary. Aside from numerous specific recommendations, I make one general recommendation: I call for a moratorium on the introduction and passage of any new legislation until (1) we have established independent, rigorous, economically verifiable methodologies by which all proposals will be tested and later reviewed for their effectiveness, and (2) we have tested all existing laws by those methodologies and have repealed or suitably amended those that fail the review.

Our current laws are the result of "lobbynomics," the continual use of exaggerated (and often false) claims and crises as an excuse to pass laws that are unnecessary and many times harmful. These laws come solely from lobbyists' entreaties, not the public's needs, or even from those of the authors whom lobbyists purport, Cyrano de Bergerac-like, to speak for.[4] We will never fix our laws unless we clean house and start all over again, this time on a sound, empirical basis: Simply adding on to a failed structure will no longer work. In the United States, the copyright law hasn't been overhauled since 1978, and even then some of the statutory provisions date back to 1909. No one should suggest that our copyright laws are rational, deliberate, unified policy instruments, carefully designed to achieve specific social and economic objectives. Instead, our copyright laws are a hapless mixture of individual provisions, worked out as political compromises among powerful special interests, taking place over large periods of time, with no continuity among policymakers, and without any effort at determining whether the parts fit into a sensible whole.[5] The result is predictable. Those who say our current laws need merely to be adapted rather than go through a top-to-bottom, systemic overhaul are dangerously denying reality.[6]

ONE

Why We Need to Fix Our Copyright Laws

Hollywood's best box office years ever were 2009 and 2010. The International Confederation of Authors and Composers Societies (CISAC), the worldwide umbrella group for over 150 musical collecting societies worldwide, declared 2010 a banner year, with revenues increasing at a rate higher than global GNP. The Association of American Publishers reported net sales revenue was up 5.6 percent in 2010 over 2008, with increases in all formats. eBooks sales had an amazing 1,274 percent growth in 2010 over 2008,[1] and they now outsell hard copy books on Amazon.com. Consistent with the fundamental changes taking place in the music industry, while the decline continued in the sale of physical recorded music (for reasons unconnected to piracy), the global performance rights market share increased an impressive 13 percent over 2009; even musical instrument sales increased 8 percent over 2009.

Yet, there is a widespread perception among copyright owners that legitimate markets are shrinking, and that copyright laws are failing to protect against their losses. Failure can be judged only in relation to purpose, against what we want our copyright laws to do. The most popular justifications for copyright laws are that they (1) put money in authors' pockets by providing them with incentives to create works they would not otherwise create, and (2) provide the public with access to cultural works the public would not otherwise have access to. These are both "but for" arguments: but for copyright, authors wouldn't create or wouldn't make money; but for copyright the public wouldn't get to enjoy those works. In many countries, especially in Europe, copyright laws also serve, via non-economic rights, a third goal: to give creators the ability to prevent their works from appearing in contexts they don't approve of.[2] Some people believe copyright laws can accomplish all three of these objectives at the same time, without conflict. I don't. Here's why. There are conflicts between authors and the distributors to whom they sell their copyrights. Those conflicts include the amount of royalty payments, reversionary rights, and distribution on new media.[3] These disputes can involve extremely large sums of money. It has been estimated, for example, that artists might receive $2.15 billion if they are successful in their current disputes with record labels over whether to categorize the deals with iTunes as involving a license (where 50 percent royalties are typically paid) rather than as a sale of copies (where royalties of 10–15 percent are typically paid).[4] If policymakers truly want to put money in artists' pockets, siding with artists in this dispute will do more for them than all copyright infringement suits ever brought, or from extending the term of copyright protection to last 1,000 years, even if the estimated amounts that might be recovered are exaggerated by 75 percent. Joyce Moore, the wife of Sam Moore of the classic soul duo "Sam and Dave," put it best: "This is life-changing. If we were paid 35 cents a download, as opposed to a nickel—that's a huge amount of money for a guy that is on a fixed income or has to run up and down the road at 75 years old."[5] The reason policymakers don't enact such life-changing laws on behalf of those they purport to protect is that doing so would put them in conflict with powerful corporate constituencies: record labels and music publishers. Substantial conflicts exist, therefore, and have a serious impact on policymaking.

There are conflicts among authors: some established artists favor extensive rights and resist new technologies that challenge their control over their works (think of Metallica and Prince), while most emerging artists tend to favor the ability to copy from established artists and eagerly explore new technologies in order to get their works before an audience. Lady Gaga and her manager Troy Carter have made brilliant use of the Internet and social media.[6] By spending more time in Silicon Valley than in Hollywood, they have been able to keep control over her future and expand it at the same time.[7]

There are conflicts between the public and authors over availability of works, pricing, and the scope of rights. One example is the 2009 dust-up over Amazon.com's text-to-speech feature for the Kindle 2. That feature allowed purchasers of lawful copies of books to have computerized voices read the text. This was of tremendous benefit to the blind and in no way competed with authorized audio books. As a father of ten-year-old twins, I happily buy many audio books at very steep prices and marvel at the performance artistry of the (human) readers. It is absurd to suggest that a computerized voice would displace such sales. Yet, the Authors Guild of America, through its president Roy Blount, Jr., objected. In a *New York Times* Op-Ed piece, Mr. Blount was quite candid in stating that the dispute was all about money—pay up for computerized voices—or else, in his words, parents "cannot send their children off to bed with the voice of Kindle 2,"[8] even

if those children are blind. Amazon bowed to the pressure, bene-
fitting no one.

There are conflicts between the public and authors' distributors over pricing, availability, and personal uses. One example is
the inability of the blind and other visually impaired people to
have access to printed (non-Kindle) copies of books. This should
be the copyright civil rights issue of our time. In the wealthiest
countries, only some 5 percent of published books are made accessible in formats the visually impaired can use; this figure drops
to less than 1 percent in poorer countries. Copyright laws are the
principal reason for this scandal. If sighted people in wealthy
countries had 95 percent of their books and other printed material taken away, the copyright laws would be amended overnight.

An international treaty is necessary to make sure all books can
be accessible by the blind. Accessibility can be accomplished
through a combination of compulsory licenses and exceptions.
Voluntary agreements among publishers, libraries, and blind
groups are certainly necessary to the ultimate success, but a global,
binding instrument is required to solve cross-border issues and to
ensure minimum standards are met. Efforts to develop such a
treaty began in 1983: almost thirty years of waiting for a solution
is unspeakably cruel to those who are denied the basic access to
the knowledge and pleasures sighted people take for granted.

Beyond this specific issue, there is a failure to realize that the
artificially high prices made possible by copyright laws, while necessary in many cases to prevent free-riding, in other cases prevent
the public from spending money on other goods, money that
would benefit the economy too. If consumers have to spend $15
on a CD album when they only want to spend $1 on a single song,
that's $14 that could have been spent on something else, say dinner
at a restaurant or buying clothes. While governments understand
they can't print money without causing inflation and thereby

reducing consumers' purchasing power, they fail to see that the same principle is at stake with copyright laws: you can't keep increasing the length of copyright or adding on new rights without taking money out of other sectors of the economy. Copyright inflation is no more desirable than monetary inflation and has the same adverse effect. Copyright law needs a monetary policy that can adjust the conflicts among the public and copyright owners.

Finally, there are conflicts between services that want to supply the public with access to lawful versions of copyrighted works and between copyright owners who object to those services. The lack of lawful, global services for music constitutes Exhibits 1–100 in this conflict.

Other than the moral issues involving the blind, the conflicts discussed above are natural, and thus are not in themselves a sign of a failed system. We do fail, though, if we pretend the conflicts don't exist and enact laws based on false, simplistic premises. And most debates about copyright take place at a simplistic level: Should we have copyright laws or not? The answer is yes we should, but at what level? Here too, the debate is usually embarrassingly simplistic: We are told we need strong copyright laws, without any evidence for why or whether strong laws are effective. The real questions arise once we insist on having an evidence-based approach to lawmaking and insist on having effective copyright laws. Hence, the title of this book is not *How to Get Rid of Copyright*, but rather *How to Fix Copyright*. My view is that copyright laws can serve valuable purposes: while they do not cause people to create in the first place and do not create economic or critical success, they do ensure that once works are created, those who wish to protect them and economically benefit can. We all should support this goal.

At the same time, proponents of ever-expanding rights have greatly over-promised what copyright laws can accomplish, and hide how copyright inflation adversely affects consumers and other sectors of the economy. My conclusions are that copyright laws successfully support investments in winner-take-all markets dominated by superstars, but do not help the majority of authors and artists in making a living. I also conclude that copyright laws have failed to keep up with fundamental changes in markets and technologies: Revenues for the core copyright industries, studied granularly, show a fundamental shift away from the selling of physical objects as possessions—CDs, DVDs and other hard copies—toward a world in which we listen and watch temporary streams of music and movies, and increasingly read books stored elsewhere. Owning is no longer the principal goal of many consumers, and therefore selling ownership of copies of works can no longer be the principal business model for the copyright industries. Since laws that are not consistent with existing markets and technologies cannot be effective, a legal regime in which the principal right is a right in copies—a *copyright*—should no longer be the principal focus of policymakers either. Copyright law without copies doesn't make sense. Instead, we must focus on the rules for access as well as on the social, interactive way people now relate to each other and to copyrighted works. Unfortunately, our laws, and much of the enforcement focus of the copyright industries, represent fruitless efforts to preserve the *ancien régime*. Laws and business models rooted in the early eighteenth century cannot be effective in the twenty-first century. Sound economic growth is occurring only in the twenty-first-century markets. But even those markets are still badly underserved by many copyright owners who cling to the ideology of property rights: "it's mine and I can say no if I want to." That attitude inhibits innovative services capable of putting the type of money in authors' pockets that they deserve. You can't eat ideology.

Beyond current disappointments, I argue more broadly that although our copyright laws have accomplished a great deal, they have *never* lived up to what has been promised of them, and can't. Copyright law has been over-promised from its inception, despite or perhaps because of its very laudable goals. Copyright laws rarely cause people to create where they otherwise wouldn't; they are also not responsible for either commercial or critical success. Even for successful works, the benefits from ownership of copyrights have always flowed disproportionately to gatekeepers who are interested in artificial scarcity and monopoly profits rather than abundance and diversity. [9] This final point was bluntly made in an April 2011 interview given by Motion Picture of Association of America Vice President Greg Frazier on a visit to Brazil. In commenting on Creative Commons licenses, which can be used by individuals to license their work on their own terms (and are very popular in Brazil), Mr. Frazier is reported to have remarked, "you're talking about democratizing culture, which is not one of our interests, it really isn't my interest." [10]

So why do so many believe copyright laws directly lead to more diversity, works and more money in authors' pockets? Because the copyright industries—which are after all in the storytelling business—have constructed a very powerful story about copyright, a story policymakers want to believe. [11] Think of copyright as a movie: we want our movies to have heroes we can identify with, and bad guys the heroes can defeat for a happy ending. Movies excel in getting us to suspend our disbelief that they are fictional. The story of copyright is that it causes amazing things to happen for the benefit of everyone, and with no conflicts or trade-offs. There are even villains: file sharers and Internet companies out to destroy the American (or fill in any other country's) way of life. Like Superman, legislators can swoop in, pass stronger copyright laws that put the bad guys in jail. The sun will come out;

there will be milk and honey in the land again. That's a great story, one that has been constructed so that we willingly suspend our disbelief about the fundamental conflicts among authors, distributors, Internet intermediaries, and the public. Frank Smith wrote: "Thought flows in terms of stories.... We learn in the form of stories.... We cannot help thinking in terms of stories.... [Stories] are the only way we can make sense of the world."[12] We need a new story of copyright, one that matches reality.

Two syllogisms and one tautology, explored in detail in chapter 3, will help explain how the current storytelling in copyright sharply diverges from reality, and therefore why our copyright laws need to be fixed. Here is their outline:

SYLLOGISM NUMBER ONE

Copyright is the basis for creativity
Creativity is the basis for culture
Therefore, copyright is the basis for culture.

This syllogism is not a straw man, but rather is directly taken from commonly made statements, especially in Europe.[13] We should all agree that creativity is one of the things around which culture is built, although perhaps it is not the most important. More important are shared practices, customs, and beliefs. Creativity can threaten these elements of culture; hence the term counter-culture to denote innovative ways of expression and acting that are contrary to the mainstream. Understanding why people create and what the actual market conditions are for works of creativity is essential if we wish to encourage creative activity.[14] People have been creating works of art, literature, and music for millennia, long before there were copyright laws. For many of these people, and many others to the present day, the instinct to create arises out of our essence as human beings: we want to make things that are meaningful to ourselves and to others. The Internet, plus simple, free or low-cost digital tools have made global creativity and global audiences possible on a scale never before seen or even imagined. We are all creators now and therefore we all have a stake in ensuring creativity thrives. Contrary to perceived wisdom, though, this does not mean we should want the high levels of copyright protection now on the books, since such laws in too many cases impede creativity.

Copyright Law Is Not the Basis for Creativity

Art, literature, and music are a creative form of communicating; to be human is to feel the desire to communicate with other humans.[15] George Orwell began "Why I Write" this way:

> From a very early age, perhaps the age of five or six, I knew that when I grew up I wanted to be a writer. Between the ages of about seventeen and twenty four I tried to abandon this idea, but I did so with the consciousness that I was outraging my true nature and that sooner or later I would have to settle down and write books.[16]

The desire to communicate is not antithetical to the desire to make money. Some works, particularly corporate works, are created solely for money. This was true even in the pre-corporate, pre-copyright era: it is said Mozart wrote mainly for financial gain,[17] which is not surprising given his break from being a servant to his necessary reliance on a mix of patronage and the free market. Dr. Samuel Johnson quipped that "No man but a blockhead ever wrote, except for money," although anyone familiar with Johnson's life is aware that he regularly wrote for purposes other than money, just as Mozart's constant financial difficulties did not lead him to take up another line of employment. Andy Warhol transformed commerce into art, calling his workplace The Factory, and declaring, "Making money is art and working is art and good business is the best art." Even those less crass than Warhol regularly mix art and commerce. John Lennon was building an extension onto his manor estate in Esher, England. When Paul McCartney showed up one day, Lennon said, "Today, let's write a swimming pool." The song was 'Help!' Paul agreed that writing a song for the specific purpose of paying for a swimming pool "was a great motivation," but he added: "We were actually writing what we considered to be art. We weren't just writing shit for a swimming pool."[18]

Happily, some works that arise out of a pure desire to create also become commercially successful. Such works should be eligible for copyright protection as much as those written only for money, but it is important to bear in mind that for all works, copyright law is not the cause of success or even a crucial enabling factor; success is determined by the marketplace or by critical acclaim. Copyright is neither the basis for creativity nor for culture. Copyright's actual role is more limited: it ensures that works once created and successful can be protected against free riding.

Certainly, few large, corporate distributors would invest substantial sums in promoting works if there was not protection against free riders, but the argument made for copyright goes well beyond this. The argument is that the protection against free riding that copyright provides also causes distributors to bring an abundance of works to market. In this argument, copyright is essential for abundance. The argument misapprehends markets and the role of law in markets. Historically, in mainstream culture, copyright law has been the legal device used by a few gatekeepers to control a winner-take-all marketplace of artificial scarcity, in which far fewer works are made available to the public than are created. This reality conflicts with the belief that copyright protection leads to an abundance of diverse works that would not otherwise have been created. Given this yawning gap between rhetoric and reality, if we are serious about having diverse cultural works, we must provide creative people with what they most need: the ability to earn a steady income. A portfolio of copyrights does you no good if you can't pay the rent, buy food, or have the time to create because you are working full-time at a different job in order to pay the bills.

Copyright protection can help you with the economic freedom to create only if you are *already* successful, but it cannot make you successful in the first place. The problem with the argument that copyright puts money in authors' pockets and is therefore a necessary incentive to create is that it leaves out the brutal fact that copyright cannot provide the necessary *initial* economic conditions most authors and artists need.

This doesn't mean we have to rely entirely on government subsidies—the marketplace is fine for works by corporations and by the popular authors they support—but it does mean we need to find non-market ways for other authors and artists to obtain the necessary initial conditions to create. Aside from government subsidies and tax breaks, one way to encourage more and diverse authors and artists is to ensure that online platforms exist where creators can post their works in order to gain an audience, run advertisements against their works if they choose, or charge for downloads, streams, or other uses if they choose. Such platforms are free to individuals and provide a way to avoid the gatekeeper lock on success. Digital distribution platforms can provide a selection that dwarfs any brick and mortar store of the past, at far lower distribution costs, and can provide a direct link between artists and fans/consumers. Such platforms need to be encouraged, not sued to death or offered license fees that make them economically unsustainable.

Creativity today is far more likely to take place outside of the established media channels than within them. By using copyright laws to keep gatekeepers in control of the spigot by which culture is released to the public, we are ensuring that the ocean of culture being created outside of the traditional media companies is suppressed. Such platforms do not mean the death of gatekeepers; indeed, as with Justin Bieber, who became known thanks to YouTube, and went on to a traditional superstar career, traditional media companies can use these platforms to find new talent.

Creativity in Copyright Has a Specialized Meaning

Also fatal to the syllogism of copyright = creativity = culture is the fact that the word "creativity" is used in a very different way in copyright laws than in popular usage. Policymakers who refer to copyright as encouraging creativity *never* use it in the specialized meaning the term has in copyright laws, and instead mistakenly refer to it in the very different, and usually misleading popular sense. Creativity, when not merely discussed as an "I know it when I see it" concept, has no agreed-upon definition in popular usage, and is usually defined by reference to synonyms, such as imagination, inspiration, ingenuity, inventiveness, and novelty. A word that has no set meaning but is only defined by diffuse analogies cannot form the foundation for evidence-based policymaking. Even worse, policymakers use creativity to refer to vastly different types of behavior, some covered by copyright laws, some covered by patent laws, and some covered by no form of protection at all. Scientific creativity is not the same as musical creativity. Creativity in software coding is not the same as creativity in making a motion picture. Saying we want to foster creativity without drilling down into the kind of creativity we want to foster and then figuring our how we can empirically foster that creativity is an empty gesture.

How does copyright law use the term "creativity"? Importantly, copyright law has rejected the subjective approach to creativity usually found in the popular usage of the term. A subjective approach—this work will be protected because critics think it is really creative, but this work won't be protected because critics don't think it is very creative—would turn the courts into judges of literary, musical, or artistic merit. United States Supreme Court Justice Oliver Wendell Holmes, Jr. pointed this out in a 1903 opinion upholding copyright in a circus advertisement:

> It would be a dangerous undertaking for persons trained only to the law to constitute themselves final judges of the worth of pictorial illustrations, outside of the narrowest and most obvious limits. At the one extreme, some works of genius would be sure to miss appreciation. Their very novelty would make them repulsive until the public had learned the new language in which their author spoke. It may be more than doubted, for instance, whether the etchings of Goya or the paintings of Manet would have been sure of protection when seen for the first time.
>
> At the other end, copyright would be denied to pictures that appealed to a public less educated than the judge.[19]

Justice Holmes' remarks about Goya and Manet point out a problem with the emphasis on creativity even in the colloquial sense: the public is slow to respond favorably to truly creative works: rejection of the unfamiliar is the rule, rather than immediate embrace. We are far more likely to reject innovation than laud it when it comes to works of authorship and art. Despite flowing rhetoric about how much we love creativity, we usually prefer things to remain the same, in safe, familiar territory, which is why all the intelligent software designed by music sites like Pandora, or Amazon.com's book recommendations cater to your existing tastes, and not to works that may challenge you.

In any event, whatever the critics or the public think the creative value of a work may be, that view is not the business of copyright laws, and rightly so. Instead, creativity in copyright (through the synonym "original")[20] means merely that (1) you didn't copy your work from someone else and (2) there is at least a minimal amount of material that goes beyond being an idea, a fact, or other basic building block. By setting the bar for copyright protection very low, and by divorcing protection from creativity in the popular sense, the coverage of copyright is vast and results in protection not just for the circus advertisements Justice Holmes approved of, but also for millions of business documents, e-mails, standardized tests, and lawyers' briefs—virtually everything anyone creates—regardless of the fact that such material is devoid of artistic content or intent. To say that copyright is designed to foster creativity is to ignore that the vast majority of copyrighted works have no creativity in the popular sense, the sense in which the word is used in discussing the effect of copyright laws. Policymakers should stop referring to copyright law as encouraging creativity since they are using the term in a totally different sense than employed by copyright laws.

Corporations and Creativity

Are the large companies that control vast numbers of copyrighted works creative? This is an important question because it confronts whether their control over so many copyrighted works furthers the type of creativity we say we want to be furthered even in the popular sense of that term. There is great diversity among companies and even within them, so the picture I paint here is at the

broadest industry level, to which there are many individual exceptions, some of them significant. For example, Viacom's Nick Jr.
television channel and videos were the mainstay of my twins' entertainment viewing for a number of years, and happily so. The
programs and videos were fantastically creative and educational,
and I loved watching them too. We still watch Aardman Anima-
tion's *Wallace & Gromit* and *Shaun the Sheep*, which appeal to children and adults alike. But new laws are advocated at the industry
level, and thus for this purpose it is fair to look at things more
broadly, understanding the points made may be inaccurate in individual cases.

Whether music publishers ever contributed to the creative aspects of the compositions they publish is highly doubtful, but if
they ever did, they certainly don't make any creative contributions
now. Music publishers are simply licensing houses. Effective licensing is valuable to authors since it puts money in their pockets,
but it is not creative activity. Two of the largest music publishers,
EMI and Warner, are owned or controlled by investment firms.[21]
Major record companies at one time had full-time producers who
influenced the sound and sometimes the content of the music
recorded, but those days are long gone. Hilary Rosen, then–CEO
of the Recording Industry of Association of America, conceded
this in testimony before Congress in 2000. In referring to the role
of record labels today, she stated: "They don't create the heart and
the passion of the artist, nor transform their music into reality.
Their sphere of expertise is really the marketplace. It is marketing,
promotion and creating the demand. Find the fans, sell the
music."[22] This role is commercially important, but is quite different from making a creative contribution.

What about large-scale motion pictures? The perception is
that one studio is the author of the film, not only creating it, but
also handling the distribution and promotion, taking all the risks,

and therefore entitled to reap all the benefits. The misconception is derived from the heyday of the studio system in the 1920s to the 1948,[23] when

> one could usually guess which studio made which film, largely because of the actors who appeared in it; MGM, for example, claimed it had contracted "more stars than there are in heaven." Each studio had its own style and characteristic touches which made it possible to know this—a trait that does not exist today. "[E]ach movie was a little different, and, unlike the craftsmen who made cars, many of the people who made movies were artists."[24] This system—which had many dark, negative aspects as well—was broken up by the Supreme Court's decision in *United States v. Paramount Pictures, Inc.*[25]

The studio system bears no resemblance to the current motion picture industry. Today, studios' principal creativity takes the form of crafting financial vehicles and devising new forms of product placement (advertisements woven into the movie, discussed below). The actual creation of the film is usually outsourced to smaller, independent production companies and directors. Edward Jay Epstein, who regularly writes about the economics of Hollywood, uses the term "clearinghouse" to describe how the studios function today.[26] He gave an illustration by describing the financing for the film *Lara Croft: Tomb Raider*:

> The budget, including Angelina Jolie's $9 million fee, was a staggering $94 million on paper. But after Paramount applied the arcane art of studio financing, of which the deal is a minor masterpiece, the studio's outlay was only $8.7 million.
>
> First, it got $65 million from Intermedia Films in Germany in exchange for distribution rights for six countries:

Britain, France, Germany, Italy, Spain, and Japan. These "pre-sales" left Paramount with the rights to market its film to the rest of the world.

Second, it arranged to have part of the film shot in Britain so that it would qualify for Section 48 tax relief. This allowed it to make a sale-leaseback transaction with the British Lombard bank through which (on paper only) Lara Croft was sold to British investors, who collected a multi-million subsidy from the British government, and then sold it back to Paramount via a lease and option for less than Paramount paid (in effect, giving it a share of the tax-relief subsidy). Through this financial alchemy in Britain, Paramount netted, up front, a cool $12 million.[27]

These transactions of course take place against the backdrop of copyright laws, which give all the various transferees the assurance that their regional rights can be enforced. Without that assurance, no financing could occur. My point here is that like most legacy businesses, studios try to risk little, and that when one hears about a $94 million budget, we should be aware that the studio did not necessarily put much of its own money on the line: indeed, through tax deductions, taxpayers may have helped to foot a healthy part of the budget.

The risk aversion starts with the content of the film itself (known as "product"). Studios regularly rely on prior works for which an audience has already been demonstrated: there are movie versions of video games, of television shows, Broadway shows, comic books, toys, and even action figures. Particularly important are the endless sequels to "tent-pole" franchises. For 2012, the following films have been announced: *Star Trek 2* (actually #12); *American Pie 4*; *Spider-Man 4*; *Batman 3*; *Madagascar 3*; *Men in Black 3*; *Cars 2*; *Clash of the Titans 2*; *GI Joe 2*; *The Hobbit 2*;

Monsters Inc. 2; *X-Men Origins: Magneto*; *The Avengers*; *Dr. Seuss*; and *Godzilla*.[28]

In a detailed look at why this is the case, Mark Harris concluded:

> For the studios, a good new idea has become just too scary a road to travel....
>
> Such an unrelenting focus on the sell rather than the goods may be why so many of the dispiritingly awful movies that studios throw at us look as if they were planned from the poster backward rather than from the good idea forward. Marketers revere the idea of brands, because a brand means that somebody, somewhere, once bought the thing they're now trying to sell. The Magic 8 Ball (tragically, yes, there is going to be a Magic 8 Ball movie) is a brand because it was a toy. Pirates of the Caribbean is a brand because it was a ride. Harry Potter is a brand because it was a series of books. Jonah Hex is a brand because it was a comic book. (Here lies one fallacy of putting marketers in charge of everything: Sometimes they forget to ask if it's a good brand.) Sequels are brands. Remakes are brands.
>
> . . .
>
> Marketing [is]...about looking at what's selling and then selling more of it.[29]

Even Hollywood insiders agree. Laura Ziskin, a legendary producer, was asked by *The Hollywood Reporter* which of her movies she thought would *not* get made today, she answered: "All of them. 'No Way Out,' 'To Die For,' 'The Doctor,' even 'Pretty Woman.' The mainstream movie business has become increasingly narrow."[30]

Branding is not concerned with creativity, but rather a lack of creativity: sell the same thing over and over again until audiences are tired of it and then move on to the next tested product that can be sold over and over again. Branding also seeps deeply into movies in the form of product placement and co-promotion deals. Product placement involves a corporation paying to have its products advertised within the movie itself, but as part of the plot of the movie and not as an identified advertisement. If such placement occurred in a newspaper or magazine, it would violate Federal Trade Commission regulations. Companies either supply free products to be shown in the movie (an actor conspicuously drinks a Pepsi-Cola) or, as typically, pay large sums of money to the filmmaker to have the products prominently displayed (in *Iron Man* there are so many Audis that the company's logo is on the screen for an amazing nine minutes).[31] In 2002, Volkswagen was reported to have paid $200 million dollars to have their cars integrated into NBC Universal films. In addition to automobiles, other products commonly integrated into movie plots include bottled water, cereals, cigarettes (and shown in ways that would be banned if they were a separate advertisement), computers, soft drinks, toy manufacturers; any product that can result in increased sales for both partners. Most movies have multiple product placement deals: Michael Bay's *The Island* had at least thirty-five individual product or brand product placements. Some movies, such as Bay's *Transformers*, are little more than extended toy commercials with gratuitous sexual content directed at sixteen-year-old males.

Product placement is worked into the story line and begins well before the shooting of the film. Steven Spielberg early on began soliciting candy manufacturers for a scene in *E.T.* where the boy coaxes E.T. out from hiding with a trail of candy. Spielberg originally wanted M&Ms, given how droppable they are, but Mars, Inc., declined, and finally the Hershey company's Reese's peanut butter cup line agreed, tying in the movie with free T-shirts. Reese's sales went up 65 percent after the film was released. Coors also bought the right to be the beer that E.T. drank.

Adam Sandler's *Little Nicky* has a blatant ad (but not presented as an ad) for Popeye's chicken in which Nicky says, "Hey . . . Popeye's chicken is fuckin' awesome," and another character replies, "It sure is. Now eat it up . . . You're gonna need your energy." PQ Media estimated the value of product placement to be $10 billion in 2010. Art for Art's Sake is thus a marketing slogan, not a business model.

The dominance of highly commercial works is hardly limited to motion pictures, It has always been the case that (with rare exceptions) the most money has been made not by the authors of literary works of great creativity, but rather by the authors of formulaic works that appeal to the broadest, most popular audience. For example, the largest-selling category of books is romance novels, a/k/a "bodice rippers."[32] One such author, Danielle Steele, has sold over 800 million copies.[33] The top ten video games by themselves sell over 1.5 million copies *every week*. No jazz or classical album has sold as many copies as either of teenager Justin Bieber's two albums. (The 17-year-old Bieber is reported by *Forbes* magazine to have made $53 million in the 12 months from May 2010 to May 2011.)[34] One need not have an excessively restrictive definition of what constitutes a creative work to agree that popular success is not necessarily synonymous with creative or enduring success.

Diverse Cultural Works Require Direct Funding

Clearly, we do not need more incentives to induce increased production of bubblegum teen stars or for the blockbuster works that dominate the market. The market is doing quite well all on its own for these works. If policymakers want to encourage culturally diverse works, works that will endure beyond whatever the current commercial fad is, works that cannot find the type of vast audiences required for commercial success, they must begin by acknowledging that culturally diverse works perform differently in the marketplace: if market incentives are all that is necessary for the production of all forms of creativity, then culturally diverse works would be doing well in the market on their own. But culturally diverse works are not doing well in the market, and they never have. They do not attract sufficient support in the market, and would not be able to do so even if copyright protection were perpetual. Stronger copyright laws cannot change market tastes.

The contradiction between policymakers' touting of copyright as a way to boost cultural heritage and the market's tendency to confine rewards to corporate and similar popular fare led economist Ruth Towse to conclude that "Governments have not been slow to see that they could easily placate artists by altering copyright law, which they could do without committing any funds, since a change in the law mostly redistributes rewards between [existing] participants...rightsholders and consumers...."[35] If we want more authors and artists, we must provide them with the economic ability to be authors and artists, above the fray for market share in a winner-take-all environment. It is not copyright for copyright's sake that matters to authors and artists, but rather a steady income.[36] If copyright is not providing such a steady income, as it is not for most authors and artists, then we have to find other sources of income for them. In addition to direct grants, there are grants through arts organizations, as well as—in the case of music—government-paid ensembles. Germany has approximately twenty-five times the number of full-time symphony orchestras than the United States, even though its population is only about 25 percent that of the United States. Most of these orchestras are supported by local or municipal German governments. Consistent with a view that classical music has to compete in the marketplace just as personal deodorant does,[37] in the United

States, government funding at a level even approaching 5 percent is unusual[38] (as compared to a typical 80 percent level in Germany).[39] There are, however, a number of U.S. military bands that employ outstanding musicians. These bands provide musicians with a steady source of income, but also give them the time and freedom to pursue other expressive opportunities. We would be better off if we spent less money on weapons systems that don't work and more money on musicians who want to.

Sometimes the necessary support for creators comes from individuals, aided by tax breaks via charitable deductions. I am the Founder and Director of the Bass Clarinet Commission Collective and a founding donor of the Clarinet Commission Collective. Both collectives are made up of individual clarinetists from around the world who pool their resources to commission new works from composers.[40] The collectives encourage as many clarinetists as possible to become involved by contributing financially *and* by performing the works commissioned. The collectives thus break with the traditional model of passive financial donors: members are expected to do their part in spreading culture by also performing.

The Kickstarter project is another example of crowd-sourced funding of creators.[41] Kickstarter is the world's largest funding platform for creative projects in the world. Kickstarter helps artists, filmmakers, musicians, designers, writers, illustrators, explorers, curators, performers, and others to bring their projects to life. Kickstarter uses Amazon.com's Flexible Payments Service so that individuals from around the world can pledge money to specific projects detailed on the site. Creators have an incentive to make their projects as appealing as possible because they are competing against other proposals, and because they do not receive any money unless the project's financial goals are met in full within a specified, short time frame.

Unlike copyright laws, such efforts directly cause the creation of works that would not have otherwise been created. They are a positive step away from gatekeepers and from the false idea that intellectual property laws are necessary and sufficient to foster new works. Governments have an important funding role too, if they believe their own statements about the importance of cultural works. Some governments are making efforts to further creativity through funding.[42] My point is that these efforts must be seen as central to creating a diverse culture and supporting authors and artists; copyright laws can't do that job.

Copyright Is a Commodity Business in Which Authors' Interests Are Secondary

The erroneous belief that copyright laws are the engine of culture and creativity (in the popular sense) is based on a misperception of the role of copyright in the marketplace. In any commodity business, the most benefits flow to gatekeepers because gatekeepers have the most leverage in contracts for the purchase and sale of the commodity. This is particularly true in the case of creative works, where there is a large oversupply of people who want to get through the gate. *American Idol* and similar reality television shows are only the most visible example of this age-old phenomenon. Contracts with such gatekeepers are hardly ever negotiable and are drafted by the gatekeepers for their own benefit. They are notoriously one-sided, sometimes to the point of absurdity. For example, in negotiations with a publisher with whom I was placing a second academic multivolume treatise on copyright I had written,[43] I tried unsuccessfully to remove a provision that meant my treatise would never go out of print, even if the publisher was not making it available in any form. The significance of this provision is that if it were to go out of print, I could get the rights back and then market it myself.

I advanced a number of scenarios where the publisher would no longer have any conceivable, remote economic interest in the work and tried, in vain, to revise the contract to reflect those scenarios. This publisher is one of only two in the United States that have online services, the dominant way legal treatise research is done in the United States. The other publisher has a competitor's book. If you want your treatise online you have to go to one of these two publishers, and in my case only one since the competitor was signed with the other publisher. As a result of the lack of competition, I had no choice but to accept the terrible language, and did.

In this real world, the world where gatekeepers most often (though not always) have superior bargaining power, the creators of copyrighted works are not guaranteed to receive substantial or even fair benefits under any contract: the existence of copyright merely means that the creators have something to bargain away, according to whatever leverage they may have, which is most often very little.[44] It is this fact that is consistently overlooked by those who claim that the stronger copyright protection is, the more benefits the actual creators will receive. This is not true today and it has not been true over the entire course of our copyright laws.

All but the most famous authors are at a strategic disadvantage. Irwin Karp, a tireless advocate for authors' rights in the United States during the long copyright reform process in the 1960s and 1970s, observed that the author assigning away all rights is not "a nincompoop, a fool, or... improvident..... [No author] would assign the copyright away unless he was forced to."[45] That the strong prevail has been a principle since ancient times. During the sixteenth year of the Peloponnesian Wars (416–415 B.C.E.), the Athenians landed warships on the island of Melos, a neutral island just east of Athens's enemy Sparta. Rather than simply kill the island's inhabitants, which their military might made easy, the Athenians called for a conference with the Melian leaders and suggested it was in the Melians' best interests to surrender and be under Athenian control. The Athenians didn't sugar-coat their argument: "[W]e shall not trouble you with specious pretences. [Y]ou know as well as we do that questions of fairness exist only between equals in power; while the strong do what they want, the weak endure what they must."[46] The Melians declined to surrender. The Athenians killed all the Melian men, enslaved the women and children, and then repopulated Melos as an Athenian territory.[47]

Those who have the leverage use it to obtain the lion's share of the money received from exploiting copyrighted works created by others. Few authors have ever made much money from their copyrights. In a May 2010 BBC interview Mick Jagger (formerly a student at the London School of Economics), noted:

[P]eople only made money out of records for a very, very small time. When The Rolling Stones started out, we didn't make any money out of records because record companies wouldn't pay you! They didn't pay anyone! Then, there was a small period from 1970 to 1997, where people did get paid, and they got paid very handsomely and everyone made money. But now that period has gone. So if you look at the history of recorded music from 1900 to now, there was a 25 year period where artists did very well, but the rest of the time they didn't.[48]

On May 30, 2011, a figure was put on this lack of payment in one country, Canada, as a result of a class action lawsuit brought by performing artists against EMI Music Canada Inc., Sony Music Entertainment Canada Inc., Universal Music Canada Inc., and

Warner Music Canada Co. Facing potential statutory damages of $6 billion, these companies agreed to pay $50 million in settlement for their failure to pay artists for what was claimed to be the unpaid use of thousands of songs.[49] The settlement is the result of what was alleged to be a longstanding practice of the recording industry in Canada, described in the lawsuit as "exploit now, pay later if at all." Performing artists claimed the record labels created and sold CDs, did not obtain the necessary copyright licenses, but instead put recorded songs on a "pending list," meaning payment was pending. Pending was, artists thought, a euphemism for never.[50]

For many years, at record labels' requests, CD plants ran what was called the "third shift": the production of large numbers of CDs that were off the books for artists. Not existing on the books, no royalties were ever paid for the sale of these CDs. Composers and artists, lacking the right or ability to audit manufacturing documents, were unable to do anything about it. This infamous practice was stopped (if it has) only by passage of the Sarbanes-Oxley law in the United States, since that law makes company executives personally liable for false statements made on financial documents, including revenue sources. The practice certainly calls into question what constitutes piracy.

SYLLOGISM NUMBER TWO

Copyright is the basis of a knowledge-based economy.
The knowledge-based economy is the basis for competitiveness.
Therefore copyright is the basis for competitiveness.[51]

The principal way policymakers justify the extraordinary expansion of intellectual property rights is by making extraordinary claims about the benefits the expanded rights are supposed to bring. An example of this is seen in a May 2011 communication from the European Commission regarding plans for harmonizing intellectual property across the European Union. The title of the communication is, "A Single Market for Intellectual Property Rights: Boosting creativity and innovation to provide economic growth, high quality jobs and first class products and services in Europe." About the only things missing are feeding the poor, curing the sick, and stopping global warming. This isn't a sarcastic remark, because in the text of the communication, we read that innovation—of the type allegedly possible only if we have a "high level" of intellectual property rights[52] not only helps the European economy to flourish, "it is indispensable to address the big challenges that humankind is facing in the 21st century: ensuring food security, containing climate change, dealing with demographic change, and improving citizens' health."

Is it any wonder that politicians across the ideological spectrum rush in front of television cameras to announce their support for protection capable of bringing to pass all these wonderful things? Who wouldn't? The reality, however, is that there are no follow-ups to see if this Nirvana has been achieved once the television cameras are long gone. The only substantial governmental follow-up I am aware of, concerning the European Union's database directive (discussed below),[53] found the objectives had not been achieved, and that the condition of European database producers was, relative to the United States, worse after the directive than before. Yet, the directive remains on the books. It should not be surprising that there is great skepticism about the alleged benefits of ever-increasing rights contained in government reports.

That skepticism is also justified regarding the increasingly extravagant claims about the relationship between copyright and the so-called knowledge-based economy. The term knowledge-based economy is not defined with any precision, and never with the precision necessary to see what role, if any, copyright plays in furthering it. The Commission's single market report doesn't even attempt a definition. It is difficult to see how copyright law can play much of a role at all in furthering a knowledge-based economy regardless of how it is defined: Copyright law excludes much material that forms the basis for those industries commonly (if imprecisely) thought as being part of the knowledge-based economy. For example, protection is denied for facts, ideas, systems, procedures, methods of operation, and many compilations of data. First-mover advantages, trade-secret law, and contracts are far more effective than copyright for protecting knowledge-based products, to the extent any protection is necessary: many prominent companies in the knowledge-based industries operate on public domain or open source software.

As discussed below,[54] U.S. database producers outperform EU database producers even though there are no database rights in the United States, but there are such rights in the EU.

Copyright Is Not the Basis for Competitiveness

Most economists regard copyright as a barrier to competition, not as a spur to competition. This is not to say they regard copyright as unnecessary; it is quite necessary to solve problems created by economically damaging free riding, but this is a very different concept from competitiveness.[55]

Copyright protection cannot be the basis for competitiveness, for at least two reasons. First, producing creative works is not the same as producing widgets, where, through productivity gains, more profit may be made by manufacturing more widgets at a lower cost. Today, assuming you are following the same metronome markings, it takes the same amount of time to play a Beethoven String Quartet as it did in Beethoven's day.[56] You cannot decrease the time it takes to write a novel, a poem, or a musical composition simply because you want to be more productive. Competition, which is based on finding more efficient ways to produce the same goods, has no application to producing more or better unique, creative works. To describe copyright as a key driver of competition is to confuse creativity with the production of industrial goods. Producing poems is not the same as producing portable toilets.

The second reason copyright cannot be the driver of competition is that there is an unprecedented concentration of ownership of copyrights in the hands of a few, mostly U.S.-based corporations. This concentration comes from acquisitions of competitors and from acquisitions of copyright catalogues. (Interestingly, when one company is attempting to buy the copyright assets of another company, the value of those assets is usually argued to be minimal.) These corporations continually press for more draconian copyright laws (e.g., cutting off Internet access, harsh criminal penalties) while arguing for more relaxed antitrust laws. They bring lawsuits against consumer electronics companies and against online platforms offering authors and performers a way around gatekeeper obstacles. The ability to demand licensing fees is viewed as much as a strategic weapon as a way to make money. Not surprisingly, these companies have a tendency to eliminate rather than to further competition.

A TAUTOLOGY

Integral to the mistaken belief that copyright laws can become the driver of world economies is the tautology that the creative industries are those industries dependent on copyright laws and that therefore copyright laws are essential to their growth.[57] In order to obtain the strongest economies possible, we are told we need the strongest copyright laws possible. As with any tautology, this is merely making an unsupported claim but masquerading it as a self-evident truth.

Aside from the fatal flaw of being a tautology, there are other, serious problems with misdescribing the copyright industries as being in the driver's seat of the world's economies, starting with (1) defining those industries which may fairly said to be the "creative industries," (2) defining how those industries differ from the "cultural industries" (another definitional problem), and (3) defining how those industries may, from a causal perspective, be "dependent" (yet another definitional problem) on copyright laws. Scholars of these industries have concluded "[t]here has been virtually no research that demonstrates the case one way or the other or that shows the responsiveness of the production of creative goods and services to the strength of copyright protection."[58]

To test the effect of copyright you need comparable markets for the same products where copyright exists and for where copyright doesn't exist. In his book *Quarter Notes and Bank Notes: The Economics of Music Composition in the Eighteenth and Nineteenth Centuries*,[59] Harvard economist Frederick Scherer attempted just such a study.

Giuseppe Verdi began his composing career before Italian copyright laws were passed. Although he and his publisher had previously developed work-arounds,[60] after Italian laws were passed, Verdi was able to amass a considerable fortune. One effect of this success should be noted, however: Verdi made so much money he stopped composing.[61] Johannes Brahms also made considerable sums as a result of the passage of copyright laws that enabled his publisher to prevent free-riding, and as a result retired early. In a letter to Clara Schumann, he told her he did not even bother collecting royalties from exploitation of his works in France because "I earn quite easily; and have no need at all to concern myself with sources of income."[62] (Brahms nevertheless continued to live quite simply in a modest apartment. He gave large amounts of money away to friends and students.) Verdi and Brahms are illustrations of how copyright laws richly—and justly—remunerated the creation of quality creative works, at least until those composers retired and stopped creating.

But beyond these superstars, most composers were not financially successful after copyright laws were passed. Reviewing the data for 646 composers in the United Kingdom, Germany, Italy, and Austria during both the pre- and post-copyright law periods, Professor Scherer concluded that the hypothesis of a positive effect in encouraging people to become composers due to copyright laws "is not supported."[63] There were positive effects from copyright law for those composers who were already successful, such as Brahms and Verdi, but Professor Scherer's study does mean that the case has not been made that establishing copyright laws had any positive impact on encouraging *more* people to become composers in the first place.

And for a very good reason: It has never been the case that laws, by themselves, create successful markets. Laws can create regimes that protect investments in markets,[64] but only demand can create successful markets. Laws cannot make people buy things they do not want to buy. Unfortunately, laws can prevent people from buying things they want to buy if the laws give incumbents the power to kill emerging businesses and business models. Reliance on copyright laws to stimulate economic growth is misplaced.

Analog Scarcity Versus Digital Abundance

The failure of our copyright laws to ever match the promises made for them has existed from their inception, but the Internet and digital technologies have fundamentally changed how copyright laws must operate in order to be effective. Our copyright laws are based on the marketplace and technologies of the eighteenth century. In that century and the two centuries following it, copyright law was the commodity concern of publishers and other distributors who acted in a dual gatekeeper role: first as the gatekeeper of who would be published, and second as the gatekeeper of price and other access issues affecting the public. The gatekeeper role is predicated on artificial scarcity. Artificial scarcity was previously possible due to the small number of distributors and to analog technological constraints: it took a fair amount of capital and labor to mass produce and distribute books, recorded music, and many other works. Unauthorized copies existed, but they were rarely of the same quality as the original, and were not widely available. Through analog scarcity, gatekeepers were able to limit distribution and to use their control to charge monopoly profits, meaning profits that are not tied to a percentage of revenue earned above the costs of production.

Even though copyright laws were enacted in the analog world to benefit authors,[65] authors typically had so little bargaining power that they accepted a one-time payment rather than ongoing royalties, and were required to assign all rights to distributors, who were responsible for determining the final content of works, producing, pricing, and selling them. Copyright was an author's right only in the sense of selling those rights on the cheap to booksellers: the great copyright dispute in England in the eighteenth century over whether copyright was a perpetual right was for good reason called the Battle of the Booksellers, and not the Battle of the Authors. Ordinary people, leading ordinary lives,[66] did not run afoul of the copyright laws: at the end of a commodity chain, ordinary people passively consumed what was offered for sale. Copyright was solely a concern of distributors.

We are now in a very different world, the world of digital abundance. Digital abundance arises from conditions almost the opposite of analog scarcity. In the world of digital abundance, one copy of a work is as good as the next, eliminating the need to source the work from a single, authorized gatekeeper. Copies of works can be made and distributed globally at no extra cost. Creators can reach vast audiences directly, without the filter of gatekeepers and without assigning rights and a big cut of the financial rewards to gatekeepers. In the world of digital abundance, to make money you have to sell more copies for lower prices, and not as, in the world of analog scarcity, sell fewer copies for higher prices.

An important error made by policymakers in grasping the role of copyright in the world of digital abundance is the failure to appreciate that the underlying issue is pricing, not technology. Technology creates new consumer expectations about markets; those expectations can either be met—in which case copyright owners will make money according to those new markets and new expectations—or, as is often the case now, copyright owners can refuse to meet the new expectations, in which case consumers will go elsewhere to have their needs satisfied by others. Technology is not the enemy but rather the means by which market expectations are created and satisfied. The chasm between consumers' expectations and the copyright industries' refusal to meet those expectations is exponentially growing due to the rapid-fire pace of technological and product development. Compounding this is the fact that young people (the prime audience for the core copyright industries) have never lived in the world of artificial analog scarcity and are voracious, intuitive consumers of every new technology. For the copyright industries (often headed by individuals two generations older) to ignore the digital DNA of their principal consumer base is suicide. As Ludwig von Mises pointed out, "producers do not produce for their own consumption but for the market."[67] Content is not king, consumers are: "The real bosses...are the consumers. They, by their buying and by their abstention from buying,...determine what should be produced and in what quantity and quality."[68] Copyright content businesses that don't respond to consumer demand should not expect to stay in business, and most assuredly no government should help them do so.

If our goal is to encourage creativity, we must adapt copyright laws to the actual ways people create and to the actual markets for that creativity. Copyright laws should not act as a bulwark shoring up outdated business models against the tide of new technologies and business models offering consumers what they want. Policy-makers readily express agreement with this statement in principle, yet turn around and pass laws whose sole purpose is to protect the failed *ancien régime*. Dr. Francis Gurry, Director General of the World Intellectual Property Organization, has rightly argued that successful copyright policy has to be based on neutrality to technology and to business models, and should not "preserve business models established under obsolete or moribund technologies."[69]

The days of artificial scarcity are gone forever, replaced by abundance. It makes no sense in a world of digital abundance to complain about the loss of revenue resulting from monopoly power made possible only by analog means of production and distribution. The changes are even more profound, though, than a mere switch from analog to digital: Ordinary people, using the Internet and digital applications in ordinary ways, are unwittingly engaging in massive copying on a daily basis simply because of the way those technologies function. For good reason, the Internet has been called a giant copying machine, copying, of necessity, every step we take.[70] Copyright laws that make everything we do an act of infringement make no sense. As Professor Ian Hargreaves concluded in his report to the UK government: "The copyright regime cannot be considered fit for the digital age when millions of citizens are in daily breach of copyright, simply for shifting a piece of music or video from one device to another."[71]

The Need to Rewrite the Concept of "Copy"

Many of these problems arise from the need to rewrite the definition of "copy." The word "copy" has two meanings. As a verb, "to copy" means reproducing content from one work into either another work (we say one song was "copied" from another song). It also means that copying into another form (you "copy" your CD onto your iPod). The verb of "copy" is what we mean by the exclusive right to reproduce a work. "Reproduce" is a synonym version of the verb to copy. The noun version of "copy" refers to a physical object, a CD or the mp3 file on your iPod that contains the intangible work (the song or the performance). When I say I own a CD "copy" of a work, I am referring to the noun.

The original use of "copy" was in the noun sense. In England, book publishers spoke of owning rights in their "copies," meaning the printed production. The 1710 Statute of Anne, in its title, also spoke of "vesting the copies of printed books in authors or purchasers of such copies. . . ." The right granted—the verb—was the right to "print" those copies. The right to print later became the right to reproduce, with reproduce being regarded as a synonym for the verb to copy. The term "copyright," though ambiguous, referred to either the noun or the verb. Most copyright acts, including the U.S. Copyright Act, combine both the verb and noun versions: the right granted in 17 USC 106(1) is the right to "reproduce the work in copies."[72] What this means is that the right to reproduce (to "copy") is a right to stop others from making permanent (or fairly permanent) versions of your work, versions that will displace sales. Unfortunately, through mistaken interpretations of the noun "copy," the reproduction right has been wildly expanded in many countries, particularly the United States, to include transitory acts such as buffering, caching, or non-consumable versions that are necessitated by the automatic operation of computers or other digital technologies. None of these transitory acts has an independent economic value; that is, they do not harm copyright owners' markets. For example, in order to ensure that the streaming of a video is not interrupted by breaks in the transmissions, websites copy ("buffer") small parts of the video so that missing pieces can be filled during the interruption. Browsers make caches of websites that you just visited in case you hit the "back" button and want to revisit a site you just left. Other caches help with latency (response) time, and managing network traffic. Other times, a cache is made in case websites are inadvertently deleted. To consider buffering or caching to be infringing "copies" is using an eighteenth-century concept to defeat necessary twenty-first-century technologies, the only purpose of which is to increase performance. Where "copies" are made as a necessary adjunct for other legitimate purposes, no liability should exist. Amending the definition of "copy" in either the noun or verb version is an easy fix that would go far in assisting musical licensing and in removing the specter of mass, unintentional copying.

Copyright Laws without Copies?

Paradoxically, we are fast approaching an era when there will be copyright laws *without* copies in the traditional sense. Consumers have shown a growing preference for works to be streamed to them, rather than buying physical media like DVDs or CDs. Accessing works stored in the cloud (on someone else's computer servers) rather than owning a copy is also now a significant business model, and is likely to be the dominant business model in many areas. This trend represents significant changes to consumer habits, and opens up the possibility for a true global distribution of culture, since streaming and cloud computing are not dependent upon brick-and-mortar stores or national boundaries. Non-physical consumption also represents a way for copyright owners to significantly reduce costs of production and distribution and to reach much larger audiences.

Yet, our copyright laws pose significant threats to these developments. The transition from selling analog physical goods to digital, non-physical consumption is not one incumbent gate-keepers favor, for obvious reasons: It eliminates their traditional role in creating artificial scarcity, and thereby receiving monopoly profits. In an effort to create scarcity in the digital environment, copyright owners have obtained rights that give them the power to regulate technologies developed by third parties and to control access to their works. Neither of these rights previously existed. Previously, the copyright laws were technology neutral: They did not regulate technologies, but rather they regulated uses of copyrighted material, regardless of the technology employed. Use of copyrighted works was the essence of copyright, not technology. The exercise of these new rights over new technologies has placed consumers at a comparative disadvantage from their experiences in the hard copy, analog world. For example, under a 1984 United States Supreme Court decision (the famous "Betamax" case), the Sony Corporation could not be stopped or fined for marketing a video cassette recorder (VCR) that permitted people to tape television programs for later viewing. Such taping was regarded as fair use: an unauthorized but permitted and uncompensated use. Copyright owners have successfully overturned the *Sony* decision in the digital era, through legislation covering digital locks.

Digital Locks

With *Sony* standing as a rejection of Hollywood's efforts to control technologies and markets, motion picture companies set out to get Congress to change the rules for the digital world, beginning with digital video disc (DVD) players. Consumer electronics companies, however, very much wanted DVD players to have the same functionality as VCRs: who wants to offer new technologies that can do less than the old technologies you are trying to replace? Yet, that is indeed what happened.

How? Through the use of "digital locks"—software code inserted into a CD, DVD, or consumer product to prevent or regulate consumer access. Circumventing the lock—"hacking" in the vernacular—was made both a civil and criminal violation in the 1998 U.S. Digital Millennium Copyright Act (DMCA) and in the laws of other countries.[73] In the case of DVDs, this is what happened. In order to sell DVD players that would play the DVDs Hollywood sold to consumers, electronics manufacturers were required by Hollywood to build into their players a key capable of de-encrypting an algorithm built into the DVD. The algorithmic key built into the DVD scrambles over the face of the DVD digital data representing the images of the film. The algorithmic key, when matched to a key in the DVD player, allows the images to play in the correct order; without the key, you get an unwatchable visual mess. To get the key, you have to play by Hollywood's rules.

Why wouldn't the manufacturers just break the algorithmic key and thereby avoid having to agree to Hollywood's efforts to cripple the new technology? The manufacturers were quite capable of breaking the key because the digital lock the industry chose wasn't at all robust: teenagers could and did break it. In a pre-DMCA world that would be the end of it: after breaking the key, manufacturers could then market players that had the functionality consumers wanted and which the Supreme Court allowed as fair use in the *Sony* case. But because of the DMCA, owners of DVD players were placed in a worse position than owners of VCRs.[74]

Here is another example of the misuse of copyright laws to place the public in a worse position in the digital world than in the analog world. A venerable principle of copyright law is the first-sale doctrine (in other countries it's called the exhaustion doctrine): Once a lawful copy of a book is sold or given away, the owner of that copy can turn around and resell it or give it away without permission or payment. This is why we can have second-hand bookstores. But what if the book is licensed and not sold? If the transaction is considered a license then the first-sale doctrine doesn't apply, as thousands of startled Amazon.com purchasers found out when their copy of George Orwell's *1984* was remotely removed from their Kindles by Amazon, after Amazon determined that its source wasn't authorized.

Digital locks govern even if the first-sale doctrine does apply because the digital lock provisions in U.S. law are not part of the Copyright Act proper and thus are not limited by the first-sale doctrine. If an eBook has digital locks, those locks can limit how many times you can read the book and whether you can loan it to family members or friends. Digital locks can be used not just with individuals, but with libraries too. In the past, libraries that lawfully acquired a copy of a book could lend it out as many times as they wanted. This may be a thing of the past: In March 2011, book publisher HarperCollins stunned the library world by announcing that a license to lend its eBooks will expire after twenty-six loans. In a world where books will increasingly be issued only in eBook format, such policies may radically change the nature of libraries.[75]

The DMCA and other digital lock laws are prime examples of our march backwards, of how our laws are used to thwart innovation and creativity. The DMCA is the reason you can't load lawfully purchased copies of your DVDs into your iPod, why you can't transfer copies of many lawfully purchased works from one electronic device to another, why DVDs bought in one country may not work in another, something that greatly embarrassed (or should have) President Obama when he gave then–United Kingdom Prime Minister Gordon Brown a set of DVDs of American movies, which couldn't be lawfully played on Brown's DVD player. The DMCA will permit copyright owners to control how many times you can read or watch a copyrighted work. In the DMCA world, both consumers and technology are treated as the enemy. This unfortunate approach ignores that consumer expectations are greatly influenced by technologies.[76] It is new technologies, not new works, that lead to new consumer expectations and therefore new sources of profits for authors. The Sony Walkman led to an explosion of new sales of audio cassettes. The same was true of the introduction of the CD, where for most of its product life, more money was made from consumers re-buying existing albums than from buying new ones.

But for new technologies, the copyright industries and authors would have starved long ago, since they have played no role, creatively or financially, in the development and introduction of the technologies that enable them to make money. Not a single penny was contributed by the music industry to the creation, manufacture or marketing of iTunes, the iPod, or the iPad. Not a single penny was contributed by the copyright industries to the development of the Internet or to any search engine even though the copyright industries could not exist without either. New technologies provide new ways to satisfy new consumer demand and to thereby make healthy profits. You would never know that from the medieval mentality of moat building represented by the DMCA and copyright industries' approach to most new technologies, an approach that has failed to grasp the simple point, proved over and over again, that new technologies create new opportunities. Whether those new opportunities are disruptive or not to existing business models is not within copyright owners' control. What is in their control is whether to respond constructively and thrive, or whether to respond destructively and fail.

The proxy battle for control of technologies and markets through copyright laws must stop. Our copyright laws must be technology neutral and based on twenty-first-century markets: those markets include a distinct and growing trend toward consumption of copyrighted works without copying them: copyright laws without copying makes no sense. A new structure must provide twenty-first-century solutions to getting authors paid and giving the public access to their creations. This will involve in many (but certainly not all) cases changing the fundamental nature of copyright from a grant of exclusive rights into a right of remuneration: a right to be paid through statutory licensing, collective management of rights, and levies.[77] Having an exclusive right does you no good if you can't get paid. The technological elimination of control over uses of copyrighted works is neither good nor bad, but it is a fact of life. As a fact of life, it requires that we rethink how we ensure that authors get paid.

There is no evidence that policymakers are willing to take the bold steps necessary to make copyright laws function effectively in the twenty-first century. We have yet to see copyright reform proposals we can believe in. Merely giving speeches about respecting copyright or about the importance of innovation and economic growth are empty gestures, unless wholesale reform is undertaken. This book offers ideas for how to construct such a new system. I begin with a review of policymakers' failure to base copyright laws on the actual conditions in which those laws operate. There is no hope for the future if it is merely a continuation of a failed past.

TWO

Replacing a Faith-Based Approach to Copyright with an Evidence-Based Approach

In 1944, conservative Austrian economist Ludwig von Mises published his book *Bureaucracy*. The book contrasts free market economies with the economies in socialist countries. Unlike those who ideologically oppose all government intervention in markets, and who view bureaucracies as inherently evil, von Mises took a more nuanced position, writing, "Bureaucracy in itself is neither good nor bad. It is a method of management that can be applied in different spheres of human activity."[1] So too with copyright laws. Copyright laws are regulation. Copyright laws may represent good regulation in some areas, but bad regulation in other areas, but copyright laws *always* regulate people's conduct. Copyright laws' regulations tell one group of people (A) they have the exclusive right to engage in X conduct. They tell another group of people (B) they can't engage in X conduct unless A says they can.[2] Governments back up those regulations with monetary damages and criminal punishment, which occasionally includes (in China) execution.

For regulations to be effective, we must be able to quantifiably measure our success (or lack thereof) in achieving the intended purposes.[3] The first step in fixing copyright laws, then, is fixing the way we enact them. Our current laws are based on rhetoric and faith, not on evidence. Unless our laws are based on empirically sound evidence tailored to meet the stated objectives, they do not stand a remote chance of achieving those objectives. In 2001, President George W. Bush concluded he could do business with Vladimir Putin because, as he said, "I looked the man in the eye. I found him to be very straight forward and trustworthy and we had a very good dialogue. I was able to get a sense of his soul."[4] The rest of us lack Mr. Bush's apparently unique abilities, and even Ronald Reagan said about Putin's predecessors, "trust, but verify."[5] You can't verify without evidence.

The obstacles to basing our laws on evidence are seen in a communication from the European Commission in May 2011 with this ambitious title: "A Single Market for Intellectual Property Rights: Boosting creativity and innovation to provide economic growth, high quality jobs and first class products and services in Europe." Without a trace of irony, the Commission made this statement, italicized in the original: "*The case does not need to be made anymore: IPRs in their different forms and shapes are key assets of the EU economy.*" Much like the expression "It goes without saying," when we read a case need not be made, we are right to suspect that no verifiable case has been made.

Alas, those who propose new copyright laws rarely go to the trouble to make a sound empirical case for their requests.

A week before the European Commission's May 2011 communication, Professor Ian Hargreaves, in his report to the British government, not only bemoaned the lack of current evidence-based policymaking, but also observed that the problem is long-standing: "In the 1970s, the Banks Review deplored the lack of evidence to support policy judgments, as did the Gowers report five years ago [2006]."[6] Policymakers have been operating in an evidence-free copyright law zone for many decades. Merely claiming that copyright laws encourage creativity, stimulate innovation, create jobs, and provide the public with access to cultural works doesn't mean copyright laws do in fact encourage creativity, stimulate innovation, or create jobs, or at least to the degree claimed. Similarly, claiming huge losses from unauthorized activity doesn't mean there are such losses, or at least anywhere near the extent claimed. Effective laws can't be based on vague claims like, "I can't prove how much, but it's substantial."

Rather than provide policymakers with data that can assist them in formulating effective laws, too often rhetoric masquerading as assertions of fact are offered up. Professor Hargreaves pointed out: "Given its importance, you would think we would have a very clear picture of the scale and dynamics of online piracy, but this is not so....There is no shortage of claims about levels of infringement, but in [our] four months of evidence gathering, we have failed to find a single UK survey that is demonstrably statistically robust."[7] The paucity of such evidence appears to have deterred few policymakers in continually proposing new, ever-harsher penalties for unauthorized online conduct—which most reports suggest has been steadily declining and is now at single-digit levels.[8] What we have now is policy motivated evidence-making, not evidence-based policymaking.

WE NEED INDEPENDENT IMPACT STATEMENTS FOR PROPOSED AND EXISTING LEGISLATION

The good news is that policymakers can base laws on real evidence, if they choose to. To make the possible real, there must be mandatory, independently-produced, impartial, empirically rigorous impact statements *before* any new copyright legislation is passed, as well as impact statements for existing laws so that we know whether existing laws need to be amended or repealed. Those impact statements must be followed, not just ignored, in the event they reveal inconvenient truths.[9] For example, an April 2008 impact assessment by the European Commission on the impact of extending the term of protection for sound recordings twenty years concluded there would be no negative price effect on consumers from that extension.[10] This conclusion was based on a single study using a very small size, performed by PricewaterhouseCoopers as part of a music-industry sponsored consultancy. An independent study showed the conclusion was dead wrong.[11] The May 2011 independent Hargreaves review agreed that term extension will have a negative impact.

Additionally, impact statements must be based on a meaningful match between the evidence and the goals, a match that must be subject to a searching review by courts or other independent bodies.[12] This is what I mean by empirically rigorous. What good does it do to have impact statements where policymakers can be found to have satisfied them by flimsy evidence or by ignoring contrary evidence? Here's an example of the failure of current impact statements to mean anything. In the UK, the Digital Economy Act of 2010 was passed by Parliament under highly controversial conditions, including a near-empty House of Commons. The law contains a provision requiring copyright owners and telecommunications operators to share in the financial burdens of complying with copyright owners' complaints about consumers' online peer-to-peer file sharing. These complaints may lead to termination of Internet service, for everyone in the house, even those who never file shared. An impact statement was prepared setting out the alleged expected costs, benefits and impact of the policy, as well as a conclusion that the benefits justified the costs. The legislation was challenged in the courts on a number of grounds, one of which was that the impact assessment failed miserably to consider important factors, including the entire dimension of social welfare. Proponents of the review also argued there should be quantitative data regarding the extent that expected new revenues from the law would lead to the creation of new works. The European Union raised concerns about the lack of any perceived benefit to telecommunications companies from the increased costs.[13] Others noted that the government had not provided robust estimates of the costs of implementation.

In reviewing the possible negative effect of the legislation on social welfare, a special committee of the House of Lords concluded that "[t]he cost imposed on ISPs will increase broadband retail prices for all consumers, leading to low income consumers being priced out of internet service." The government, in replying to the committee, acknowledged this would occur, but took the position that while "This is regrettable, [it] needs to be balanced against the wider benefit to the UK's digital economy."[14] One would expect that where the poorest elements of society are dramatically and negatively affected by a copyright law, the "wider benefits" to the economy would have to be clearly demonstrated. But one would be wrong in holding that expectation.[15]

In upholding the impact assessment, a judge in the High Court of Justice rejected the very idea that Parliament had to make *any* calculation of the costs and benefits of new legislation.[16] To the judge, the existence of copyright legislation already on the books meant that Parliament had already achieved the correct balance for all time. This approach renders all impact statements meaningless, as well as all evidence-based policymaking. The judge went further, questioning whether Parliament *could* ever calculate increased productivity from stronger laws, even though this is precisely the basis on which copyright laws are argued to be necessary. But the judge went further yet, writing that if Parliament were to consider social welfare losses, it would make copyright owners angry and would thus put Parliament in a tough political spot. So what? Aren't legislators elected to do the job of making tough choices? And apparently, making the public angry by having its Internet service disconnected means so little that it need not even be a factor.

What is baffling about the judge's willingness to forego any inquiry into the basis for the impact assessment is that such inquiries are routinely conducted by the courts when a private copyright infringement lawsuit is brought. In such lawsuits, there is a rigorous examination of experts offering opinions on the economic impact of the defendant's conduct. Where the conclusions offered by the experts on the economic effect of the use do not meet the requisite standards,[17] the testimony is excluded. Numerous courts have excluded expert testimony on this ground. I set out some of these in the note,[18] but here is one example. In *DSU Medical Corp. v. JMS Co., Ltd.*,[19] the Court of Appeals for the Federal Circuit explained: "To prevent the hypothetical from lapsing into pure speculation, this court requires sound economic proof of the nature of the market and likely outcomes with infringement out of the picture ... Indeed, the concept of sound economic proof requires some grounding in 'sound economic and factual predicates.'"

Such court opinions are commonplace. Copyright infringement litigation between parties is an evidence-based exercise. Yet, when the copyright industries come to Congress, Parliaments, or government agencies, seeking sweeping powers over entire industries and classes of works, claims with no basis in the evidence are blandly accepted with none of the fundamental evidentiary controls found in private litigation affecting only two parties. Governments are routinely told that the content industries face a "catastrophic decline in future markets," or that they face a "mortal threat to the economic and creative processes which underpin our business, and consequently to the economic growth."[20] The copyright industries repeat, year after year, discredited figures on lost sales and lost employment. Elected and government officials frequently repeat those figures as "evidence" of why stronger copyright laws are necessary. Such evidence would be laughed out of any courtroom. They should be laughed out of the halls of government too.

Given the important societal implications of our laws for creators and consumers of copyrighted materials, we must hold our copyright laws to standards at least as high as those to which private parties are held in litigation. The failure to do so in the past has been a principal factor in copyright law's failure to act as an effective vehicle to accomplish its lofty goals. It is not asking too much to have our laws supported by empirical data and to match current markets and technologies. After all, policymakers routinely claim that copyright laws encourage the creation and distribution of new works, create hundreds of thousands of jobs, foster innovation, and benefit the public. These are very broad claims. Those who make such claims in order to pass new laws should offer the best empirical support that can be marshaled in support of their claims.[21]

Most people become lawmakers because they want to make a positive difference in others' lives. But you can't make a positive difference in others' lives if the laws you pass are ineffective, if they are based on outmoded markets and outmoded technologies, and if they are contrary to consumers' reasonable expectations and interests. Merely claiming laws are effective can fool some of the people only some of the time, and many are never fooled.

The need for effective lawmaking applies not only to national laws, but internationally as well. The Berne Convention for the Protection of Literary and Artistic Works, the preeminent international copyright convention, is expressly based on the need for effective laws, its preface stating that the convention was founded on the desire "to protect in as *effective* and uniform a manner as possible the rights of authors over their literary and artistic works...." We fail authors and the public if our laws are ineffective.

For too long, copyright laws have been a faith-based enterprise, passed according to theological claims and slogans that are contrary to both common sense and independent economic studies. As a result, our copyright laws have as much chance of being effective as astrological predictions. Professor James Boyle has described copyright legislation as existing in an "evidence-free zone,"[22] although, as we shall now see, in many instances there *is* evidence; it is just ignored.

IGNORING EVIDENCE: EXTENDING THE LENGTH OF COPYRIGHT

One area of copyright law where there has been a willful refusal to base policymaking on easily available evidence is in determining the proper length of copyright. This issue goes to the heart of the debates about copyright, because claims about what copyright laws do in practice revolve around the argument that creators will not create unless they believe that a sufficiently long term of copyright is in place. I examine this issue in depth in Chapter 8, but the issue is also relevant for this chapter because there are empirical studies demonstrating what an effective term of protection should be.[23] Unfortunately, such studies are routinely ignored, supplanted with vague moral claims. I will explore

two examples: the first in the United States, the second in the
United Kingdom.

The United States

In the mid-1990s, the United States began debating whether to
extend the term of copyright an additional twenty years. At the
time, copyright lasted for the author's life plus fifty years after
death.[24] The proposed extra twenty years could not conceivably
lead to the creation of a single new work. Was there a single author
in the entire world who said, "A term of copyright that only lasts
for my life plus fifty years after I die is too short. I will not create
a new work unless copyright is extended to last for my life plus
seventy years"? There is no such person. Studies conducted after
the length of copyright was extended confirm this. In 2009, professors Ivan Png and Qiu-hong Wang reviewed the production of
motion pictures, books, and music in twenty-three Organization
for Economic Co-operation and Development countries that had
extended the term of copyright in the years 1991 to 2005.[25] They
found no evidence that longer term of copyright caused the creation of more works than the prior, shorter term. Yet, term extension remains on the books.

The term of copyright was extended not only for new works,
but also retroactively to large numbers of already-created works
that would otherwise have passed into the public domain,[26] and
whose owners long ago gave up any financial interest in them.
The inability to distribute these works, to preserve them, or use
them as the basis for creating other works has led to a locking up
of our cultural heritage.[27]

The inability of a longer term to inspire the creation of a single
new work, and to inhibit the use of older works were facts known to
Congress before passage of the term extension, thanks to a study

done by Congress's own research service, the Congressional Research Service, which concluded that even the shorter length of copyright then in effect was too long for most works.[28] Copyright term extension in the United States was a triumph of rhetoric over reality.

The United Kingdom

In his November 2006 report to the Chancellor of the Exchequer (then Gordon Brown), Andrew Gowers conducted a thorough economic inquiry into sound recording sales and the distribution of royalties to performers. Mr. Gowers' goal was to develop data that would permit lawmakers to determine whether increasing the term of copyright in sound recordings by twenty years would increase performers' production and income. (The existing term is fifty years from first release of the album.)

Increasing performers' production and income are worthy objectives. How to achieve those goals can be empirically determined, and that's what Mr. Gowers set out to do. Based on his inquiry, Mr. Gowers concluded that even for those performing artists who do receive royalties—many receive only a one-time flat fee—the "distribution of income [is] highly skewed, with most income going to the relatively small number of highly successful artists whose work is still commercially available after 50 years."[29] He also observed: "Evidence suggests that most sound recordings sell in the ten years after release, and only a very small percentage continue to generate income, both from sales and royalty payments, for the entire [current] duration of…50 years." Highly successful artists have no need for a longer term of copyright: they neither contemplated nor relied on such a windfall when they did their work. If they truly care about the many who are worse off than they are, they would support reform of artists' contracts and other steps that would actually put money in performers' pockets.

This is not a form of wealth distribution. I do not propose taking money away from the rich to give to the poor, whether the rich are performers or anyone else. Rather, I want to ensure that the money goes *in the first place* to the intended beneficiaries.

The economic benefits of copyright, while real, are short-lived and generally flow to a small group of creators and distributors, an economic fact of life that has held true regardless of the century and regardless of the type of work.[30] Copyright laws have, in practice, functioned as a way for government officials to placate authors, artists, and performers with the promise of monetary rewards, while throwing them on the mercy of the free market. This process of privatizing the creation of cultural heritage is a timeworn political tactic for giving the appearance of working for the benefit of all.

Based on the inability of a longer term of copyright to help the vast majority of performing artists, but its ability to harm the public through reduced access and higher prices, Mr. Gowers sensibly recommended against adding twenty more years of copyright. Having the government step in and take money out of the public's pockets to give those whose incentive to create cannot be increased by such beneficence is neither good policy nor good economics. Mr. Brown accepted Mr. Gower's recommendation.

Upon becoming Prime Minister, and after intensive lobbying by celebrities and the copyright industries, Mr. Brown changed course 180 degrees, led by his Secretary of State for Culture, Media, and Sports, Andy Burnham.[31] Since Mr. Burnham could not challenge any of the empirical conclusions in the Gowers report, he instead relied on a previously unarticulated and undefined "moral case at the heart of copyright law."[32] We are truly at sea if our laws are to be enacted according to a moral case espoused in the face of unchallenged economic evidence refuting the minister's brief. We will not help those we claim to be helping, but will instead help those who don't need it. As the Hargreaves review noted in criticizing

Mr. Burnham and the government's *volte*-face, independent research "suggested that the benefits to individual artists would be highly skewed to a relatively small number of performers."[33] Term extension will also injure the public through restricted access and higher prices. We cannot have effective laws under such conditions.

Regrettably, the same process occurred in the European Union, when the European Parliament ignored both of the studies the European Commission had ordered, as well as the opinions of a large number of independent academics and consumer organizations. For some reason, it is the arguments of those seeking greater rights for themselves that are always credited over the public's.

Not extending the term of copyright doesn't mean needy performers should be abandoned—they shouldn't be—but it does mean adopting different policies, in particular long-overdue reforms in music-industry contracts. Here are two possible reforms: (1) a use-it-or-lose-it provision where an album,[34] though given by the performers to the record label, is not released, in which case all rights would be returned to the performers; (2) a use-it-or-lose-it statutory provision where an album, having been released, has not been commercially exploited for ten years. Again, all rights would be given to the performers.[35]

In the case of the first type of use-it-or-lose-it reversion, contractual provisions in record label contracts typically do not require an album[36] that has been recorded to ever be released. When an album is not released, the labels do not have to reassign the rights to the performers so that the performers can then release it. If an album is not released, the performers cannot make money; even worse, they are in debt, given costs charged against their account for the creation of the album, but with no ability to pay those costs back through sales of the album. The public loses as well since it cannot hear the album. That performers sign such contracts is a testimonial to their weak bargaining power.

Here is why the second type of use-it-or-lose-it provision is necessary too: Lack of access to albums that have been made but not released is the tip of the iceberg. The larger problem is the vast number of previously released recordings that are no longer available for purchase and that, due to the extremely long term of copyright, cannot be sold by those who are willing to do so. For example, even though Motown Records is a very valuable music catalogue, 95 percent of its recordings are no longer available. Similar figures exist for other labels. Giving the rights back to performers would give them the economic incentive to release the albums, leading to greater income for them and greater access by the public. It is baffling that policymakers talk so frequently about the importance of culture but propose only to strengthen penalties for alleged infringement of a small body of existing works, while ignoring the vast trove of culture that is at risk of being lost forever.

INACCURATE DATA

Sometimes the problem with drafting effective copyright laws results not from ignoring data but from using inaccurate data. The one-sided, heavy reliance of government officials on the copyright industries' inaccurate claims of financial harm is extremely common. Inflated figures, unsupported assumptions, and false correlation-to-cause arguments are used to gain greater control over the public's access to culture and knowledge, and to divert public monies for the benefit of the private sector through misguided enforcement efforts. Wildly exaggerated claims of the importance of copyright owners to the overall economy are the vehicle by which this agenda is pursued: policymakers are led to believe that they are acting not for the benefit of private interests but instead to protect the broader economy. The data are, however, farcically false and have always been so: the errors have been going on for so long and are so well-documented that there is no excuse for policymakers to continue to rely on them. The Social Science Research Council noted the problem in its 2011 report "Media Piracy in Emerging Economies": "[W]e see a serious and increasingly sophisticated industry research enterprise embedded in a lobbying effort with a historically very loose relationship to evidence."[37]

Here are a few illustrations of the use of grossly inflated loss figures. In an April 2010 report to US congressional committees,[38] Congress's General Accountability Office (GAO) noted that the Business Software Alliance (BSA), in calculating losses from unauthorized copying of software, questionably assumed a one-to-one rate of substitution for unauthorized and authorized copies and simply guessed about the rates of piracy in some countries. For example, in May 2010, BSA, in arguing for changes in the South African copyright law, stated that 35 percent of the software in South Africa is pirated. Where did this figure come from? Not from surveying any actual copying of software in South Africa because the BSA hadn't attempted to learn the actual practices in that country. Instead, the figure was made up.[39] A similar report in Australia, commissioned by content owners estimating losses of $900 million a year, also appears to have been fabricated.[40]

The BSA's misuse of figures is not anomalous within the copyright industries. Regarding a 2006 Motion Picture Association of America (MPAA) study, Congress's General Accounting Office concluded, as it had with the BSA, "It is difficult, based on the information provided in the study, to determine how the authors handled key assumptions such as substitution rates and extrapolation from the survey sample to the broader population."[41] There is a good reason for such ambiguity: MPAA has employed an economist who applies multipliers—extrapolation from the survey sample, in the technical jargon of the GAO—to already inflated figures to inflate them even further. An alleged $6 billion in losses for the motion picture industry became $20.5 billion to the general economy using multipliers that took inflated losses and then tripled them. The alleged total loss to the overall U.S. economy from all forms of piracy for 2007 was thus put at $58 billion using the multipliers.[42] In such circumstances, not only do the figures offered provide no guidance for assessing the extent of the problem, but they make year-to-year calculations of whether the problem is increasing or decreasing impossible. Rational decision-making is impossible in such situations. As the Hargreaves Review wrote, "At this moment, given our state of knowledge, no-one in the UK could make an informed assessment of what is the right level of resource for online enforcement in the UK."[43] This sad state of affairs is not accidental, but is a deliberate result of what may be called the Piracy-Industrial Complex.

The Piracy-Industrial Complex

Why would the copyright industries risk laws based on inaccurate data? Because they have correctly judged that lawmakers will accept their figures without question, and will therefore continually ratchet up the laws: a continually increasing problem requires, it is argued, a continually tougher response. This explains why, despite sound year-to-year economic growth and profits, as well as numbers suggesting that the level of peer-to-peer file sharing is now in the single digits,[44] the level of piracy must always be stated to be on the upswing.

Such a conjuring up of an ever-present external enemy is reminiscent of the Cold War period, which saw the rise of what President (and former General) Dwight Eisenhower called the military-industrial complex[45]: a symbiotic relationship between government and the private sector. In copyright, we have the piracy-industrial complex, a symbiotic relationship between government officials, who genuinely want to protect creativity and jobs, and the private sector, which seeks government benefits. The private sector supplies the existential threat to creativity and jobs—piracy—while the government steps in as the white knight to vanquish that threat by granting new rights to the private sector and by committing public resources. Such actions can only be defended by accepting the false figures offered up year after year by the private sector.

In this respect, there is no better skirmish for a political white knight to engage in than a battle to protect jobs; for this reason, copyright owners have gone to great lengths to claim that reductions in piracy will lead to job creation. In doing so they engage in the same multiple false equations they do for revenue losses. The same multipliers used to generate inflated monetary losses have been used to inflate job losses. The MPAA's economist estimated that piracy resulted in job losses of some 373,000 jobs in 2005 alone, a figure which, if held constant, would mean a stunning loss of 2,238,000 jobs from 2005 to 2010, inclusive. The implication is that if we solve piracy we will solve the worldwide recession. In my earlier book, I debunked other claims of job losses,[46] yet these claims continue to be made today. Repeating false claims doesn't make them true.

Not to be outdone, in 2010, the International Chamber of Commerce, using the same methodology, guesstimated that there will be a cumulative loss of between 611,000 and 1,217,000 jobs in Europe between 2008 and 2015 due to piracy.[47] Leaving aside that the Chamber left itself a margin of error of 100 percent, no lists were provided of actual job losses due to piracy; no lists are ever provided that state that these many people at these companies in these positions lost their jobs. Yet, year after year wild claims are made. Since enough years of making such claims have passed, and no actual data have been provided, we can only conclude the claims are bogus.

This is the conclusion of Dr. Ben Goldacre, an English physician who has a column in a British newspaper called "Bad Science,"[48] in which he debunks spurious assertions of fact. Dr. Goldacre has no ax to grind with copyright laws or the copyright industries. Yet, he concluded, "as far as I'm concerned, everything from this industry is false, until proven otherwise."[49] Here's why. Dr. Goldacre had read statements that "Downloading costs billions. More than 7 million Brits use illegal downloading sites that cost the economy billions of pounds, government advisers said today. Researchers found more than a million people using a download site in ONE day and estimated that in a year they would use £120bn worth of material." He noted £120bn is a tenth of the entire GDP of the United Kingdom. If the figure is true, then there is indeed a serious problem. But the figure is false. Dr. Goldacre explained how he discovered the errors:

> So where do these notions of so many billions in lost revenue come from? I found the original report. It was written by some academics you can hire in a unit at UCL [University College London]...On the billions lost it says: "Estimates as to the overall lost revenues if we include all creative industries whose products can be copied digitally, or counterfeited, reach £10bn (IP rights, 2004), conservatively, as our figure is from 2004, and a loss of 4,000 jobs."
>
> What is the origin of this conservative figure? I hunted down the full...documents, found the references section, and followed the web link, which led to a 2004 press release from a private legal firm called Rouse who specialise in intellectual property law. This press release was not about the £10bn figure. It was, in fact, a one-page document, which simply welcomed the government setting up an intellectual property theft strategy. In a short section headed "background," among five other points, it says: "Rights owners have estimated that last year alone counterfeiting and piracy cost the UK economy £10bn and 4,000 jobs." An industry estimate, as an aside, in a press release. Genius.

Dr. Goldacre then discovered that the £120bn was off by a factor of ten, so that the figure, even if implausibly correct, should have been £12bn. There are many, many other such exposures of the copyright industries' false figures.[50] These figures are churned out by a large lobbying effort whose existence depends on creating the false impression that the creative world as we know it will end unless their constant demands for ever-stronger laws are met. Think of it this way: how is the productivity of a trade association head located in a national capital measured by those paying the head's salary and benefits? The answer is by the number of new laws or regulations passed, and by the enemies vanquished. The heads of these associations – who are prominently quoted as authorities on copyright laws and the business of their organizations – are usually politicians, not business people nor experts on copyright. Their expertise is in politics, the politics of delivering new laws and regulations. The head of the Motion Picture Association of America is former U.S. Senator Christopher Dodd. The head of the American Association of Book Publishers is former Congresswoman Patricia Schroeder. The head of the Recording Industry Association of America is Mitch Bainwohl, who was a Republican Party staff member and lobbyist for twenty-six years (lastly for Senator Bill Frist) before he became RIAA's chairman and CEO. David Israelite, head of the National Music Publishers Association, was a former staffer for Senator Kit Bond, and then a staffer for Senator John Ashcroft when Ashcroft went to the Justice Department. Trade association heads' ability to keep their very healthy multi-million dollar incomes is based on success in lobbying and not success in business innovations. In the environment in which copyright laws are enacted, those laws are products.

The effects of the very well-funded efforts by lobbyists pushing copyright laws as products are devastating to sound copyright policy, policy that should be based on economics and on effectiveness, but are not. Professor Ian Hargreaves, in his May 2011 independent review for the British government, made the same point, illustrating the global nature of the problem:

> On copyright issues, lobbying on behalf of rights owners has been more persuasive to Ministers than economic assessments.[51] ...It is impossible to avoid the conclusion that there is something deeply and persistently amiss in the way that policy toward IP issues in the UK is determined and/ or administered.[52] ...[T]here is no doubt that the persuasive powers of celebrities and important UK creative companies have distorted policy outcomes.[53] There can be no doubt that the perspective of consumers has played too small a part in the work of the UK's IP policymakers.[54]

Professor Hargreaves' sentiments are not unique to the UK.

THE PROPER MEASUREMENT OF GAINS AND LOSSES IS SOCIETY'S, NOT INDUSTRY'S

False figures on monetary and job losses importantly ignore that whatever the correct figures are, those losses are **not** losses to the larger economy. A loss of revenue in one sector of the economy is not lost to the economy as a whole: the money does not fall into a black hole, never to be recovered or spent. Instead, a loss to one sector is a gain to another sector (or in consumers' savings). As the Social Science Research Council points out:

> Within a given economy, the piracy of domestic goods is a *transfer* of income, not a loss. Money saved by consumers or businesses on CDs, DVDs, or software will not disappear, but rather be spent on other things—housing, food, or other entertainment, or other business expenses, and so on. These

expenditures, in turn will generate tax revenue, new jobs, infrastructural investments, and the range of other goods that are typically in the loss column of industry analyses.[55]

The same analysis holds true in the case of declining revenue through changes in consumer consumption: the record industry has been complaining for over a decade about its "losses" from the decline in CD sales. It is true that CD sales have markedly declined, but the number of digital singles sold has dramatically increased. The decline in CD sales and the increase in digital singles sales have nothing to do with piracy, and is instead a reflection of record companies' inability to continue their long-standing practice of forcing consumers to buy CDs and therefore albums. Here are two charts illustrating the real, economic facts.[56] The first chart shows where the record industry has historically made its money:

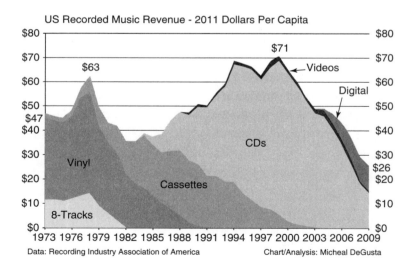

US Recorded Music Revenue - 2011 Dollars Per Capita

Data: Recording Industry Association of America   Chart/Analysis: Micheal DeGusta

FIGURE 2.1

The second chart shows the decline in per capita income for album sales:

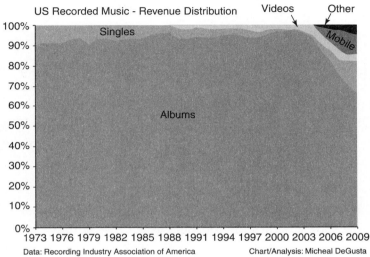

FIGURE 2.2

This chart shows the natural product cycle decline in every format that has occurred for the last thirty-eight years. CDs are no different. What is different now—and which has nothing to do with piracy—is that consumers can buy the one or two songs they want, in a digital form, resulting in the obvious decline in album sales. Even if record labels make less money from the increase in sales of digital singles than they did from the peak year of CD sales (an unfair comparison in any event), the difference is a *positive* social benefit: Consumers are now able to spend money on what they do want and not on what they don't. Record labels may have less money but we have more, and that's a great thing for us and for society. Technology has accomplished what our anti-trust laws should have—they have prevented a seller from tying the sale of an unwanted product to the sale of a much-desired product over which the seller has monopoly power. We should cheer the decline in the record industry's sales: not because of any hostility to record labels, but because in this case, their loss is truly society's gain.

GETTING THE RIGHT DATA **BEFORE** LEGISLATING

Figuring out whether proposed legislation will achieve the benefits it claims has been a concern of diligent legislators for a long time. In 1841, in Britain, Lord Thomas Macaulay successfully blocked a bill to lengthen the term of copyright by pointing out that it would not benefit authors:

> Dr [Samuel] Johnson died fifty-six years ago....Now, would the knowledge that this copyright would exist in 1841 have been a source of gratification to Johnson? Would it have stimulated his exertions? Would it have once drawn him out of his bed before noon? Would it have once cheered him under a fit of the spleen? Would it have induced him to give us one more allegory, one more life of a poet, one more imitation of Juvenal? I firmly believe not. I firmly believe that a hundred years ago, when he was writing our debates for the Gentleman's Magazine, he would very much rather have had two pence to buy a plate of shin of beef at a cook's shop underground.[57]

Lord Macaulay—himself a famous author—also pointed out that not only would we not have had more works from Dr. Johnson from a longer term of copyright, but the costs to the public from that longer term would be greatly increased. A similar empirical approach to legislating was advocated in the legislative committee reports to the 1909 Copyright Act in the United States: "In creating a copyright law Congress must consider…two questions: First, how much will the legislation stimulate the producer and so benefit the public; and, second, how much will the monopoly granted be detrimental to the public?"[58] These questions cannot be answered unless the relevant data is gathered first.

The European Database Directive: A Case Study in What Not to Do

The common sense approach to legislating found in the 1909 committee reports has been honored more in the breach rather than in the observance. One example of such a breach is the European Union's 1996 Database Directive. On March 11, 1996, the European Union adopted a directive that had two goals, the first laudable, the second not. The first goal was to harmonize the level of originality required for a database to be protected. As a single market, the rules in that market should be consistent. Databases covered under this part of the directive include compilations of literary material, musical compositions, and audiovisual material. The second goal was to create new, sui generis (non-copyright) rights over unoriginal databases: databases of facts, numbers, and other material that require investment to produce but which are not the result of creative activity.

This new right to prevent others from copying without permission was made available to database compilers outside the European Union, but only on a reciprocal basis; that is, only if the non-EU country of origin extended the same rights to EU database compilers.[59] This provision was directed squarely at the United States, which, as a result of the 1991 Supreme Court opinion in *Feist Publications, Inc. v. Rural Telephone Services Company*,[60] cannot, as a constitutional matter, extend copyright to non–original databases.

The *Feist* Court held that there was no author of facts and that arranging facts in alphabetical or similar lock-step ways did not meet the constitutional requirement of originality. (*Feist* involved a copyright claim in the white page listings of a telephone book.)

In an attempt to get around the *Feist* opinion, database compilers in the United States attempted for many years to convince Congress to grant sui generis rights, but eventually gave up. The database industry in the United States has continued to thrive nevertheless. Recital 12 of the EU Directive asserted, without support: "Whereas such an investment in modern information storage and processing systems will not take place within the Community unless a stable and uniform legal protection regime is introduced for the protection of the rights of makers of databases." This is illogical: if investment in database production was greater in the United States, but the United States lacked a sui generis right, why would establishing sui generis rights for EU database producers lead to increased production in the European Union? It wouldn't, and it didn't, as we shall see. Once the European Union established sui generis rights, there was a *decrease* in the production of databases within the Community, as well as an *increase* in the relative gap between production in the United States and the European Union.

The directive required a post-enactment impact statement in which the Commission would evaluate whether the goal of increasing the production of databases had been met.[61] The first evaluative report was to have been submitted no later than January 1, 2001. It was not submitted until December 12, 2005,[62] and as of the writing of this book in early 2011, there has been no second report. The first report is, though, remarkable in its candor, declaring that although "[i]ntroduced to stimulate the production of databases in Europe, the 'sui generis' protection has had no proven impact on the production of databases."[63] The evidence pointed in the opposite direction, to a reduction in the number of databases produced within the European Union. The report noted that the number of EU-based database entries in the Gale Directory of Databases dropped from 4,085 in 2001, to 3,095 in 2004, the year before the evaluation report was issued.

The number of EU databases also declined relative to the United States. Recall that the sui generis right was conditioned on the United States granting reciprocal rights to EU databases. The United States did not, however, grant sui generis rights. Not only did the number of EU databases decline in absolute numbers, but so too did the relative global market share of EU databases to U.S. databases. In 1996, two years before the database directive went into effect, the EU worldwide market share was 22 percent. In 2004, the share was 24 percent, an increase of two points. That's good news. But here's the bad news: In 1996, the U.S. market share was 69 percent. In 2004, the U.S. market share was 72 percent, an increase of three points.[64] Clearly, market share is not driven by protectionism.

Notwithstanding the evidence, the report recites how EU database producers continue to believe, incorrectly, that the sui generis right "has helped Europe catch up with the US in terms of investment."[65] The report disagreed, noting "there has been a considerable growth in database production in the US, whereas, in the EU, the introduction of 'sui generis' protection appears to have had the opposite effect. With respect to 'non-original' databases, the assumption that more and more layers of IP protection means more innovation and growth appears not to hold up."[66]

Based on the dismal performance of the directive in achieving its objectives, the logical approach would have been to repeal it. This was the first option discussed in the report, but it was quickly dismissed—not on empirical grounds, since the evidence supported repeal—but instead based on the false insistence of EU database producers that the right was necessary:

While [EU database producers'] endorsement of the "sui generis" rights is somewhat at odds with the continued success of
US publishing and database production that thrives without
the "sui generis" type protection, the attachment to the new
right is a political reality that seems very true for Europe.[67]

The database directive shows the danger of enacting legislation
that departs from economic reality: once enacted, even failures are
continued due to political pressure.[68] The most essential step in
having effective laws is effective lawmaking, where effective means
laws based on the actual business practices of and evidence about
the relevant industries *before legislation is passed.*

A MORATORIUM ON NEW LAWS AND A REVIEW OF EXISTING ONES

The long-standing failure of policymakers to base their decisions
on empirically rigorous evidence, and the need for a thorough
remaking of our copyright laws to match existing markets and
technologies, demonstrates the need for a moratorium on new
laws. Passing new laws that lack any basis in existing markets and
technologies will only make a bad situation worse. Leaving on the
books laws that are equal failures is equally terrible. We need a
fit-for-purpose review of old laws, hopefully coupled with a
start-from-scratch mentality. With that mentality, we would ask
ourselves, "if we could start from scratch, what should our copyright laws look like?" I doubt anyone in the world would answer,
"just like they do right now."

THREE

What Are Copyright Laws Supposed to Do?

Laws are effective only if they do what we want them to. What do we want copyright laws to do? The most popular things policymakers say copyright laws should do are (1) provide incentives for authors to create works they would not create in the absence of that incentive; (2) provide the public with access to those works; and (3) provide respect, via non-economic rights, for those who create cultural works. Sometimes policymakers throw in the kitchen sink. The European Union's 2001 Information Society directive states that copyright laws "foster substantial investment in creativity and innovation, including network infrastructure, and lead in turn to growth and increased competitiveness of European industry." To accomplish these ambitious goals, we are told there must be a "high level of protection, since such rights are crucial to intellectual creation."[1]

No definition of a "high"[2] level of rights is offered, no empirical evidence is offered in support of why such an undefined high level of rights is, in actual practice, crucial to intellectual creation, nor how such rights benefit authors, performers, producers, consumers, culture, industry, and the public at large all at once.

Due to our faith-based approach to legislating, it is impossible to effectively allocate rights and responsibilities among the broad swaths of society affected by copyright laws. To be able to effectively allocate rights and responsibilities, we need realistic premises and solid empirical data. The three popular justifications for copyright noted above are difficult to pull off individually, and even harder in combination: granting rights to one group of authors places them at odds with later authors who want to build on their predecessors' works to create new works; granting exclusive rights to copyright owners gives them the ability to protect their investment, but it also gives them the ability to charge monopoly prices and restrict access; granting authors the right to prevent uses for non-economic reasons protects reputational interests but also gives them the ability to suppress satirical works or uses that are socially beneficial but of which the author does not approve. One person's rights are the next person's barrier to creation and competition. You can't have effective laws unless these inherent problems are effectively dealt with.

That there are difficulties doesn't mean there is always failure. There *are* archetypal cases where the system works well, and we need copyright laws for these archetypal cases. But the archetypal cases are not the typical cases, and even if they were, laws necessary to cover the archetypal cases would look very different from the laws we have now: The length of copyright would be much shorter, there would be formalities such as a copyright notice and a requirement to register a claim to copyright with the government, plus, the scope of the right to stop derivative works—works based on the original—would be far more limited.

Beyond over-strong laws, there is a more fundamental problem: the unproven assertion that copyright is the basis for creativity.

COPYRIGHT IS NOT THE BASIS FOR CREATIVITY

The decision by legislators whether to grant new rights and at what level has never been the result of studying how the creative process actually works, or of studying the actual market conditions for authors and artists. There is a great deal of literature on these issues, none of which appears to have been consulted before the passage of copyright laws. That research reveals an unpleasant truth: the production of creative goods and services is not positively affected by the relative strength of copyright (as contrasted with a complete absence of protection).[3]

Beyond the need to understand how markets for creative works generally function, we must also understand how markets actually behave for *each type of work* we want to encourage the production of. To date, discussion of copyright and creativity has been mostly limited to meaningless macro numbers: the percentage that large media corporations (allegedly) contribute to the Gross Domestic Product (GDP). Although these figures are wholly unreliable, even if they were reliable, the market value of all goods and services produced within a country in a given period of time (which is what GDP is) tells us nothing about how to incentivize the production of particular goods and services. Nor do the aggregate figures for a large, diversified, multinational media company tell us anything about the incentives necessary for one of its divisions to produce a particular copyrighted work. Policies that may help create more novels will not work for sculpture; policies that may create more poetry will not work for video games. Creativity takes place at the micro level.

If we are serious about encouraging creativity, our policies must be reformulated for the micro level. Copyright laws currently ignore all of these important differences by imposing the same solution on everything. One size fits none.[4]

There is no substitute for the hard work of figuring out the complexities of creativity, including the very different markets for different types of works and the different cultural approaches taken around the world.[5] It is not enough to say the free market will figure it out so we don't have to.

Can Creativity Be Increased By Passing Laws?

Policymakers are told they can increase the production of creative works simply by passing new, stronger laws. This assertion is based on the unproven and implausible idea that there are people sitting around either doing nothing or doing something else, and that once a new, stronger law is passed, they will automatically switch to producing copyrighted works. Another version of this idea is that people are producing some works but if the laws were stronger, they would produce more. This too is silly: how could a law be strong enough to cause people to create some copyrighted works, but not others? Beneath all of these suppositions is the belief that creativity can be increased through external forces.

There is a long-standing debate about whether creativity can be externally influenced. This is the nature versus nurture debate.[6] Some people believe creativity can be learned, and that therefore the greater the expenditure on teaching children and others to be creative, the greater the supply of creative works. If this is the view you share (the "nurture" view), then the right approach is assuredly not more copyright laws, but rather increased funding in schools and other programs that can teach people to be creative.

Certainly, it is grotesquely hypocritical to be eliminating or severely cutting back school arts and music programs while making children sit through "Respect Copyright" fear propaganda written by motion picture and record companies but peddled as educational curriculum. If we truly value creativity as a society, we must put our money where our mouths are and fund those school programs in which children learn to be creative.

Some people believe that creativity is inborn, and can't be learned. They argue this is what separates the great from the rest of us, and greatness can't be taught; it just is. If this is your view (the "nature" view), then you can't increase the number of great authors and artists, but you can take steps to support and protect them once their talent flowers.[7] This is the romantic view of authors and artists, and it is not surprising that it is the most consistent with copyright laws, even if this view fails to admit that it is inherently contradictory to also believe copyright laws can increase creativity. Copyright laws can protect the fruits of that creativity, but they are not responsible for their existence.

There are clear examples of astounding young prodigies, and these instances support the nature theory, although even here prodigies need to be carefully nurtured: the sheer mechanics of producing art must be learned. There are examples of children who had some abilities but whose abilities were greatly increased through nurturing. There are also people who are talentless in particular areas and simply cannot acquire the necessary creative skills no matter how much they try. It is quite possible there is not one answer to how people are creative, and but rather a mix of answers. Policymakers, however, do not get into such fine points of human nature and instead simply declare that copyright laws are the reason people create, and therefore passing more copyright laws will lead to more works and will put more money in creators' pockets.

There is no basis for such declarations. Whether intentionally or not, this legalistic approach to the nature of creativity results in outsourcing our cultural heritage to the private sector.

Reliance on a marketplace controlled by a few gatekeepers backed by a government-created monopoly is a particularly poor choice for fostering cultural diversity and for aiding those who have little or no bargaining leverage.[8] As cultural economist Ruth Towse concluded, "what evidence there is, is consistent with the other data on artists' earnings—that the top superstars benefit considerably from royalty and remuneration income but the 'ordinary' artist does not."[9] This has been true since 1710, with the passage of the first modern national copyright act, the UK Statute of Anne. Technologies change, but economic laws do not.[10]

I shall now explore why copyright laws have principally helped superstars and distributors. The point of this inquiry is not to argue for the abolition of copyright—something I disfavor—but rather to help create an evidence-based approach to how our copyright laws can work better in practice. Our copyright laws are, and have always been, a winner-take-all system. If that is the desired policy, then our copyright laws are working fine. If, however, the policy is to create diverse works by diverse members of our society in order to create a rich cultural heritage, then it is important to realize copyright laws never have accomplished that purpose. Indeed, our current laws on steroids are impeding creativity. A different approach is needed.

WHY COPYRIGHT HAS ALWAYS BEEN A WINNER-TAKE-ALL SYSTEM

Most musicians, like most authors and artists, live in obscurity. According to Nielsen research, only 2.1 percent of the albums released in 2009 sold over 5,000 copies.[11] This doesn't stop an overabundance of those willing to make substantial sacrifices, as John Pareles noted in an article called "1,700 Bands, Rocking as the CD Industry Reels": "There's never a shortage of eager musicians. Many bands drive cross-country by van or cross an ocean to perform an unpaid showcase at South By Southwest, and the most determined ones play not only their one festival slot but also half a dozen peripheral parties as well, hoping to be noticed."[12]

Why would people do this? There are a few reasons: first, the thrill of performing in front of others and getting back the audience's appreciation. While this should never be discounted as an emotional reward, in economic terms, grinding road trips are a tough way to make a living for up-and-coming bands. As Mr. Pareles observed, the purpose of subjecting yourself to such hardships is to be noticed, and to be noticed among everyone else who is vying to be noticed too.

There has always been an overabundance of those who wish to make their livelihood from creative endeavors, relative to the opportunities to do so. As Robert Frank and Philip Cook wrote in their book *The Winner-Take-All Society*:

> Winner-take-all markets attract too many contestants in part because of a common human frailty with respect to gambling—namely our tendency to overestimate our chances of winning. Becoming a contestant in a winner-takes-all market entails a decision to pit one's own skills against a large field of adversaries. An intelligent decision obviously requires a well-informed estimate of the odds of winning. Yet people's assessments of these odds are notoriously inaccurate.[13]

We ignore the odds not only because the potential payout is so big but also because of the "optimism bias": the systematic tendency to overestimate the likelihood of positive outcomes and to downplay the likelihood of negative events, especially failure.[14] The market for creative works, like all markets, is structured to take advantage of this phenomenon. An oversupply of authors, artists, and performers eager to work for little or no money depresses the odds of making a steady, decent living, and also decreases the odds against any one person hitting it big. A winner-take-all approach to success funnels vast sums of money to a few, leaving little left for the many. If a seventeen-year-old like Justin Bieber can make $53 million in one year—as he just did—that's $53 million in consumer spending that is not going to other artists. This has been the case for centuries, and can't be changed—you can't tell tweenies they have to spend money on a celebrity they don't like. The point is to understand how the market works so that if the market doesn't fulfill all our policy goals, we can then find alternate ways to do so.

Gatekeepers and Limiting Production

Oversupply leads to gatekeepers. Sometimes gatekeepers perform a valuable function by weeding out lower quality works in favor of "the best." As we shall see, though, the best need not correlate to the best quality: A gatekeeper's objective is to find the works that have the best chance of being *commercially* successful. Commercial success can just as easily be the result of clever marketing as it can be the result of the most talented making their way to the top. Moreover, contrary to a foundational belief that copyright protection leads to the production of many works, gatekeepers negate this possibility by publishing[15] fewer works by fewer authors. By permitting fewer works into the market and by controlling the distribution channels to the market, gatekeepers minimize competition and create artificial scarcity in order to drive up demand for those works they do publish, thereby permitting them to charge monopoly prices. The combination of the gatekeeper role and the enforcement mechanisms provided by copyright laws make it possible to avoid the common economic fate of falling prices that occurs when competitors enter the same market.

The theoretical belief that copyright laws lead to more works by more authors is thus at odds with how the market works in the real world. Some examples from the early days of our copyright laws follow. Although I begin with the eighteenth-century England book industry, I do so not out of antiquarianism, but because the same dynamics at play then are found today in global markets: In place of a small number of London booksellers trying to control a luxury market of book sales, we have a small number of multinational corporations attempting to control the lucrative major markets. In place of renegade Scottish and Irish book publishers we have local producers and distributors in developing countries, as well as global peer-to-peer (P2P) networks.

THE EARLY ENGLISH EXPERIENCE

While some have misdescribed the 1710 English Statute of Anne as landmark legislation favoring authors over booksellers because the right vested initially in authors rather than in booksellers,[16] the facts on the ground were that authors benefitted no more after the Statute of Anne than they had before it was enacted. Dr. Isabella Alexander has written:

> Authors always had at least the right to consent to publication by virtue of their physical possession of the manuscript.
>
> Practically speaking, the right to print was of little use to authors, unless they happened to own a printing press and have access to a distribution network.[17]

After the Statute of Anne, as before, the only purchasers of authors' works were a small group of London booksellers. The language of the title of the act hints at this: "An Act for the Encouragement of Learning, by Vesting the Copies of Printed Books in the Authors *or Purchasers* of such copies, during the Times therein mentioned."[18] The "learning" in the title was not the general learning of society as a whole (as is commonly but mistakenly believed), but rather, only of the wealthy members of society, due to the pricing of books, pricing made possible by copyright laws. Even aside from pricing, the literacy rate in England was low;[19] there was no mass market for books, much less cheap books. There were no public libraries. Bookselling instead served a luxury market,[20] deliberately limited to the upper classes, from which legislators and many booksellers were drawn (five members of the Stationers Company, the book industry's association, served as Lord Mayor of London). William St Clair, in his deep study of the book industry and of reading in the relevant period observed:

> The high monopoly period regime not only suited the producer interest of the book industry: a powerful political constituency in England liked the results on reading and mentalities. Among the main arguments put forward in the parliamentary bill that introduced a stamp duty on periodicals in 1701 was that the resulting higher prices would keep such print from the "poorer sort of people," and so reduce the allure and enticement of reading among their children. In 1757, Soame Jenyns argued that to "encourage the poor man to read and think, and thus to become more conscious of his misery, would fly in the face of divine intention."[21]

Copyright, through the control it gave publishers over supply and the pricing of books, played a critical role in severely limiting the type of works made available to the middle and poor classes: "Comparatively high prices encouraged the rationing of supply to the market, and there is clear evidence of booksellers in the mid-eighteenth century keeping prices high and abandoning lower price tranches."[22] A printer, testifying before the House of Commons in 1818 stated forthrightly, "books are a luxury, and the purchase of them has been confined to fewer people."[23] This remained the case 60 years later, in the 1878 Report of the Select Committee on Copyright's Report to Parliament, where Sir Louis Mallet observed, "It may indeed be said that new books are a luxury, the possession of which is confined to the wealthy class, and that they are placed by price altogether beyond the reach of the great bulk of the people."[24] Reading the lofty goals of the Statute of Anne from the vantage point of 300 years later leads one to entirely miss the reality of copyright on the ground.

The grip that copyright exerted over what was read by whom was loosened for a period of time beginning in 1774, when the House of Lords, in *Donaldson v. Beckett*, rejected book publishers' claims of perpetual copyright. (One year before, Scottish judges reached the same conclusion in a dispute over the same work and the same defendant, with Lord Kames writing: "I have no difficulty to maintain that a perpetual monopoly of books would prove more destructive to learning, and even to authors, than a second irruption of Goths and Vandals.")[25]

As a result of the rejection of booksellers' claims, "a huge, previously suppressed, demand for reading was met by a huge surge in the supply of books, and was soon caught up in a virtuous circle of growth."[26] The new, powerful demand not only lowered dramatically the cost of classic texts—reestablishing the link between manufacturing costs and profit margins—but it also led to the invention and spread of new technological ways of printing, paper production, and binding, resulting in considerable economic and cultural changes.[27] There was a sharp increase in output in the quarter century following the House of Lords' decision, including children's books.[28]

Even with the understanding that, as in any industry, consumption patterns are multi-faceted, data compiled by the English Short Title Catalogue[29] make a compelling case that passage of the 1710 Statute of Anne led to a *decrease* in the number of works available. That decline began to turn around only at the end of the 1740s, due to the advent of the first generation of commercial circulating libraries, and the wider use of new, innovative forms of printing. The most dramatic increase in publishing came in the two decades following the House of Lords' decision in *Donaldson v. Beckett*. Rejection of perpetual copyright led to an almost 54 percent increase in first editions alone, as seen below:

Number of First Editions since 1700

Year	Number of First Editions
1700	3,407
1710	3,649
1720	3,016
1730	2,816
1740	2,962
1750	4,454
1760	4,677
1770	5,052
1780	6,152
1790	9,196[30]

Source: Adapted from James Raven, *The Business of Books: Bookseller and the English Book Trade.*

People of all classes were reading after the House of Lords' *Donaldson* decision:[31] Daniel Defoe's *Robinson Crusoe*, which had been published in 1719 and therefore should have gone into the public domain in 1747, but didn't authoritatively until the 1774 decision, sold more copies in the five-year period from 1774 to 1779 than it had in the entire period before the decision.[32]

THE MYTH OF THE SOLITARY GENIUS AND THE SUPERSTAR SYSTEM

Publishing fewer rather than more authors implicates another foundational element of copyright: the myth of the solitary genius: a solitary romantic figure whose creativity burns in his or her soul. Copyright is believed by some, especially in Europe, to be a form of respect for authors, a recognition of authors' romantic genius. While this view has led to grants of non-economic rights (*droit moral*) designed to protect the author's honor and reputation,[33] in practice the greatest application of the myth of the solitary genius is in supporting the economic superstar system. Superstars are not just stars, they are the top of the top, the most unique of the unique, self-made geniuses.[34] We idolize them, carefully follow their personal lives, and most importantly, we give them our money—not directly, because they are beyond our personal reach—but to the marketers who have helped create them as superstars. Yet, despite their personification of the romantic genius that has supplied much of the ideology of copyright for the last 200 years, superstars are merely commodities, to be consumed by us, and to be eventually discarded for the next superstar in a cycle of endless consumer purchases.

Copyright is the legal protection for the superstar commodity, much like trademark law is the legal protection for the commodities we purchase on grocery shelves. But unlike grocery commodities, where money is made from mass reproduction and sale of the same object, superstar commodities make money through scarcity. Gatekeepers ensure that only a few become superstars and copyright ensures that such artificial scarcity is legally enforceable. The myth of the solitary genius provides philosophical cover for the superstar system, a convenient way to justify a decidedly commercial enterprise. Contrary to the belief that copyright laws lead to a diversity of offerings, the myth of the solitary genius and the superstar system support a choking off of diversity in favor of the winner-take-all approach that leaves the few with almost everything and the many with little. There is, of course, no shortage of individuals who are quite eager to be commoditized in this way because it promises them fame and fortune. Justin Bieber is just a product, and very happily so.

The ability of distributors to charge monopoly prices for superstars was a phenomenon noted by Adam Smith way back in 1776:

> The exorbitant rewards of players, opera-singers, opera-dancers, &c are founded upon those two principles; the rarity and beauty of the talent, and the discredit of employing them in this manner.[35]

Whether the talent displayed by superstars is in fact rare is questionable (especially in the area of popular culture), but the purpose of *proclaiming* a superstar's talent to be rare is easy enough to understand. It is a zero sum game, where the more people vie for the top, the fewer make it, but the rewards are disproportionately greater.[36] Since rare talent must, by definition, be uncommon, there can only be a few who succeed. Those who succeed take it all: superstars get all the product endorsements, the clothing and perfume lines, the magazine covers, the television appearances, and most of our money.

The winner-take-all market dominated by superstars also plays out in the argument that superstars need protection from those imitators who would, by copying from them, try to pull themselves up by pulling the lone geniuses down. If we permit others to copy from lone geniuses, the argument goes that we will have fewer of them. We therefore need the strongest copyright laws possible in order to provide the strongest protection for our superstars. Moreover, we need distributors to own the copyright in superstars' works because it is distributors who know the markets and marketing, and know how to effectively make money for the superstars.

The myth of the Lone Genius is a distributors' myth that some artists buy into, but it ill-serves copyright and the majority of artists.[37] Creativity is furthered not by limiting success to a few superstars, but by opening up audiences and the channels of distribution to the many. Culture is the result of sharing creative experiences, not walling creativity off as the province of only a select few. The hostility of gatekeepers to platforms like YouTube stems not from the existence of some unauthorized content on them, but rather from such platforms' direct challenge to the superstar system. Creativity by the Great Unwashed[38] is said not to be creativity at all, and if permitted, the large corporations who manufacture superstars argue, such platforms will crowd out quality works—that is superstars' products. Superstars themselves come to believe in the marketing hype. In a statement that defines irony, the Walt Disney–created product Miley Cyrus dismissed thirteen-year-old songwriter and performer Rebecca Black (whose song "Friday" achieved a worldwide audience thanks to YouTube) by claiming, "It should be harder to be an artist. You shouldn't just be able to put a song on YouTube and go out on tour."[39]

This posture against creativity by the many shows how the "marketplace is egalitarian" argument is false. The marketplace for copyrighted products is one of deliberate scarcity, in which our place is as passive consumers, not as creators. We are supposed to show our respect for the lonely geniuses by consuming their products, and by recognizing that their genius requires us not to create and certainly not to copy from them, since we cannot be like them. Creativity is served, however, not by prohibiting copying, but by encouraging it: as often as possible, by as many as possible. The myth of the Lone Genius drives a stake through the heart of the central, *actual* requirement for creativity to flourish: the ability to copy. If policymakers truly want to increase creativity, then they must greatly liberalize the ability of one person to transformatively copy from another.[40]

CREATIVITY IS BASED ON COPYING

If we genuinely want to encourage creativity, we must encourage copying. This approach is consistent with copyright's history, although one would never know this from current perceptions. Current conceptions are the result of media corporations' efforts to recast the limited privilege of copyright as real property, and to thereby equate all copying with theft. These efforts have been remarkably successful and demonstrate the power of ideas, especially bad ones. John Maynard Keynes observed that ideas, both correct and incorrect, "are more powerful than is commonly understood. Indeed, the world is ruled by little else."[41] The idea that copying equals a lack of creativity is powerfully harmful and ahistorical.

The right to prevent unauthorized copying was, for the first three hundred years of our copyright laws, determined not by property rules, but by reference to whether the defendant's work added new insights, whether it too was a creative work.[42] Verbatim copying, mere paraphrasing, or a qualitative copying of the heart of the work were prohibited since such copying did not provide new insights or evidence any creativity,[43] but instead acted as a substitute for the original. Outside of substitutional copying, though, there was considerable leeway for unauthorized copying by subsequent authors. In the 1803 English case of *Cary v. Kearsley*,[44] Lord Ellenborough nicely summed up the policy:"That part of the work of one author is found in another, is not of itself piracy, or sufficient to support an action; a man may fairly adopt part of the work of another: he may so make use of another's labours for the promotion of science, and the benefit of the public... [W]hile I shall think myself bound to secure every man in the enjoyment of his copyright, one must not put manacles on science." Science here referred to the eighteenth-century conception of knowledge.

There can be no question that literature, music, and the arts flourished under this policy, and for good reason: All works exist only in context with past and present authors and culture: readers can only understand contextually; that is, within shared communal understandings. This is what Hans-Georg Gadamer meant when he wrote:"Understanding is to be thought of less as a subjective act than as participating in an event of tradition, a process of transmission in which past and present are constantly mediated."[45] This is equally true of authors, as T.S. Eliot wrote in his essay "Tradition and the Individual Talent":"The historical sense compels a man to write not merely with his own generation in his bones, but with a feeling that the whole of literature from Homer and within it the whole of the literature of his own country has a simultaneous existence and composes a simultaneous order."[46] Even those who purport to rebel against tradition do so in relation to that tradition. The late Canadian pianist Glenn Gould— who upset many traditions of his own in the classical world—made this point in discussing the music of Arnold Schoenberg, "whenever one honestly defies a tradition, one becomes, in reality, the more responsible to it."[47] Creativity requires the breathing space necessary to permit all authors to draw on the whole of culture.

Regrettably, we have undergone a sea change in the policy that worked so well since the inception of copyright law, a change that works against the very nature of the creative process as it has existed since the "Time whereof the Memory of Man runneth not to the contrary."[48] The current trend toward finding even minimal uses to be infringement is based on a very different approach than that which formed the basis of copyright. Instead of a policy of encouraging new works, we are fast adopting a property-based theory of ownership—"it's mine, every bit of it."

An example of this is the way hip-hop music changed after a series of court opinions finding infringement for the creative copying and alteration of tiny amounts from recorded performances. The most important of these opinions is from the United States Court of Appeals for the Sixth Circuit.[49] The case arose out of the unauthorized use of a very short sample from a sound recording of "Get Off Your Ass and Jam" by the immortal George Clinton and the Funkadelics. The use first occurred in the rap song "100 Miles and Runnin," the second in the sound track of the movie *I Got the Hook Up*. The use consisted of a two-second sample of an arpeggiated guitar chord copied from "Get Off." The defendant lowered the pitch and then looped the sample to last sixteen beats. The sample was used in five places in the movie, with each looped segment lasting approximately seven seconds. In light of the *de minimis*, transformative copying, the district court observed, without apparent denial by the defendants, that "even one familiar with the works of George Clinton would [not] recognize the source of the sample without having been told of its source."[50] The district court correctly found no infringement.

The court of appeals reversed in an opinion that is a compendium of almost every error that can be made in construing the U.S. Copyright Act, beginning with adopting a different approach to infringement of a musical composition than for infringement of the recorded performance of it (called the "sound recording"). For musical compositions, the court acknowledged there is no infringement from *de minimis* copying. For sound recordings, however, the court held there is no *de minimis* threshold; the copying of any amount is infringing.[51]

The result of this terrible decision has been an unwillingness of record companies to put out albums[52] unless each and every sample is cleared. Producers of records must certify that all samples have been licensed when delivering the masters. Since previous hip-hop albums used hundreds (and sometimes thousands) of samples, licensing that number of samples is out of the question due to financial and transactional cost reasons. As a result, the creative process of hip-hop has changed.[53] Here is an explanation by Public Enemy's Chuck D and Hank Shocklee in interviews with *Stay Free! Magazine*:

> *Stay Free!*: When you were sampling from many different sources during the making of "It Takes a Nation," were you at all worried about copyright clearance?
>
> *Shocklee*: No. Nobody did. At the time, it wasn't even an issue. The only time copyright was an issue was if you actually took the entire rhythm of a song,....But we were taking a horn hit here, a guitar riff there, we might take a little speech, a kicking snare from somewhere else. It was all bits and pieces.
>
> ...
>
> By 1990, all the publishers and their lawyers started making moves. One big one was Bridgeport, the publishing house that owns all the George Clinton stuff....
>
> *Stay Free!*: There's a noticeable difference in Public Enemy's sound between 1988 and 1991. Did this have to do

with the lawsuits and enforcement of copyright laws at the turn of the decade?

Chuck D: Public Enemy's music was affected more than anybody's because we were taking thousands of sounds. If you separated the sounds, they wouldn't have been any-thing—they were unrecognizable. The sounds were all col-laged together to make a sonic wall. Public Enemy was affected because it is too expensive to defend against a claim. So we had to change our whole style, the style of "It Takes a Nation" and "Fear of a Black Planet," by 1991.[54]

The issues with sampling are endemic of a fundamental transfor-mation that has overtaken copyright. Once a tool for creativity, copyright law has been infested with a permission mentality in which all uses, no matter how trivial or remote from impacting on artists' wallets, are declared licensable and therefore must be li-censed. Culture, however, can be built only out of a shared ap-proach to knowledge, including a generous use of each others' creations. Culture is behavior, creatively duplicated.[55]

Here are some examples of the importance of copying (whether of copyrighted works or not). Children and adults who wish to learn how to play a musical instrument *must* do so by listening to the sounds their teachers make and then trying to replicate those sounds as closely as possible. Many times you play the same pas-sage in unison so that you can keep your teacher's sound stored in your brain along with yours. Tricky rhythms can only be learned by listening to others and by copying their playing. For most mu-sicians, this process of copying continues throughout their lives, as you seek out new sounds you want to copy.

People pay a great deal of money for instruments[56] (and in the case of clarinet players like myself, mouthpieces as well) owned by famous performers, in the hope that if we play on them, we too will sound like our mentors, although we always end up sounding like ourselves. We do it anyway because it is the process of copying from others that allows us to gain the skills to find our own voice. I am very fortunate to own a (thoroughly restored) set of early Buffet R-13 clarinets and three Kaspar mouthpieces that Robert Marcellus, the principal clarinetist with the Cleveland Orchestra from 1953 to 1973,[57] previously owned and played on. Marcellus's sublime 1961 recording of the Mozart Clarinet Concerto with George Szell conducting has long been an icon for classical clarinetists, who seek to replicate Marcellus's expressiveness. Here is a comment by one person about how important it was for him to copy Marcellus's sound:

> I was 12 years old. I hadn't formed any opinion of Mozart, and had never heard of Robert Marcellus. But when I heard that recording for the first time, I knew I wanted to be the one playing that piece someday. His tone was what hooked me. Marcellus had a haunting clarity, a round, dark ring to every note. I couldn't get that sound out of my ear, and I still strive for it.[58]

To deny people the ability to copy—whether from a book, a recorded performance (as in the Marcellus example), or from any source—is to deny them their dream of becoming who they want to be. This applies to groups of people, not just to individuals: European jazz exists only because European musicians have been able to copy American jazz musicians. The British rock groups of the late 1960s to early 1970s were successful because they copied from American blues artists and Elvis Presley.[59] A 1971 note from John Lennon to *New York Times* reporter Craig McGregor explains why. McGregor had written a piece called "The Beatles Betrayal," accusing the group of "ripping off" black artists. Lennon responded: " 'Money', 'Twist 'n' Shout', 'You really got a hold on me' etc, were all numbers we (the Beatles) used to sing in the dancehalls around Britain, mainly Liverpool. It was only natural that we tried to do it as near to the record as we could—I always wished we could have done them even closer to the original. We didn't sing our own songs in the early days—they weren't good enough." This is the way it works for all creators: you absorb the sounds of those you love until you are able to find your own voice. Lennon was admirably candid in admitting the Beatles didn't sing their own songs yet, because they weren't good enough. Lennon also made the direct connection between copying and love for those you copy: "People like—Eric Burdon's Animals—Mick's Stones—and us drank ate and slept the music, and also recorded it, many kids were turned on to black music by us. It wasn't a rip off, it was a love in."[60] Keith Richards, guitarist for the Rolling Stones, agreed: "Our thing was playing Chicago blues; that was where we took everything that we knew."[61] (Muddy Waters recorded a song with white guitarist Johnny Winter called "The Blues Had a Baby and They Named It Rock and Roll.") Elvis's music would not have been possible had he not copied from blues singers like Big Joe Turner, including covering recordings of Turner's like "Shake Rattle and Roll," "Corrine Corrina," and "Sixteen Candles." Blues artists freely copied from each other.[62] That copying went well beyond unprotectable elements like style and included remakes of others' songs under different names.

It has been a tradition for hundreds of years for aspiring painters to go to museums and faithfully copy works hanging there. Henri Rousseau (1844–1910), who painted magical works such as "The Hungry Lion Throws Itself on the Antelope," "The Dream," and "The Sleeping Gypsy" was self-trained and learned much of his technique from camping out at the Louvre and copying from the works on exhibit. Poets, choreographers, and novelists find their voice only after a long period of imitation. This is why Northrop Frey wrote: "Poetry can only be made out of other poems; novels out of other novels."[63] George Orwell confirmed this in "Why I Write," by stating that his first poem was, as he put it, a plagiarism of Blake's "Tiger, Tiger," and that he then moved on to imitating Aristophanes.[64] Creating your own poems and novels only occurs after you have thoroughly assimilated others and have created your voice out of theirs. James Joyce's *Ulysses* is closely patterned after Homer's *The Odyssey*, yet at the same time it was so closely of its own time that it has been said to be a "demonstration and summation of the entire [Modernist Literature] movement."[65]

Here is world-famous clarinetist Buddy DeFranco, who has been playing for over seventy years, giving advice on "How to Develop Your Own Voice on Clarinet":"[I] recommend[] repeated listening to recordings, transcribing the solos of these players, and playing along with the solos....[You] should begin to develop patterns and phrases based on these players' styles....[You] should strive to internalize aspects of the masters' styles and incorporate [them] into [your] own playing."[66]

Ray Charles, described how he set out deliberately to copy Nat King Cole:

I knew...that Nat King Cole was bigger than ever....Funny thing, but during all those years I was imitating Nat Cole, I never thought about it, never felt bad about copying the cat's licks. To me it was practically a science. I worked at it. I enjoyed it. I was proud of it, and I loved doing it.

Mr. Charles later decided to move to a different style, but even here he copied from gospel music: His famous 1954 composition "I Got a Woman," was unabashedly copied from the 1904 hymn "My Jesus Is All the World to Me" written by a white composer from East Liverpool, Ohio, William Lamartine Thompson.[67] Ray Charles regularly copied (without permission) from other hymn composers:"This Little Girl of Mine," was taken from Clara Ward's "This Little Light of Mine," much to her annoyance.[68] Martin Luther King, Jr.'s constant copying from multiple sources for his speeches, including in his "I Had a Dream" speech, is well-documented;[69] far from being regarded as immoral, King's copying was accepted as an effective way to bring the audience into a communal, historical dialogue.

The process of copying and imitation, although often deliberate is, at least from a young age, also often unconscious, and is why musical historian Richard Taruskin wrote in his essay, *The Limits of Authenticity* "a performer schooled in the mainstream (any mainstream) receives his basic training before he has reached the age of consent[;] ...his musical responses and tastes will have been formed at a preconscious level—will be vested, so to speak, in his spinal column."[70] Here is a real life example of that process, taken from rap artist Jay-Z's book *Decoded*:

> When I was a kid, my parents had, like a million records stacked to the ceiling in metal milk crates....If it was hot in the seventies my parents had it....I remember those early days as the time that shaped my musical vocabulary. I remember the music making me feel good, bringing my family together, and more importantly, being a common passion my parents shared. That music from my childhood still lives in my music. From my very first album, lots of the tracks I rapped were built on a foundation of classic seventies soul.[71]

To deny people the right to copy, intimately, from others, is to deny the essence of what it is to be a creative person. George Orwell put this point even more strongly, "if [a writer] escapes from his early influences all together, he will have killed his impulse to write." Orwell is making the point that we all carry our earlier selves with us: those selves include imitating others.

The most damaging consequence of the movement to turn culture into private property is the largely successful change in attitude toward creativity and copying. Creative people are supposedly those who do not copy or imitate others. As we just saw, this is false; creative people must copy and must imitate others. Treating transformative copying as theft, as laziness, or as being non-creative is counter to human nature. All learning is social; copying is an essential form of social learning. Our copyright laws must be changed to reflect this fact.

Copying, Mash-Ups, and the Derivative Right

For much of history, and long before appropriation art became a vogue,[72] authors and artists had either no control, or at best, very limited control over other authors' or artists' use of their works.[73] Such unauthorized copying was not usually done by the talentless; quite the opposite. One of the most famous Renaissance composers, Giovanni Pierluigi da Palestrina, wrote fifty-three parody masses, of which thirty-one were based on music by other composers. Josquin de Prez's *Missa Malheur Me Bat*, *Missa Mater Patris*, and *Missa Fortuna Desperata* are further examples of masses based on others' music, as is Antoine Brumels' *Missa de Dringhs*. It has been estimated that by the middle of the sixteenth century, most masses were parody masses. Parody masses did not make fun of the original,[74] but were instead designed to show respect for and appreciation of the original music while simultaneously showing off the second composer's own skills. The use of the first composer's work was not use of a mere single line or two, but rather involved copying of "an entire texture...."[75]

There were also paraphrase masses,[76] in which the original music appeared in many voices of the second composer's mass. Several of Josquin's masses feature the paraphrase technique, including one of the most famous mass settings of the entire era, the *Missa Pange Lingua*, which was based on the hymn by Thomas Aquinas for the vespers of Corpus Christi. The mass uses Aquinas's theme in all voices and in all parts of the mass.[77] The great Renaissance composers could have written few of their masterpieces under our current copyright laws. In the Baroque, Classical, and Romantic eras, composers freely composed variations on each other's works, without requesting permission and without payment, since neither were expected. Think of the scene in the movie *Amadeus*, when Mozart first meets Salieri and informs him that he had composed piano variations on the theme of Salieri's aria "Mio caro adone."[78] Salieri is surprised, but not because Mozart had done so without asking permission or without paying him. Johannes Brahms freely copied the theme of the finale of Beethoven's Ninth Symphony in the finale of his own First Symphony, so blatantly that when a critic pointed this out, Brahms rejoined that "jeder Esel" (any ass) could hear the similarities.[79]

The modern form of the Renaissance parody and paraphrase masses is the mash-up,[80] or if one prefers a fancier name, pastiche: highly creative compositions that take pieces from other works and combine and transform them to result in a new work that gives us fresh insights.[81] Mash-ups take many forms: literary, graphic, cinematic, and musical works, and even maps, as in Google Maps, which permits people to layer other works on top of Google's maps. Permitting people to create such overlays permits an explosion of useful information that would never be possible if Google insisted on controlling all uses. The "Google Maps Mania" blog (not affiliated with Google)[82] has a world map showing where all the mash-ups are, and dividing them into categories like

Art, Crime, Fun & Games, History, News, Real Estate, Real-Time, Tourism, Traffic, Weather, and Wining & Dining. You can find instant mash-ups of things like the March 11, 2011, Japanese earthquake, traffic jams, crime in a neighborhood you are thinking moving into, and almost any subject that might interest someone in the world.

A good example of an audiovisual mash-up is Israeli musician/producer Ophir Kutiel, performing as Kutiman.[83] For his audiovisual composition "The Mother of All Funk Chords," Kutiman took hundreds of clips from YouTube and spent three months splicing samples of singers and various instruments, as well as a cash register. He then made seven tracks in various genres, including R&B, Funk, Reggae, and Jazz. His work was a worldwide sensation and demonstrated tremendous originality.[84] Gregg Gillis, performing as Girl Talk,[85] has also made new compositions from samples of others' works. The laptop computer is his musical instrument. An infamous example, due to EMI's efforts to ban its distribution, is Danger Mouse's *Grey Album*,[86] which sampled from The Beatles' *White Album* and from an a cappella version of Jay-Z's *Black Album*. As Danger Mouse (a/k/a Brian Burton) explained:

> A lot of people just assume I took some Beatles and, you know, threw some Jay-Z on top of it or mixed it up or looped it around, but it's really a deconstruction. It's not an easy thing to do. I was obsessed with the whole project, that's all I was trying to do, see if I could do this. Once I got into it, I didn't think about anything but finishing it. I stuck to those two because I thought it would be more challenging and more fun and more of a statement to what you could do with sample alone. It is an art form. It is music.

Jay-Z, whose album was used in making the *Grey Album*, had a response consistent with those who create, rather than with corporations that merely buy rights from creators. He was interviewed by Terry Gross on National Public Radio's "Fresh Air" program:

> TERRY GROSS: I've got to ask you how you feel about the Grey Album, which is the mash-up that Danger Mouse did of your Black Album and the Beatles' White Album, without any copyright permission. So, how do you feel about it musically and how do you feel about the fact that he did it?
>
> JAY-Z: I think it was a really strong album. I champion any form of creativity and that was a genius idea to do it, and it sparked so many others like it...
>
> TERRY GROSS: Did you feel ripped off by the fact that he used your music on it without paying for it? Or did you think it doesn't matter, it's really good art.
>
> JAY-Z: No, I was actually honored that, you know, someone took the time to mash those records up with Beatles records. I was honored to be on, you know, quote-unquote the same song with the Beatles.[87]

Performer RZA from the group Wu-Tang Clan put the creative process involved in sampling this way: "I've always been into using the sampler more like a painter's palette than a Xerox."[88] Saying you want to protect authors but ignoring the way authors now create doesn't make sense.[89] We do performers, composers, and authors no favor if we cut them off from the very culture that gives rise to their creativity: "viewing humans as existing within a context does not diminish the individual but adds richness to the picture and makes experience not less unique, but more human."[90]

The type of works discussed in this section, plus many others, such as James Joyce's *Ulysses*, are called in copyright law derivative works, works that are based on other works; e.g., translations, musical arrangements, motion picture versions of novels, and three-dimensional versions of two-dimensional works.[91] As Judge Posner and Professor Landes wrote with considerable understatement: "The case for giving the owner of a copyrighted work control over derivative works is a subtle one. It is not, as one might think, to enable the creator to recoup his cost of expression. By definition, a derivative work is an imperfect substitute; often it is no substitute at all."[92] Yet, the increase in derivative rights represents the biggest expansion of rights in the last century,[93] and the most harmful because it suppresses works that tend to be the most creative and the most culturally significant. In Anglo-American copyright, a general derivative right did not exist until 1909 (United States) and 1911 (United Kingdom). Previously, courts had taken a case-by-case approach, examining whether the derivative work provided new creativity and insights, or, by contrast, whether it was a mere substitution for the original, copyrighted work.[94] This was a much sounder approach, and is one we need to return to.[95]

One anomaly of the vast expansion of rights is that they are disproportionate to copyright owner's actual use of them, a topic I now explore.

HISTORY SHOWS COPYRIGHT PROTECTION HAS BEEN RELATIVELY UNIMPORTANT FOR MOST AUTHORS

Even under our current system of automatic, formality-free copyright,[96] the vast majority of creators have no use for copyright. This has always been the case. Prior regimes in the United States, which required compliance with formalities such as affixing a notice or registration in order to either obtain or maintain copyright, provide empirical evidence of the relatively minor importance of copyright protection to many creators. In the legislative committee reports to the 1909 Copyright Act, Congress examined the effectiveness of the copyright laws passed in the 1800s. Those laws required an initial registration with the government and then a second application to be filed after the first twenty-eight-year term of protection in order to enjoy another, fourteen-year renewal term of protection (called the "renewal term"). In other words, unless you filed the renewal application, your work went into the public domain after twenty-eight years. Filing the application was cheap and easy.

In examining how many copyright owners availed themselves of this easy ability to get another twenty-eight years of protection, Congress noted that only "a very small percentage of the copyrights are ever renewed."[97] Why? Not because of the difficulty of renewing, but rather because Congress found that the economic value "ceases in most cases long before the expiration of the [first] twenty-eight years."[98] The percentage of copyright owners who bothered to file for renewal under the governing acts in the 1880s was a mere 15 percent.[99] Keep in mind that this is not 15 percent of all works, since the majority were never registered in the first place and therefore could not be renewed. Copyright was of value to the owners of less than 5 percent of all works that could have received protection. If copyright is such a necessary incentive, why did more than 95 percent of those who could have obtained protection never bother to get it?

We can also see proof of the limited importance of copyright to creators in other government records. Records assembled by the Library of Congress and private researchers indicate that more than 21,000 books were published in the United States between

1790 and 1800, but only 648 copyright registrations were made in this same period,[100] resulting in a registration rate of 3.28 percent at a time when registration was mandatory to get protection in the first place. Of this paltry 3.28 percent, an unknown percentage was renewed, but based on other data, the number renewed of those published must have been tiny, less than 1 percent. The lack of interest of most authors and publishers in copyright led Congress to reject, in the 1909 Act, a proposal that would have granted a term of life of the author plus thirty years.[101] Such a term would have extended copyright well beyond what copyright owners had themselves shown they needed by their failure to renew after the first, twenty-eight-year grant.

Nor did the picture change appreciably in the intervening 100 years. In a survey of renewal rates from 1910 to 2001, Judge Richard Posner and Professor William Landes found a range of renewals from 3 percent in 1913 to 22 percent.[102] Project Gutenberg, a nonprofit organization that makes public domain works available to the public for free (and which thus must be quite sure about the public domain status of works on pain of being sued), has estimated that only 10 percent of works published between 1923 and 1963 were renewed.[103] In 1960, the Copyright Office did a study of renewals in 1958 through 1959, and found an average rate of 15 percent, the exact rate that Congress had found in 1907—as shown on page 106.[104]

These data are not "old" in the sense of not being relevant; to the contrary, the data are remarkably consistent for over a century, and demonstrate, under actual business conditions, that for the vast majority of copyright owners, twenty-eight years is a sufficient period of protection. That remains true today.

Aside from registration records, one can also look to other indicia demonstrating that a very long term of protection and extensive rights imposes enormous costs on the public by keep-

Copyright Renewal Rates 1958–1959

Type of Work	Renewal Percentage
Books	7%
Periodicals	11%
Lectures, Sermons and other oral works	0.4%
Dramatic Works	11%
Music	35%
Maps	48%
Works of Art	4%
Technical Drawings	0.4%
Art Prints	4%
Movies	74%

ing works unavailable for use that copyright owners have no interest in exploiting. Jason Schultz did a study of 10,027 books published in the United States in 1930 and therefore still under copyright until 2025.[105] The study showed only 174 books, or 1.7 percent, are still in print. A study in 1998 by the Congressional Research Service showed a 1 percent renewal rate among books first published between 1923 and 1932 with only 11.9 percent of that 1 percent being in print as of that year.[106] The tiny number of books still in print does not mean the public is free to use such works: To the contrary, the threat of infringement suits renders use of them economically unfeasible.

The reason most publishers and other creators either did not use copyright at all or used it only for a limited time is that the economic value of most works is short-lived: the money is made soon after publication or not at all. Granting a term of copyright longer than the market value cannot change that value. A work that people don't want to buy after fifteen years is not valuable in year sixteen because it still is under copyright.

The fact that copyright is valuable for only a few[107] doesn't mean we should abandon copyright. But the fact that copyright has been of limited utility for most people does mean we cannot have wildly expansive laws that benefit the few at the expense of the many.

Trickle-down Copyright Economics: Where Is the Money Going?

The strained correlation of copyright to creativity and culture is mostly made by corporations that purchase copyrights from the actual creators. Such corporations want the warm feelings we have toward the actual creators to be transferred to them, and they therefore portray themselves as "standing up for artists." But, as in Rostand's *Cyrano de Bergerac*, authors are merely the beard for a different interest, an interest in commodities not creativity.

It is an old tactic: Edward Thurlow, then Attorney General and later Lord Chancellor,[108] stated in his argument before the British House of Lords in the 1774 case of *Donaldson v. Beckett* that booksellers had introduced authors into the equation "to give a colorable Face to their Monopoly."[109] One hundred and twenty-nine years after *Donaldson v. Beckett*, things had not changed. In a memorandum to a committee of the House of Commons examining unauthorized copying of musical compositions, MP James Caldwell wrote that publishers, who had been spending large sums of money lobbying the government for new rights, "have been putting in the forefront the interests of the Composers of Music, thereby attempting to arouse sympathy in favour of the Bill—a proceeding somewhat analogous to that of putting a row of women and children in front of a line of soldiers."[110] The same tactic is used today at legislative hearings and press conferences on extending copyright.

The second step is to treat individual creators' contributions as if they were industry contributions. Individuals who create and then sell their copyrights to companies are creative. Companies that buy the copyrights and then sell commodities embodying someone else's creativity hopefully provide essential marketing skills and a revenue stream, but they are not engaging in creative activity themselves.[111] Not everything that goes on in a media company can fairly be characterized as reliant on copyright. The largest purchasers and sellers of copyrighted works are large, vertically integrated multinational companies that generate revenue from thousands of sources, many of which have nothing to do with copyrighted works, including trading in monetary fluctuations, trading in financial instruments, real estate ventures, and operating theme parks. Counting total revenues at such companies as dependent on copyright because some of the revenues involve selling copyrighted works is poor economics.

It is also poor economics to assume that just because we need distributors to market works created by others, that increasing revenue to distributors means increasing revenue to artists: however false the aggregate industry numbers on the wealth created by large media companies, policymakers are never told about the *distribution* of that wealth *within* those industries: how much of this value to national economies makes its way back to those who created the works, who created the wealth in the first place. The actual living conditions of those who created the works are apparently either irrelevant, or, it is erroneously believed, the wealth will trickle down from the corporations who own and exploit the works to the individuals who created them.

Every study of the actual living conditions of those in the traditional cultural areas—authors of literary works, artists, musicians, performers sculptors, illustrators—shows that individuals engaged in these activities have lower incomes than others with similar training and education, have episodic employment, and fewer benefits such as health care.[112] Trickle-down economics works just as poorly in the copyright market as it does in the general economy.

The term "trickle-down" has been attributed to humorist Will Rogers, who said during the Great Depression of the late 1920s to 1930s that the "money was all appropriated for the top in hopes that it would trickle down to the needy. Mr. Hoover didn't know that money trickled *up*. Give it to the people at the bottom and the people at the top will have it before night, anyhow. But it will at least have passed through the poor fellow's hand."[113]

Trickle-down economics is based on an ideology that reducing taxes on the already wealthy will cause them to re-invest the saved amount in new productive endeavors, especially hiring new workers, leading in turn to long-term higher economic growth for everyone. The data are to the contrary. During Ronald Reagan's first term, when large tax cuts were made (see below), job creation increased 1.5 percent. This should be contrasted with the 3.2 percent increase during his predecessor, Jimmy Carter's four years. Carter's increase was not only more than double Reagan's, but occurred under much higher tax rates. The next significant tax cuts came under the eight years of President George W. Bush. In those eight years, job creation increased a miniscule 0.1 percent, the lowest figure since the statistics began to be collected in 1921 (with the obvious exception of Herbert Hoover's term during the Great Depression, where there was a 9 percent loss of jobs).[114]

As with many issues, people's perceptions of the facts are quite different from the facts; that gap interferes with the ability to formulate effective policy. Figure 3.1 sets out (1) the actual distribution of wealth in the United States; (2) what Americans think the actual distribution is; and (3) what Americans say they would like the distribution to be.

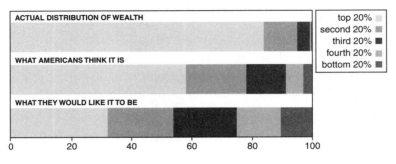

FIGURE 3.1   Actual Distribution of Wealth in the United States

Source: Michael I. Norton, Harvard Business School; Dan Ariely, Duke University

Here are a few facts about how the income gap came about and how trickle-down economics is simply redistribution of wealth upwards. When Ronald Reagan began his Presidency in January 1981, the top marginal tax rate was dramatically reduced from 69.125 percent to 39.1 percent.[115] The effective tax rate for a head of household earning the equivalent of $1 million on non-investment income in 2010 dollars is now 32.4 percent.[116] Where did the money saved from lower taxes go? In the late 1970s, right before the Reagan presidency, the top 1 percent of the population took in less than 9 percent of the total national income. By 2007, the second-to-last year of the Bush II presidency, that figure had increased to 23.5 percent.[117] The Clinton years were no different; his policies on Wall Street, such as repealing the Glass-Steagall Act, were indistinguishable from Reagan and the Bushes. Indeed, the steepest increase in income for the top 1 percent occurred during the Clinton Presidency. Figure 3.2 is a chart that graphically shows the income redistribution that has occurred as a result of the change in taxation.

INCOME GROUP	TOTAL LOSS/GAIN IN ANNUAL INCOME*	AVERAGE LOSS/GAIN PER HOUSEHOLD PER YEAR*
Top 1%	$673 billion more	$597,241 more
96–99	$140 billion more	$29,895 more
91–95	$29 billion more	$4,912 more
81–90	$43 billion less	$3,733 less
61–80	$194 billion less	$8,598 less
41–60	$224 billion less	$10,100 less
21–40	$189 billion less	$8,582 less
BOTTOM 20%	$136 billion less	$5,623 less

FIGURE 3.2   Income Redistribution Resulting from Changes in Taxation.

*Compared to what incomes would have been had all income groups seen the same growth rate in 1979–2005 as they did during previous decades.
Source: Jacob Hacker, Yale University; Paul Pierson, UC–Berkeley

The largest gains have gone to those who have the most already, namely top executives. In 1965, top executives earned twenty-four times the average worker's pay; that figure rose to 122 times in 1990, and to 550 times in 2009.[118] The last time there was such a concentration of wealth at the top was in 1928, the year before the Great Depression.[119]

Just as there has been a tremendous concentration of wealth at the top 1 percent of the population—the wealthiest 400 own as much as the bottom 125 million—we have an unprecedented concentration of ownership of copyright in the hands of a few, mostly U.S.-based corporations. Four record labels, Sony BMI Music, Warner Music Group, EMI Music Group, and Universal Music control around 85 percent of the U.S. market for recorded music and 70 percent worldwide. Five motion picture studios—

Walt Disney, Paramount, Sony, Twentieth Century Fox, Universal Pictures, and Warner Brothers—all part of larger, highly vertical conglomerates, control 80 percent of the U.S. market and 75 percent of the world market for motion pictures. And of course, the executives at these companies are in the top 1 percent of the general population in income. Moreover, their income is going up even as they complain about how their companies are (allegedly) being damaged by those they call copyright pirates. Figure 3.3 is for one company, Warner Music Group, and for only the top two executives at that company, Edgar Bronfman Jr. and Lyor Cohen, both of whom have been very vocal about copyright issues.

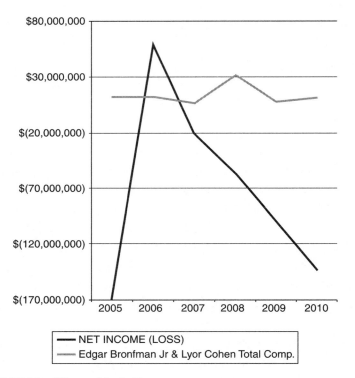

FIGURE 3.3   Warner Music Group

The data is from Warner's own SEC filings.[120] To sum up, since 2005, Warner Music Group lost $429 million while these two executives alone made $83.8 million. The year 2005 is important as a milestone because the company was taken public in that year, but right before it was made public, the investors, which included Mr. Bronfman, were paid back all of their investment. Rather than being a way to raise money to invest in the company's development and future, the IPO served merely as a cash-out for the original investors, with no new money being put into the company. In 2010, the stock declined by 2.9 percent but Mr. Cohen received a 30 percent increase in compensation, to $6.5 million.[121]

The trends in the national economy, the tremendous concentration of wealth and power in a few top media executives, and how money at those companies is distributed, are directly relevant to the goal of furthering creativity by putting money in authors' pockets. Policymakers must be concerned with *who* is making the money, not just the overall amount being made. We do not need stronger copyright laws if the effect of those laws is principally to benefit those executives making astronomic amounts of money: for example, in 2010, Viacom's CEO Philippe Dauman received the largest compensation package in corporate America: $84.5 million. This was a 149 percent increase over 2009, which wasn't shabby either.[122] If it is true, as copyright theory goes, that wealth creation begins with individual authors, that wealth does not end up with them, thereby presenting a crisis in copyright policy. After decades of studying authors' and artists' actual living conditions, economist Ruth Towse concluded that "strengthening copyright has not apparently resulted in boosting royalty payments."[123] Copyright is a trickle-up system in which increasing rights results in more money flowing up, away from creators.

Trickle-down Economics and Restoration of Cultural Works

One justification for the current, almost perpetual, term of copyright concentrated in large corporations is that longer rights will cause them to invest in restoring cultural works. Here is a version of the argument given by Jack Valenti before the U.S. House of Representatives in 1995, in advocating for extending the term of copyright for twenty more years for existing motion pictures. He begins by attacking studies showing extending the term would not cause the studios to engage in more restoration:

> The academics…assert that when copyrighted works lose their protection, they become more widely available to the public….[W]hat the academics do not know are the marketplace realisms [sic] which exist. Whatever work is not protected is a work that nobody preserves. The quality of the print is soon degraded. And there is no one around who is going to invest the money for enhancement. Why? Because there is no longer a financial incentive to rehabilitate and preserve because it belongs to everybody and therefore it belongs to nobody.
>
> A public domain work is an orphan. No question about that. No one is responsible for its future life. But everyone exploits its use until that time certain when it becomes soiled and haggard and barren of all of its former virtues. Who then—who then will invest the funds required to renovate it and to nourish its future when nobody owns it?
>
> How does the consumer benefit from that scenario? The answer is the consumer has no benefit. What the academics offer in numbing detail are the arcane drudgeries of

graphs and charts and arithmetical lines that cross a page. But the fact is that all of these scholarly works are separated from the real world in which realism [sic] exists.

Mr. Valenti manages to reject the real world—the graphs, charts, and data that show the film industry has historically done a poor job in preserving and restoring its own works[124]—while making the false assertion that copyright ownership by itself will lead the motion picture industry to preserve and restore works. According to Mr. Valenti, a work in which there is no copyright allegedly has no value, and thereby "becomes soiled and haggard and barren of all of its former virtues." This is false. A work in which copyright has expired but for which consumer demand remains high is a work that will attract a number of possible investors, all of whom are eager to make a profit off their investment. A work still under copyright but for which there is no consumer demand will attract no investment, including that of the original studio. The works whose term of copyright Hollywood had extended were never in danger of needing to be restored, and thus Mr. Valenti's remarks were simply an attempt to divert attention away from the real agenda: getting longer protection for those few popular movies that were about to go into the public domain, principally Disney animated films.

The real preservation concern is with the vast number of works for which Hollywood doesn't own copies. Most of these are held in large public archives. Other copies are in private hands or small public collections.[125] A study by the European Union showed approximately 355,000 films for which rights clearance was believed not possible.[126] In the United States, a study was done in 2002 on the availability of films from the era then covered by term extension (1927–1946). Here are the data:

36,386 titles were released from 1927–1946; of those:
only 2,480 were available on VHS;
only 871 were available on DVD;
only 114 were available on television/pay-per-view
only 113 were available in theaters.[127]

If term extension does, in fact, result in copyright owners investing in older works, these numbers would look very different. There is no reason to believe that extending copyright will induce corporate copyright owners to spend more money on preservation than would the vast number of entrepreneurs who would have access to films but for their failure to go into the public domain.[128] The decision of studios whether to invest in any film is based on a perceived ability to turn a profit from that particular movie. The same is true of any other copyrighted work. The only obligation of the media corporations that dominate the ownership of copyrights is to their shareholders, and that obligation is to maximize shareholder value. If a better return on investment can be made on real estate, that is where the money will go. If the money is better spent on the latest blockbuster rather than restoring a movie from the 1940s with no chance of another theatrical release, that's where the money will go, and understandably so.

Here is another example. The failure of corporate copyright owners to reissue historically important works despite the extension of the duration of copyright for twenty more years has been extensively studied in the recorded music field. In 2005, Tim Brooks wrote to the U.S. Copyright Office to endorse a request for the Copyright Office to issue a Notice of Inquiry examining out-of-print sound recording copyrights:

I first became aware of this issue during the research for my book *Lost Sounds: Blacks and the Birth of the Recording*

Industry, 1890–1919. I identified approximately 800 commercial recordings made in the U.S. by African-Americans
during this period, of which 400 appeared to be still under
the control of a present-day rights holder....Of these 400
exactly two—or one-half of one percent—had been reissued by the rights holder, or licensed to be reissued, during
the entire CD era....This situation did not come about
through any lack of interest, as evidenced by the fact that
more than one hundred of these recordings have been
reissued in foreign countries—where our laws do not
apply—or by small, unlicensed (and therefore illegal) enti-
ties in the U.S. Far more would be reissued, and those reis-
sues would be more widely available, under a more rational
legal structure.[129]

Mr. Brooks was then commissioned to conduct a study by the
National Recording Preservation Board at the Library of Congress
on the number of historic pre-1965 sound recordings controlled
by an existing rights holder, as well as the number of such recordings rights holders have made available, either directly or through
licensees. Here are his conclusions:

For most periods prior to the Big Band Era the percent
reissued dropped to less than 10 percent, and for the early
part of the twentieth century it was nearly zero. This, re-
member, is not a percent of all recordings but rather a percent of those recordings in which present-day scholars and
collectors have the greatest interest, as documented by
widely used discographies and other publications. The study
also showed very uneven treatment by genre of music. Historic blues and gospel recordings (10 percent reissued) and
recordings by U.S. ethnic minorities (1 percent reissued)
were particularly poorly treated by rights holders.[130]

Record labels may well have made a rational economic decision that reissuing such works was not profitable for them. The scale on which they operate may require issuance only of the most popular songs or albums. The problem lies with their reliance on copyright to prevent those who *will* take the risk of reissuing such works. As noted by the National Recording Preservation Board of the Library of Congress, "while rights holders may deem that there is insufficient market for them to even meet the expenses of reissuing their historic catalog, interest in their early catalogs is still sufficiently high to encourage non-rights holders to try to make the material available,"[131] but of course at the risk of being sued.

Giving large corporations more money in the form of a longer term of copyright or additional rights will not incentivize them to take more risks; it will not lead to innovation or edgier works; it will not lead them to reissue more historically important music; it will not lead to furthering the public interest. If a record label thinks it can make more money on the next manufactured teen sensation, that's where the investment will go, and not on the reissue of culturally important earlier works by jazz musicians, blues performers, or anyone else.

Corporations should be able to decide what makes the most financial sense for themselves, rather than for society at large. My objection is two-fold: (1) their lobbying legislatures for a longer term of copyright is based on the misrepresentation that a longer term is for the benefit of society at large because it will cause them to reissue works they don't reissue or would have anyway; (2) their use of extended copyright protection to block those entrepreneurs who would take the risk of reissuing works the major labels refuse to. Trickle-down copyright economics works just as poorly as general trickle-down economics does.

CULTURAL INDUSTRIES VERSUS CREATIVE INDUSTRIES: THE PROBLEMS WITH DEFINITIONS

Then-former Arkansas governor Bill Clinton's first, 1992 presidential campaign was built around the slogan "It's the economy, stupid." This slogan was based on the truism that politicians' fates rise and fall on whether people are working or not. Corporate copyright owners have seized on this truism in marketing their campaign for ever greater rights as a campaign for job creation and job loss. Their slogan might as well, be, "It's the copyright law, stupid."

An important part of this rebranding is a switch from copyright's previous concern with furthering culture to a new concern with furthering the "creative industries." Rebranding requires a new idea, and the new idea is "the creative industries are the driver of 21st century economies."[132] One must marvel at the cleverness of rebranding eighteenth-century solutions to eighteenth-century problems as the solutions to twenty-first-century problems, but the assertion that the creative industries are the drivers of twenty-first century's economies is backed up with allegedly impressive figures. I shall examine these false figures below, but first I need to discuss how the creative industries have so quickly come to be seen as a critical part of national economies.

This new role did not come about through a change in the economy: The economic contribution of the music industry has been declining. The contributions of the traditional cultural industries even as a whole have not dramatically increased. So why the claims of great economic importance? The claims are based on a change in language: the "cultural industries" have been replaced with the "creative industries."[133] The creative industries are based on a different group of industries than those copyright laws have traditionally been concerned with. This linguistic sleight-of-hand is critical to avoiding bad policy decisions, decisions that are based on helping one group but which in fact help another. In order to understand the consequence of this linguistic shift for copyright policymaking, I shall first separately examine the words "creative" and "culture."

"Creative" is a wonderful word, with only positive associations. It connotes novelty, progress, intelligence, and artistic skill, even genius. There is no agreed-upon definition of "creative" (one scholar identified 100 different definitions)[134] and it can't be measured. It is, therefore, the perfect vehicle for grandiose claims. "Creative" is so porous it can be all things to all people and do all things for all people. These associations are then placed on the "creative industries," even though creativity in an industry is very different from creativity in individuals.

"Culture" is also a word with different uses, although it has interesting roots, noted by David Throsby:

> The original connotation of the word 'culture'...referred to the tillage of the soil. In the sixteenth century this literal meaning became transposed to the cultivation of the mind and the intellect. Such figurative usage is still in active service today; we refer to someone well versed in the arts and letters as a 'cultured' or 'cultivated' person, and the noun 'culture' is often used without qualification to denote what, under a more restrictive definition, would be referred to as the products and practices of the 'high' arts. But since the early nineteenth century the term 'culture' has been used in a broad sense to describe the intellectual and spiritual development of civilization as a whole. In turn, these characteristics when evidenced in particular societies, such as nation states. In due course, this humanistic interpretation was supplanted by a more all-encompassing concept whereby

culture was seen to embrace not just intellectual endeavour
but the entire way of life of a people or society.[135]

In line with the last sentence, today, "culture" is largely seen
through a sociological viewpoint, as the "totality of socially
transmitted behavior, patterns, arts, beliefs, institutions of human
work and thought."[136] Alongside this very broad usage, intellectual property laws are said to further a "culture of improvement"[137] or a culture of "innovation." When words are widely
used in so many different contexts, they lose their ability to form
the basis for precise meanings, although as we shall see this im-
precision constitutes their very appeal to the private sector and
governments.

The current use of the conjoined term "cultural industries" is
ironic given the focus of culture on the behavior and beliefs of
peoples, rather than the production of commodities, and given the
origins of the term. The term was coined in 1944 by Marxist
writers Max Horkheimer and Theodor Adorno, out of concern
that culture was becoming a commodity.[138]

Horkheimer and Adorno were convinced that popular culture
was being transformed into an endless stream of factory-produced
standardized entertainment goods. The new creators of culture
were not the people, but rather industrialists; the people's role was
dumbed down into being passive purchasers of commodities.
Much like Marx's view of religion as the opiate of the masses,
Horkheimer and Adorno worried that this new trend was shifting
people's attention away from their economic exploitation. Culture was becoming the equivalent of the Ancient Romans' *panem
et circenses* ("bread and circuses"), entertainment to appease the
masses.[139] Traditional creativity, produced by individuals, was increasingly being left to state-subsidized programs and could therefore hardly be said to be an industry.

Eventually, budgets for state programs were cut back. Rather than declare they were no longer interested in furthering culture—an option not open to countries with ministries of culture—governments simply declared that the marketplace was already supplying people's cultural needs: The marketplace magically became the creative industries. The creative industries were then defined as those industries dependent on copyright—a necessary tautology since a marketplace solution was required and copyright, although a government grant, does not involve the expenditure of money along with the grant: the magic of the marketplace was said to create the value. This is the birth of the tautology that copyright is essential for the growth of the creative industries.

The tautology comes at a very high cost, though: a previous agenda of encouraging the direct creation of works by individuals was replaced with an economic policy of encouraging industries dominated by large companies whose agenda is the production of commodities. Authors and artists are a necessary supply cost in this effort, but are not an end in themselves. The switch from culture generally being what individual authors and artists do to culture being generally what the creative industries do is an important shift; a move away from a focus on cultivating diverse expression and toward the sale of commodities, as industries are in the commodity, not creativity, business.

The shift to the "creative industries" is also profound because of the industries included within that term, many of which are not historically associated with traditional cultural works. In 2009, KEA, a Brussels-based consultancy group, prepared a report for the European Commission.[140] The KEA report defined culture-based creativity as "a form of innovation that essentially helps businesses and institutions (whether public or private) to drive marketing, communication, human resources, or product/

service innovation."[141] These are not the traditional forms of culture or of copyright law. Advertising is said by the report to be a "creative trade," and thus a part of the definition of creative industries.[142]

When we speak of copyright as being essential to the creative industries, we must pay a great deal of attention to the businesses considered to be within those industries. This is particularly the case when we speak of the global importance of copyright. Different countries include different businesses within the creative industries, making comparisons among countries impossible. In some countries literature, performing, and visual arts are part of the creative industries, but in others, inexplicably, they are not.[143] In such countries, it is a stretch indeed to say creative industries are those industries dependent on copyright laws and that therefore copyright laws are essential to their growth.[144]

So how then is it decided which industries form the creative industries? A common approach is to use economic data based on International Standard Industrial Classification (ISIC) codes. Unlike building codes or regulations, these codes are classifications. They can be quite granular, going down to different levels of specific types of employment. The choice of what level of granularity to choose greatly determines what data you will generate, with more general classifications lumping together diverse activities, few of which are directly related to producing copyrighted works. Lying with statistics is custom-made for such exercises.

Economist Ruth Towse has shown how figures in a 2007 report commissioned by the UK Department of Culture, Media and Sport resulted in inflated figures due to the use of very general classifications: using more accurate, granular classifications reduced the asserted contributions of the "core creative activities" to the GDP from 3.4 percent to 2.7 percent and revealed over 40 percent of the contributions came from the computer software and games industries.[145] Yet further granularity would have altered these figures even more. Relying on very general classifications to create exaggerated figures leads to bad policymaking.

Here is one example, from remarks by the then-Secretary of State for Culture, Media and Sport, made in the UK Work Foundation's July 2007 publication, "Staying ahead: the economic performance of the UK's creative industries":

> The size of the creative industries is comparable to the financial services sector. They now make up 7.3 per cent of the economy, and are growing at 5 per cent per year (almost twice the rate of the rest of the economy). Including those working in related creative occupations, the creative economy employs 1.8 million people.
>
> The UK creative industries outperform every other European state and in the 21st century they have moved to the centre stage of the UK economy. It is vital to the whole economy that Government works with industry to create a framework in which these sectors can flourish.[146]

The errors in this passage could fill an entire book twice the size of this one. Here are a few highlights from just the final paragraph, and leaving aside the just discussed inflated figures for the economic contributions of the creative industries made possible by using very general, non-granular ISIC classifications. If it is true that the UK creative industries outperform all other European countries and are at the center of the UK economy (a comparison that is impossible due to different definitions of the creative industries), why would those industries need government help, and why would they need even stronger laws since there is no correlation between stronger copyright laws and better economic performance.

The attempt at quantifying the creative industries in order to serve as the basis for empirical policymaking has, to date, been an exercise in the manipulation of data. To recap, there is the highly result-oriented initial classification of some industries, but not others, as being part of the creative industries. Then, the aggregate figures for those industries are derived by attributing all revenues generated as being dependent on copyright, as if nothing would have been done without copyright protection, as if every revenue-generating part of every company in the industry is directly involved in producing works dependent on copyright, and without ever specifying what level of copyright is required even for those few works that may remotely be said to be copyright dependent. These are vast, vertically integrated multinational companies, with revenue sources from thousands of activities, many of which have nothing to do with the production or distribution of copyrighted works.[147]

Creativity Can't Be Measured

Beyond all this, no efforts are ever made to measure creativity even by those who loudly assert that copyright is necessary to increase creativity.[148] If we want to increase creativity levels we have to be able to measure those levels; otherwise we can't tell if creativity is being increased or decreased. As the EU's consultant on culture and creativity KEA observed: "The role of creativity remains difficult to quantify. Intangible inputs are difficult to measure and do not explicitly appear in companies' accounts or terms of additional sales."[149] The Xerox corporation's famous Palo Alto Research Center (PARC), home to some of the most important innovations of the digital era, put the matter more bluntly: "Inventive creativity can't be measured by spreadsheets."[150] Nor do those who so rhapsodically warble about copyright's alleged tremendous impact on increasing creativity ever offer empirical evidence that it does. If those who stand the most to benefit from the assertion and who are in the position to know whether the assertion is true fail to provide any data, how, in the absence of any relevant data, are policymakers to make effective policy?

The economic models typically used for such matters are not only so theoretical as to be practically worthless, but they assume away the very issue to be proved. Harold Demsetz, a major figure in the Chicago school of economics, whose pioneering work in property rights provided a key foundation for the law and economics movement, argued in 2009 that the dominant neoclassical approach had sought to understand the exploitation of privately owned resources wholly in terms of prices.[151] Meaningful creativity, he wrote, "necessarily involves differences between a new work and old works, and this implies that the new and the old are imperfect substitutes."[152] Neoclassical economics is centered, however, on perfect competition, and therefore "does not and cannot embrace creative activity."[153] In plain English, Professor Demsetz was admitting that neoclassical economics can't measure creativity, yet neoclassical economics underlies much of the current economic copyright theorizing.

If we want to focus on increasing creative works—art, literature, movies, and music—because we think they are areas where economic growth is possible, we need to figure out why people produce creative works, we need to be able to measure growth in the production of those works, and we must then figure out how to increase that growth. It is questionable whether these tasks are possible, but if the tasks are important, we have to begin to figure them out. Some academics have undertaken this task. Professor Jessica Sibley has begun a book-length project that involves face-to-face interviews with artists, scientist, engineers, their lawyers, agents, and business partners, in an attempt to learn why artists create and innovate and what the role of those interviewed is in the process of creation and distribution of creative products. The first part of her study, the result of forty-five hours of interviews, has been published.[154]

Consistent with the position taken in chapter 1 of this book, Professor Sibley found that for those interviewed,[155] copyright law does not act as economic incentive for creating works in the first place. Intrinsic, not extrinsic, motivations were the driving force. The point is not that we don't need copyright; we do need it for those who do want to make a living from their works regardless of why they created them in the first place. The point is that the need to have some level of protection cannot support current claims that we need a very high and ever-increasing level of protection. Those levels have nothing to do with furthering creativity, and we should be honest about that.

Syllogism Number Two

Copyright is the basis of a knowledge-based economy.
The knowledge-based economy is the basis for competitiveness.
Therefore copyright is the basis for competitiveness.

In 2006, this syllogism was expressed by the then-EU Commissioner for the Internal Market: "The protection of intellectual and industrial property—copyrights, patents, trademarks or designs—is at the heart of a knowledge-based economy and central to improving Europe's competitiveness."[156] More recently, in calling for a single market for intellectual property rights, the European Commission made this extraordinary statement: "all forms of IPR are cornerstones of the new knowledge-based economy....IP is the capital that feeds the new economy."[157] This is a novel, and incomprehensible use of the term "capital."[158] While human development theorists will sometime use the term "individual capital" in referring to inherent personal abilities—in contrast to more traditional economists, who refer to labor as a form of intellectual capital—copyright and patent rights are not capital in either sense: they do not create value and are not based on labor. Instead, they are a form of legal insurance protecting value otherwise created (by satisfying consumer demand for products and services).

In any event, there is no causal relationship between creativity and competitiveness. In 2009, KEA, a Brussels-based consultancy group, prepared a report for the European Commission[159] questioning the asserted link between creativity and competitiveness: "[T]raditionally, culture is not seen as a motor for better management or for honing a competitive edge in product development, learning or human resources."[160] In Europe (and many other regions), for example, there is intensive competition and innovation in developing cuisines, the recipes for which are not protected by copyright.[161] Yet, despite occasional calls for such rights,[162] chefs continue to innovate, much to diners' delight.

Just as the shift from the cultural industries to the creative industries led to a shift away from the expressive nature of authors' and artists' contributions and toward commodity sales, so too culture is now seen as merely another aspect of the "knowledge economy,"[163] judged by how it performs in an invisible hand marketplace. But you can't economically measure how an increase in knowledge will lead to productivity gains. If we want more creative works and more knowledgeable citizens, we will have to disassociate these goals from commodity markets, and focus on why people create and learn. We must then be willing to commit public monies to their encouragement where market forces have proved inadequate to the task. While there are many wonderful educational products available from the private sector, and as a father of young children I am an avid consumer of them, I have never thought that the copyright in those products was driving competition. What drives competition is the ability of different companies to offer better and cheaper products, characteristics quite at odds with the artificial scarcity and monopoly profits made possible by copyright laws.

FOUR

The Public Interest

In all copyright systems, furthering the interest of the public is said to be an important goal. The public interest will not be the same in all countries or in all cultures, just as the nature of creativity varies across the world.[1] In order to further any type of interest, you have to identify it, study its characteristics, and then figure out empirically how to ensure it thrives.

Unfortunately, these necessary steps are rarely taken in crafting the public interest in copyright laws. Sometimes the public interest is dismissed as being automatically served by the granting of copyright. This is seen in James Madison's 1788 Federalist Paper Number 43, where he asserted that the "public good fully coincides" with the claims of individuals in copyrighted works.[2] Under Madison's approach we needn't worry about including public interest provisions in our copyright laws because whatever individuals do is in the public interest. Madison didn't go into his reasoning for this view, but if it was based on a belief that the enlightened self-interest of individuals will, collectively, always work to benefit society. John Maynard Keynes—purportedly—had a response: "Capitalism is the astounding belief that the most wicked of men will do the most wicked of things for the greatest good of everyone."[3]

A contemporary view of the public interest is equally dismissive: when we say that the public interest is in getting access to copyrighted works, this usually means access as a passive consumer. The public's interest is extinguished once payment is made. If no payment is made (where requested) there is no public interest and therefore no access.

The public interest need not be so narrowly considered: Authors are part of the public too, and as discussed in chapter 3, authors have a compelling interest in being able to copy from other authors in the creation of new works. The interests of these later authors may conflict with the interests of earlier authors as later authors seek to build on, or even attack, the work of their predecessors.[4] There are also interests of book reviewers, parodists, satirists, libraries, archivists, preservationists, consumer electronics manufacturers, and Internet service providers, to name only a few. Contrary to Madison's cheery view, it is not true that the interests of everyone in society fully coincide with each other. The history of the copyright laws is rife with pitched battles over proposals for change, as competing interest groups face off before legislatures and parliaments, each of which claiming that they—but not the other side—represent the public interest.

Contrary to Madison's views, first courts and then legislators have developed public interest rights to use copyrighted works without authorization and without payment. Some statutes have a detailed list of public interest uses. Others, such as the fair use provision of the U.S. Copyright Act, list some permissible uses, but also act as a general safety valve so that copyright law does not "stifle the very creativity which that law is designed to foster."[5]

Is there a different public interest apart from such specific exemptions or privileges? There are a few such interests typically identified. I will examine two: (1) the public interest in works once under copyright passing into the public domain; (2) the public interest in certain material not being protected at all.

THE PUBLIC INTEREST AND THE PUBLIC DOMAIN

Although it is often stated that the ultimate purpose of copyright is to place works into the public domain so that they may be freely used, I do not share this view, which is akin to saying that the purpose of life is death. It is true that once a work formerly protected by copyright is in the public domain, it can be freely adapted to create other works, and it is true that such re-uses perform a valuable public purpose furthering the goals of copyright. It is also true that older works have importantly formed the basis for modern adaptations. All of these are significant public interests.

My disagreement is practical: Statistically, we benefit the most from our ability to have access to works during their copyrighted existence for the simple reason that few works of authorship have staying power beyond a decade. If the public interest is confined to the ability to freely use works that retain their currency only after the authors of them have been dead for fifty or seventy years, that interest will be limited mostly to scholars and to the creation of derivative works based on (the few) public domain works. Access to works remaining under copyright is therefore a critical public interest.

THE PUBLIC INTEREST AND
UNPROTECTABLE MATERIAL

The term "public domain" is also used to refer to unprotectable parts of a protectable whole; for example, unprotectable math equations in a mathematics textbook. The textbook would be protectable, but the equations aren't. The United States Supreme Court has noted this type of public interest: "The public interest in the free flow of information is assured by the law's refusal to recognize a valid copyright in facts."[6] The public interest in the non-protection of unoriginal material was recognized in the United States Supreme Court's 1991 *Feist Publications, Inc. v. Rural Telephone Service Company* opinion,[7] where Justice O'Connor wrote for a unanimous Court: "It may seem unfair that much of the fruit of the compiler's labor may be used by others without compensation.... This result is neither unfair nor unfortunate. It is the means by which copyright advances the progress of science and art."[8] It is creativity, not labor, that the copyright laws seek to further.

THE FALLACY OF THE BALANCE METAPHOR

In determining the proper level of copyright, it is often said we must balance various policy considerations, such as "promoting the public interest in the encouragement and dissemination of works of the arts and intellect and obtaining a just reward for the creator." The 1996 World Intellectual Property Organization's Copyright Treaty declares the treaty arose from a "need to maintain a balance between the rights of authors and the larger public interest, particularly education, research and access to information...."[9]

We frequently use metaphors in discussing legal principles.[10] There is said to be a "marketplace of ideas" and a "wall of separation" between religion and the State. The "law as a person" metaphor is used when we speak of the "long arm" of the law, the "conscience of equity," a "body" of case law, and when we say that a statute "contemplates" a particular result. Abstract concepts such as copyright can only be understood metaphorically because the rights that comprise copyright do not exist as tangible things: You cannot kiss a copyright or tuck it into bed at night.

When we fail to recognize a metaphor is at work, we do not realize we have bought into the powerful associations they embody. The balance metaphor is one such metaphor. Mark Johnson, who has done the most in-depth study of the balance metaphor, wrote:

> The experience of balance is so pervasive, and so absolutely basic for our coherent experience of the world... that we are seldom aware of its presence. We almost never reflect on the nature and meaning of balance.... [B]alance, metaphorically interpreted... holds together several aspects of our understanding of the world.[11]

The balance metaphor evokes notions of harmony, of everyone being taken care of by "weighing" the "balance" to achieve a desirable equilibrium for all interests. Yet, the balance metaphor presumes opposing forces;[12] in the case of law, the metaphor presumes legislators or judges objectively "weighing" the interests of those opposing forces and then coming to the correct result based on a determination of what is right and just.[13] This is why Justice is depicted as a blindfolded figure holding scales. In real life there is no blindfold.

Those who wish to preserve the status quo will argue that things are nicely balanced just as they are, and that any change will unfairly disadvantage them. Those seeking the change will argue that things are out of balance and that only change will restore fairness, thereby mindlessly conflating fairness with balance. In practice, policymaking almost always involves making choices that benefit one group at the expense of others.[14]

Our task in achieving effective copyright laws should be to measure, empirically, whether this policy or that policy increases or decreases the output of cultural products, assists in the promotion of knowledge, or otherwise promotes the public's interests, including authors' interests. We cannot measure—and therefore should not attempt to measure—whether that increase or decrease restores some mythical balance between the interests of competing parties. Calls for "high levels" of rights have nothing to do with achieving a balance since constant increases destroy any existing "balance" to the disadvantage of some party, and an upward arc is graphed quite differently from weighed scales at equilibrium.

Things are in balance or out of balance only in relation to other things. We have a balanced diet, for example, if we have the right number of different foods and in the right amounts. But such a judgment is possible only by reference to external criteria: some authority declaring what are the right foods and the right amounts of those foods. These prescriptions change over time and are usually controversial since they involve judgment calls.

Balance in copyright laws is also relational and determined by external criteria: that's why people say "copyright has to preserve the balance *in* . . . ," with the ellipses constituting the underlying, external policy objective the underlying balance is supposed to achieve. We therefore always "balance" from an initial ideological bias, a bias that guides you to your preconceived idea of what is the right result, that will guide you to the result that will, for you, restore things to the right balance.

Balancing is completely subjective, and therefore use of the balance metaphor in copyright disputes does not involve a mathematical weighing of interests on twin scales, with equilibrium being achieved when each side's rights are identical. Balance is a metaphor used to mask a result that accords with one's own view of a correct result, that view being determined by other factors, mostly subjective value judgments. One's own ideological-oriented claims are weighed very favorably, while the other side's interests are weighed unfavorably if they are considered at all. There is no balancing but instead only one side or the other prevailing.

From an innovation perspective, balance is precisely the wrong objective. Indeed, it is a dangerous objective since invocation of the balance metaphor is often done in order to maintain the status quo, as in "why upset the balance?" or as in descriptions of the status quo as containing a "delicate balance." Balance conflicts with the dynamic disruption that creatively pushes us forward no matter how reluctantly: that's what is behind Austrian economist Joseph Schumpeter's theory of creative disruption, which was not named, it should be noted, "creative balance."

The balance metaphor should be abandoned in favor of simply asking, "what is the result we want?" What we want, however, cannot be separated from the political arena in which rights and privileges are granted or changed. In that arena, there are serious impediments to the balancing that lawmakers routinely invoke as descriptive of the political process. If we want to fix copyright, we have to recognize the political obstacles.

POLITICAL IMPEDIMENTS TO BALANCING

The balance metaphor presumes that lawmakers are objective, neutral judges of the various interests' claims. The reality is quite different, and I do not say this as a criticism. Legislators generally pursue interests that are important to their constituents or to their own intellectual interests. We want legislators to be engaged in the issues at hand; it is hard to be engaged in those issues without forming a view of the merits of the arguments advanced by the parties. But being involved is not the same as being closed to the facts and arguments of those who take an opposing position. Being involved effectively means basing decisions on the data, not on rhetoric or for the benefit of those who offer the largest campaign contributions.

There are formidable obstacles for those legislators who wish to pursue good policy. One is an asymmetry between the resources and information possessed by lobbyists and the resources and funding possessed by legislatures. Even those who believe in a good government model in which legislatures objectively balance competing interests in order to achieve the maximum public good have long recognized reality is often to the contrary. Maffeo Pantaleoni (1857–1924),[15] an Italian neoclassical economist, believed that legislatures should, as the elected representatives of all the people, empirically determine benefits versus costs, but he acknowledged that "these are calculations which require far more time than is available to any Parliament and which far exceed the intellectual capacities of the great majority of mankind."[16] Such bounded rationality, to use Herbert Simon's term,[17] can lead to substituting ideology and slogans for evidence. In such an environment, effective lawmaking is serendipitous.

Another impediment to effective copyright policy is copyright's relative unimportance when considered against the greater scheme of issues governments deliberate and decide, such as whether to go to war, whether to bail out banks or car makers, whether to reform health care, as well as dozens of other pressing societal concerns that not only affect society, but determine the fate of elections and which party ultimately governs. In this context, copyright issues are trivial, so there is every incentive for individual lawmakers to hope the problem will go away or somehow otherwise be solved, whether by the parties, the courts, or by a regulatory body. This lack of relative importance may explain the 1995 remark by the press secretary for then-Presidential candidate Bob Dole that "people are more interested in a strong economy than someone who can tell you if Hootie and the Blowfish are going to have a strong album next time."[18] There is little incentive (outside of constituent interest) for individual lawmakers to take on controversial copyright issues.

REPLACEMENT OF THE BALANCE METAPHOR
WITH THE PROPERTY METAPHOR

Despite all the flaws in the balance metaphor, at least it is premised on the existence of competing, valid interests. For this reason, it has fallen out of favor with those who wish to exercise total control over all uses, regardless of how trivial, and regardless of the lack of any economic harm from those uses.[19] The property metaphor is the chosen vehicle for this agenda.[20] There is, after all, no need to balance others' interests if you have an absolute right in your property.

The property approach is dependent on an initial categorization of the claim as constituting property. Once this claim is accepted, a great deal follows, as English writer and member of Parliament Augustine Birrell pointed out in a series of lectures on copyright in 1898:

> To be allowed to enter this sacrosanct circle is a great thing. None but the oldest families need apply.... Once inside this circle your rights were supposed in some romantic way to be outside the chill region of positive law—they were based upon natural rights, existing previously to the social contract, and without which Society was deemed impossible. Neither were these romantic conceptions mere jeux d'esprit. Consequences flowed from them. If your right to turn your neighbor off your premises, to keep your things to yourself—was property, and therefore ex hypothesi founded on natural justice, he who sought to interfere with your complete dominion was a thief or a trespasser.[21]

The property metaphor falsely assumes that property is not the *creation* of society, but is nevertheless an *obligation* of society to enforce. There are, however, no natural rights, rights that aren't created by society.[22] Rights are created by laws, and laws are created by society, including property rights. As Jeremy Bentham recognized, property "is entirely the work of law. . . . Property and law are born together, and die together. Before laws were made there was no property; take away laws, and property ceases."[23] Bentham's remarks place property in the correct context—a right created by society to further social goals. As important as many property rights are, they do not exist automatically as part of the human condition, but rather as social creations, to further social goals.

Use of the property ownership metaphor is meant to persuade us that owners of the property have no obligations to others, precisely because to be an owner[24] of something supposedly means an obligation only to yourself. This is, however, a rhetorical position, offered not out of a genuine belief that government cannot regulate at all—a position not even the most ardent libertarian takes. Rather, the "I can do what I want with it since it is my property" argument is made in an effort to place a heavy burden on those who seek government regulation in the public interest. By contrast, when a government is bestowing a privilege rather than enforcing a property right, the onus of establishing entitlement to the privilege is on the person seeking it.[25] Copyright is a privilege granted by governments on everyone's behalf.[26]

The balancing of everyone's interests, if balancing is the right metaphor, must be done without the heavy hand of property rhetoric on the scales. The only helpful approach is to ask ourselves what conduct we wish to permit and what conduct we wish to prohibit. Affixing labels *before* we figure out the answers to those questions does not assist us. Copyright laws can be helpful in ensuring that the interests we wish to further are, in fact, furthered. But there are real limits to how much copyright laws can do, as we shall now see.

FIVE

Law Is Not the Solution to Business Problems

Laws are not the answer to all problems. Laws are useful for solving only those problems laws can solve. If there are non-legislative ways to solve whatever the problem is, the last thing we should want is for lawyers, courts, or governments to get involved. Many businesses that rely on copyrighted material have a problem: not enough consumers are paying for their works. While copyright owners like to portray this as a legal problem—a problem of piracy—the problem is a market problem, arising from the continual failure of copyright owners to respond and adapt to changing markets and the technologies that drive consumer demand. As the Hargreaves review for the UK government found: "Where enforcement and education have so far struggled to make an impact on levels of copyright infringement, there has been more evidence of success where creative businesses have responded to illegal services by making available lower priced legal products in a form consumers want."

I review below data from a study of file sharing during times when there were lawful purchase options and during times when those options disappeared. The results should not be surprising: the ability to buy lawful goods at fair prices significantly drives down the levels of unauthorized copying. Taking away the ability to buy lawful copies increases unlawful copying. It is in everyone's interest to have the market flooded with lawful choices, yet this is not the case: a recent study in Europe by Forrester Research found that fewer Europeans bought lawful digital content in 2010 than in 2009, even though 20 percent more wanted to do so in 2010 than in 2009. Why? Forrester found that the number of lawful options "far from growing, is actually stagnating.... The [lawful] content market...is simply failing to meet consumer demand."[1] Denying consumers what they want cannot succeed as a business model, and no law can save copyright owners who refuse to satisfy consumer demand. The problem is as old as it is ignored. In June 2000, eleven years ago, *The Economist* magazine, hardly an anti-property rights publication, criticized the record industry for its failure to capitalize on the consumer demand tapped into by Napster, writing that consumer response to Napster showed "that online distribution of music is feasible. If record companies are not making greater use of the Internet, it is because they have chosen not to.... Their delays have merely left the field open to nimbler pirates.... Given this, a better response to Napster would be not to sue but to defeat it in the marketplace.... It is time for record companies to take the plunge and change their pricing and business models to reflect the new Internet environment." As *The Economist* pointed out, denying consumers what they want cannot succeed as a business model. No law can save copyright owners who refuse to satisfy consumer demand.

Technology is frequently cited as the culprit for copyright owners' woes, but most of the problems attributed to technologies—such as the decline in sales of CDs, DVDs, and print newspapers—are the result of the natural end of product cycles. Laws cannot prevent ordinary operation of product cycles any more than they can stop the ordinary operation of business cycles: You can't outlaw recessions and you can't make it a violation of the copyright act not to buy a CD or a DVD.

THE NANCY REAGAN JUST SAY NO BUSINESS MODEL

In 1982, Nancy Reagan launched the "Just Say No" approach to the drug problem. It didn't work. Too often copyright owners think if they just say no to any new business models, they can hang on to their old ones. Too many in the copyright industries persist in the misguided view that copyright is the key to the success of their just say no approach because copyright equals control, and control equals sustainable profits, despite the end of product cycles and despite changing consumer demand. Long-run profitability is the result of satisfying consumer demand, not satisfying legal commands. Copyright provides the legal framework for both healthy and unhealthy business models. In a healthy market, copyright owners make their works available in formats and at prices consumers desire. Consumers then pay copyright owners money and everyone wins. There will still be some bad guys but the copyright laws provide remedies to go after them. We need copyright laws to protect healthy business models. In the unhealthy model, new technologies and the new business models that flow from those technologies are opposed, seen as an existential threat to the old business model of vertical control. In the unhealthy model, copyright owners don't respond to consumer demand; acting like ostriches, they expect that their refusal to fulfill the market demand means that no one else will. They are shocked, shocked, shocked! when unauthorized supply sources crop up. They then insist that the courts and legislatures protect them from their own failure to understand the basics of how supply and demand works. When they ultimately see they cannot kill off the new technology, they grudgingly accept it, change their business models, and then profit from it.

This pattern of fighting every new technology that comes along as an existential threat and then profiting from it is the defining relationship of gatekeepers to copyright law. The only mystery is why policymakers are taken in over and over again by gatekeepers' "sky is falling" routine. No good and a lot of bad happens when they are taken in. As Dr. Francis Gurry, the Director General of the World Intellectual Property Organization cautioned: "History shows that it is an impossible task to reverse technological advantage and the change that it produces. Rather than resist it, we need to accept the inevitability of change and to seek an intelligent engagement with it. There is, in any case, no other choice—either the copyright system adapts to the natural advantage that has evolved or it will perish."[2] There are many natural and highly beneficial advantages for individual creators over the analog world. The analog world was one of fragmented markets, each controlled by gatekeepers, with overall access controlled by a central gatekeeper: in the case of music, the record label or music publisher (often divisions of the same media corporation) to whom the composer or performer had to assign rights. Royalties were received, if ever, only after cost recoupments, including recording studio time, as well as manufacturing and promotion costs. CDs were in record stores or big-box stores like Wal-Mart which exercised content control. MTV provided the outlet for music videos. Radio play was controlled by large companies such as Clear Channel.

Today, bands or individual performers can be their own studio technicians, manufacturers, distributors, retailers, and promoters, through no- or small-cost websites and social networks. YouTube provides a free platform for music videos and live performances and the ability to monetize against an audience larger than ever possible before, one that is global. Here is another way the Internet provides immediate financial benefit to artists: One of the keys to success as an artist is knowing as much as possible about your audience. If you want to plan a tour, you need to know where your fans live and where they don't. Free online analytical tools track where website visitors are geographically located. This information allows artists to plan where they should and shouldn't play, whether they should try for a bigger venue because they have a larger concentration of fans than they thought, and where they should try to do radio interviews. There is no time in history that has been more favorable to individual creators to control their own destiny and make money. Many creators are wholeheartedly embracing these new outlets.

Newspapers unfortunately provide an example of a failure to adapt, and of the use of calls for new laws as an excuse for not adapting.

Newspapers: A Failure to Adapt

There is no question newspapers have serious problems, but those problems are business problems and cannot be solved by additional legal rights. To listen to some in the newspaper business, the industry was destroyed by Internet search engines. As we shall see, the decline in the newspaper business has been going on for a long time, well before the advent of the Internet, and involves loss of advertising revenue made possible by artificial, analog scarcity.

Newspapers' revenue losses, while substantial, have nothing to do with copying their content, and therefore nothing to do with copyright laws. If all search engines stop crawling and indexing newspapers' websites, is there anyone who doubts newspapers would receive *less*, and not more advertising revenue? Similarly, if all search engines stop crawling newspapers' websites, is there anyone who believes there would be a resurgence in the purchase of print editions?

Yet, policymakers are told that we face the end of investigative journalism, and therefore (it is alleged) the end of democracy. The end of democracy will not, apparently, occur if news organizations are granted new rights over the very facts of events, and if search engines are obligated to pay them money for the privilege of crawling their websites. Democracy seems easily preserved by money changing hands.

Calls for new rights must be rejected; they will not solve newspaper organizations' problems, they are impossible to implement in practice, and if implemented would enmesh the courts in harmful efforts to suppress speech on behalf of elites who did not generate that speech. Moreover, the claims about the death of investigative journalism are greatly exaggerated. In Washington, D. C., alone, there has been an explosion in the hiring of journalists covering Congress. The number of journalists credentialed to troll the halls of the Capitol seeking out stories has increased every year for the last five years, to the highest ever: over 6,000, roughly eleven journalists for every member of Congress. The Hill newspaper has switched from being a weekly to being a daily, doubling its staff, and providing all day web coverage. Bloomberg News has added 150 staffers for the launch of its $5,700-a-year Bloomberg Government Service. Congressional Quarterly and Roll Call, owned by Britain's Economist Group have, according to the chief executive, begun an "unprecedented" hiring spree, adding thirty-five new editorial positions alone.[3]

Democracy flourishes from the participation of the many, not from the reporting of a few legacy newspapers. Today, news reporting is also done by citizens or by journalists who have struck out on their own via websites. The popular Politico website is an example of this latter type of reporting. Citizen journalism can be as good quality or better than that done by people at established newspapers, and is certainly faster. Many breaking stories are reported by citizens on Twitter, Facebook, or on individual's websites or blogs. Ordinary citizens, armed with cell phones that have camera and video capabilities, post stories with pictures as events are happening and now constitute an essential element of news reporting. News organizations copy these individual sources with abandon, without payment, and sometimes even without attribution.

Websites and blogs also provide in-depth coverage of complicated stories that are as good as and usually better than those found in established newspapers. With few exceptions, newspaper reporters are generalists with no hands-on experience in the areas they cover. For coverage of an issue about search engines, I will take Danny Sullivan at www.searchengineland.com over any newspaper journalist. But we don't have to choose; choice is a false decision tree advanced by newspapers in an effort to retain their gatekeeper role. We can have both investigatory journalism in newspapers and investigatory journalism by citizens, and we should.

But if we lost investigatory journalism in newspapers we might not notice. Investigative journalism has always been a very small part of the overall creation and distribution of news in the United States or in other countries by those newspapers. Most reporters and correspondents employed by newspapers are not doing, and have never done, investigative reporting. While news organizations like to talk about how war correspondents and photographers are frequently in danger and are sometimes killed, the truth is that many of these brave people are stringers and freelancers, who live assignment to assignment on one-time payments, who do not own copyright in their reports or photographs, and who are not given health or death benefits for their families. (The fate of locals who provide much of the intelligence, translating, contacts, and transportation is much worse.) If news organizations cared as much as they profess to about these people, they would give them what they need most: a full-time job with benefits.

The history of newspaper content going back over 150 years consistently shows very little investigative journalism content. Long-time newspaperman Alex Jones[4] sought to quantify how much "iron core" style news newspapers actually have—with "iron core" representing a broader category than investigative journalism.

After an extensive review of newspaper content going back to the nineteenth century, Mr. Jones concluded that the average amount of iron core style news is 15 percent of a given paper, and that this number has remained consistent for 150 years: "The iron core style of news may have been the ostensible heart of newspapers, but the reality was that both advertising and lighter, racier content outpaced serious news from the start."[5] Mr. Jones added with understatement, "it seems reasonable to think that if there had been clamor for more serious news by newspaper readers, they would have been accommodated."[6] The historical lack of investigative journalism in newspapers is a function of the marketplace. Newspapers have understandably responded to the marketplace by having a low rate of investigatory journalism. New laws cannot accomplish what the marketplace has failed to do for 150 years: create a demand for greater investigative journalism. It is understandable why news organizations put investigative journalism front and center in their lobbying efforts, but if one reads the newspapers themselves, investigative journalism is a distinctly minor affair.

Nor is the plight of newspapers itself news. Newspapers have been in a long decline well before the Internet: Newspaper circulation has been on a steep decline since 1950; the peak year for the number of newspapers was 1914. Circulation per capita has been declining at a steady rate since the 1960s, although circulation per household has been declining longer (since the 1940s) and at a much steeper rate, as seen in Figure 5.1.

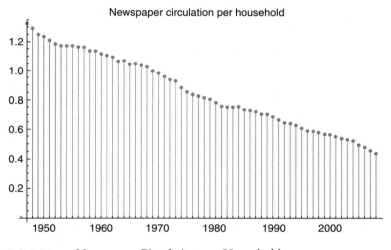

FIGURE 5.1   Newspaper Circulation per Household
Source: Newspaper Association of America

In the competition for advertising dollars, the media share of U.S. advertising for newspapers has declined from around 36 percent in 1949 to 13 percent in 2009, with the steepest short-term decline being in the ten-year period of 1949 to 1959, as a result of the increased popularity of television. The next big short-term drop occurred in the period 1989 to 1993, the latter date being the date the World Wide Web was opened up for free to the public. Television, both over the air and cable, by contrast, began with zero advertising market share in 1949, and went up to 26 percent in 2009. Direct mail has also gone up, from 15 percent in 1949 to 22 percent in 2009. The decline in newspaper advertising thus occurred most sharply *before* the introduction of the Web, while other media, especially cable television, have gained at newspapers' expense.

One important reason for newspapers' decline in advertising revenue versus other media is the decline in the amount of time consumers spend with newspapers. Advertisers follow the eyeballs, and if the eyeballs go someplace else, advertisers go to that other place too. No law can make advertisers stay with newspapers if, in advertisers' judgment, newspapers do not have the most eyeballs. In 2005, people spent 187 hours a year reading newspapers. In 2009, that number had declined to 162, and is projected to decline to 154 hours in 2011. By contrast, in 2005, consumers spent 1,659 hours watching television. In 2009 that number had increased to 1,714 and is projected to increase to 1,742 in 2011, with the biggest growth in viewership being in cable television, matching the growth in advertising on cable.

Media Usage and Consumer Spending

Media	Unit	2005	2006	2007 projection	2008 projection	2009 projection	2010 projection	2011 projection
Total	Hours	3,543	3,530	3,532	3,559	3,569	3,596	3,624
Television	Hours	1,659	1,673	1,686	1,704	1,714	1,728	1,742
Broadcast Television	Hours	679	676	676	678	673	673	669
Network stations	Hours	582	599	603	604	598	598	593
Independent stations	Hours	97	77	73	74	75	75	76
Cable, Satellite & RBOC TV Services	Hours	980	997	1,010	1,027	1,041	1,055	1,073
Basic cable, satellite & RBOC TV	Hours	807	835	849	865	877	891	913
Premium cable, satellite & RBOC TV	Hours	173	161	161	162	164	164	159
Broadcast and satellite radio	Hours	805	778	769	768	760	758	751
Recorded music	Hours	196	186	171	165	168	174	185
Out-of-home media	Hours	130	133	137	141	145	149	154
Consumer magazines	Hours	124	121	119	117	114	112	110
Consumer books	Hours	107	108	108	108	109	109	110
Videogames	Hours	73	76	82	90	91	94	100
Home video	Hours	63	62	64	66	68	70	70
Yellow Pages	Hours	12	13	13	13	13	12	12
Box office	Hours	12	12	13	13	13	14	14
Pure-play mobile services	Hours	9	12	16	21	28	33	38
In-flight entertainment	Hours	1	1	1	2	2	2	2

It should be no surprise that advertisers have gone with media that have an increase in consumer viewing rather than with media that are declining in consumer viewing. Newspapers are in decline and therefore so are their advertising revenue. This is the market at work, and is not the fault of others, especially Internet companies. Laws cannot force people to spend more time reading newspapers. People are estimated to spend somewhat over one minute a day reading news online versus twenty-five minutes a day reading hard copy newspapers. Magazines readership is up, with readers (young and old) spending an average of forty-three minutes per issue. Why the vast disparity? Is it because search engines are encouraging people quickly to flit from one site to the next? No. It is because the basic unit of news consumption has changed, from an entire hard copy paper, to individual articles.

Newspapers, like record companies selling only full-length albums, used to be able to force consumers to buy far more than they wanted. The basic unit that consumers want has been called the atomic unit of consumption. For music this is usually the individual song. For newspapers, it is the individual article. As with the music industry, fundamentally changing the unit of consumption that you charge consumers for is disruptive, requiring businesses to develop radically new models. As Google's Marissa Mayer noted in 2009 testimony before the U.S. Senate:

> Changing the basic unit of content consumption is a challenge, but also an opportunity. Treating the article as the atomic unit of consumption online has several powerful consequences. When producing an article for online news, the publisher must assume that a reader may be viewing this article on its own, independent of the rest of the publication. To make an article effective in a standalone setting

requires providing sufficient context for first-time readers, while clearly calling out the latest information for those following a story over time. It also requires a different approach to monetization: each individual article should be self-sustaining. These types of changes will require innovation and experimentation in how news is delivered online, and how advertising can support it.[7]

Well beyond these points, the nature of the way online news is created, presented, and consumed has dramatically changed even in the last ten years. Google News did not exist ten years ago: it was the idea of one person, Krishna Bharat, who, created it in response to his inability to get fast-breaking news on the 9/11/2001 attacks. Mr. Bharat was dissatisfied with Google's search engine, but rather than blame others, he set out to solve the problem by starting from scratch. Today, Google News has over seventy editions in thirty languages, and sends over one billion clicks a month to news publishers worldwide. This expansion came as a result of changes in the larger online news environment, and includes the integration of video, images, and social media. As a result of these changes and the vast expansion of individuals becoming both participants and reporters in critical events (think of the 2011 "Arab Spring" and the role played by Facebook and Twitter), consumers demand more news and faster. News organizations have to respond to these changes or be left behind.

There are two ways to get to a news company's website. The first way is for the news company to make its site attractive so that people come there as a destination site, and then stay there. The task of attracting consumers to, and keeping them on, newspapers' websites is the sole responsibility of newspapers themselves. Another way people get to a newspaper's website is by formulating a web search query in researching a particular topic; the search engine then provides links to news websites that carry the story. Consumers then choose which link to follow based on their own judgment about the quality and relevance of the site. Once at the news company's site, it is the news company's responsibility to keep consumers there. If they can't, they have no one to blame but themselves. If I refer you to a restaurant and you go there but don't like the food, is it my fault you won't go back again? If you like the food and go back again, it will be because you like the food and not because I recommended the place.

Newspapers are the masters of their own websites and have to take responsibility for how consumers interact with them, as well as how advertisers choose to place ads on them or not. Magazines have managed to figure this out by providing high-quality, in-depth niche stories that appeal to educated, and generally wealthier, consumers. But what advertiser is willing to place an advertisement on a news organization's website that generates low amounts of traffic and is only able to keep people there for a very small amount of time? The task for any content owner is to find a business model that matches consumer expectations. Who is the consumer in this context? In any discussion of revenues, the consumer is the person who pays. In the case of advertising and newspapers, the advertiser is the consumer and the product is advertising space and audience share. Eighty percent of newspapers' revenue comes from advertising. Of this 80 percent, 40 percent is from retail advertising, 32 percent is from classified advertising, and 8 percent is from national advertising. The remaining 20 percent of revenue is from sales, with newsstands making up 17 percent and subscription revenue 3 percent. Erecting pay walls in order to increase the 3 percent revenue figure is truly nibbling at the margins.

In 2000, classified advertising accounted for $19.6 billion in newspapers' revenue. Since 2000, that amount has decreased over

70 percent. In 2008, the amount declined to $10.2 billion, and to $6 billion in 2009. None of that revenue will come back: It was lost to online services like Craigslist and other local or specialized online advertising platforms. Those platforms provide a far more appealing platform for advertisers, both in terms of audience size and focus. There is no reason the government or anyone else should make up for advertising that has been lost due to a change in the market, a market that is, moreover, characterized by fair competition. The loss of classified advertising to Craigslist and other online advertisers has nothing to do with copying or free-riding. The loss had nothing to do with search engines or news aggregators. Many businesses do not place classified ads with a newspaper for the simple and economically sound reason that the people they want to reach would never dream of looking in the classified section of a newspaper. I recently and quickly sold a car on Craigslist. I never thought of placing it with my local paper, as much as I love that paper and read it every morning. The reason: my local paper is local and is not read by some of those who might be interested in buying the car. This proved to be true: the person who bought the car lived well outside the circulation area of my local paper.[8]

Cold, economic facts of life cannot be changed by laws. Laws cannot make advertisers place ads where they don't want to and laws cannot create audience share. If newspapers want to make money from search engine advertising, they have to develop an attractive product for advertisers that works for that medium. The real money in search engine advertising is in highly commercial verticals such as shopping, health, and travel. Most of the search clicks that go to newspapers are in categories like sports, news, and local events, which don't attract the biggest spending advertisers. This should not be surprising: newspapers have never made much money from news. They've made money from the special interest sections on topics such as automotive, travel, home & garden, and food. These sections attract contextually targeted advertising, which is much more effective than non-targeted advertising. Someone reading the automotive section is likely to be more interested in cars than the average consumer, so advertisers will pay a premium to reach those consumers.

Traditionally, the ad revenue from these special sections has been used to cross-subsidize the core news production. Internet users go directly to websites like Edmunds (cars), Orbitz (travel), Epicurious (food), and Amazon.com to look for products and services in specialized areas. Advertisers follow those eyeballs, which makes the traditional cross-subsidization model that newspapers have used far more difficult to sustain today. That cross-subsidization was possible in the past only because of the monopoly power newspapers had in their market. That monopoly power derived from artificial scarcity of print advertising space in given markets. If you wanted to place a print classified advertisement, you had at most two—and usually only one—newspaper to go to outside of large metropolitan markets. The prices set were monopoly prices. With the Internet, that scarcity and monopoly power have been taken away, replaced by abundance. Any recommendation that has as its goal the restoration of newspaper revenues to the days of lost print monopoly power is simply not feasible. It is not a question of analog dollars versus digital dimes, but rather a realistic assessment of how to make money in a world of abundant competitors.

Rather than adapt to this changed world of abundance, a few generally powerful news organizations, both in the United States and abroad (especially Germany), have taken on the mantle of victim: things have happened to them, bad things for which other people are to blame. It is no doubt emotionally satisfying in the short-term to blame others for your own failures, but it is unhealthy in the long-term; one's failures can only be cured by admitting them and finding a way to solve them. Newspapers are not victims in any sense; a robust future is possible only if newspapers decide to take their own fates into their own hands, rather than ask for legal handouts.

You Can Compete with "Free"

One argument copyright owners frequently make for why stronger enforcement laws are necessary is the prevalence of unauthorized free material on the Internet.[9] If copyright owners withhold their works, it is only because letting things out "in the wild" will lead to massive piracy by consumers who won't pay anyway because they have grown accustomed to getting things for free on unauthorized online sites. This is a common but false belief. Here is an excerpt from a February 2011 interview with the prolific and successful science fiction and comic book author Neil Gaiman. (Gaiman by the way has been a plaintiff in copyright infringement suits over his characters and is not shy about asserting his rights):[10]

> When the Web started I got really grumpy with people
> Because they put my poems up, they put my stories
> up....
>   Then I started to notice that two things that seemed much more significant. One of which was that places where I was being pirated....I was selling more and more books. People were discovering me through being pirated. And then they were going out and buying the real books.....
>   I thought that was fascinating and I tried a few experiments, and some of them were quite hard—persuading my publisher to take one of my books and put it out for free. We took "American Gods"—a book that was still selling and selling very well. For a month they put it up, com-

pletely free on their website. You could read it, you could download it. What happened was that sales of my books....went up the following month 300%.[11]

Even more dramatic increases were seen by the comedy group Monty Python, whose series appeared on the BBC from 1969 to 1974. Fans of the Pythons had been uploading segments to You-Tube. The Pythons could have blocked them, but instead chose a different route: in 2008, they launched their own free YouTube channel offering high-resolution versions of the series, along with new interviews and rare archival footage. They also added a "Click to Buy" button, allowing viewers to purchase DVDs of the shows (and their movies) from authorized retailers. As a result, sales of the DVDs increased 23,000 percent. Aside from individual experiences such as Neil Gaiman's and Monty Python's (which, it should be noted, aren't unique), are there systematic data that test whether copyright owners can compete with "free"? There are, and empirically rigorous data at that. Economist Michael D. Smith and colleagues conducted two studies, one on the presence or absence of authorized audiovisual works on iTunes, the other on the presence or absence of authorized audiovisual works on broadcast channels. The results of these studies are available online, both in printed form[12] and on YouTube in a presentation by Professor Smith.[13]

The iTunes study was possible because of a fortuitous event: a dispute between Apple and NBC. In August 2007, NBC refused to extend its contract with iTunes, under which Apple had been selling NBC shows. Apple in turn refused to sell any NBC shows. By December 2, 2007, Apple had removed all NBC content from iTunes. A new agreement was later reached; NBC content was restored to iTunes on September 9, 2008. The researchers wanted to know what happened when NBC's works were removed and when they were restored. Did the removal of the content lead to more copying of NBC works from unauthorized sites? Did the restoration of the works reduce unauthorized copying? Was there an effect on unauthorized copying of non-NBC works from the withdrawal and later restoration of NBC content? Was there an effect on sales of DVD copies of NBC works?

The researchers engaged in extensive data gathering during the period November 2007 to November 2009. They gathered data for CBS, ABC, and Fox, and for DVD sales on Amazon.com. They gathered data from the Mininova bit torrent site for unauthorized downloads. They did comparisons for all of these sources during the entire period. This is what they found.

Before the removal of NBC content on December 2, 2007, the level of unauthorized copying was the same for all the networks surveyed. The copious data gathered demonstrate that there was an 11.4 percent increase in unauthorized copying of NBC content during the period that NBC shows were not on iTunes. The data were even broken down by genre, in order to test the theory that those using torrent sites for unauthorized copying tend to be (although are not exclusively) younger males. The theory was supported: the amount of unauthorized copying in this group's favored genres (comedy and science fiction)[14] increased 20 percent, while the increase for their least favorite genre, drama, was statistically insignificant.

Torrent copying of non-NBC content still available on iTunes also rose during this period, increasing 5.6 percent, and leading the researchers to suspect that once people were on Mininova copying NBC content, they stayed there to copy non-NBC content too. Sales of DVDs on Amazon.com were not affected, however, leading the researchers to suspect that the DVD market is separate from the digital download market.

What happened when the NBC content was restored to iTunes? The level of unauthorized copying diminished for NBC and for non-NBC content alike (although not to pre-removal levels), and again DVD sales were not affected. The lesson from the iTunes experience is that copyright owners *can* compete with free, but if they don't, they will increase the amount of unauthorized copying across the board: it is in *all* copyright owners' interests to have authorized material available.

The researchers also tested this hypothesis with a positive control group: on May 1, 2009, ABC announced it was adding its content to Hulu. The content was streamed for the first time on July 6, 2009. The same approach to data gathering as with the NBC/iTunes dispute was used, resulting in a finding that the amount of unauthorized downloads of ABC material decreased 37 percent once that content was made available on Hulu, again with no impact on DVD sales.

Here is a third set of data: the BitTorrent news blog TorrentFreak published a list of those TV shows most copied in 2010 using its service; in other words, those shows, in short, that copyright owners describe as being the most "pirated." Interestingly, number 1 on the list was ABC's *Lost*. For several months of 2010, the series was available for free on Hulu: not just the last five episodes, but the whole series, and for free. The obvious question is, why did people copy via BitTorrent when they could get it for free from Hulu? One answer is most copying was from outside the United States. Why? Because Hulu is available only inside the United States. The interesting data point here is not only the obvious one that those outside the United States have to download from unauthorized sites, but also the data that the availability of shows on Hulu has reduced by 50 percent the amount of unauthorized downloads from within the United States.

The iTunes, Hulu, and BitTorrent data show that contrary to received wisdom, the solution is not more laws, but more authorized content, at correct pricing, and in forms that are the most useful and convenient to consumers. Copyright owners will never be able to eliminate piracy, but they can effectively compete with it and make good profits with correct pricing and convenience. Reliance on laws as a deterrence to unauthorized behavior is possible, but only under conditions that do not presently exist. I shall now examine the belief about the effectiveness of copyright laws as a deterrence to unauthorized copying.

SIX

Does Deterrence Work?

Much like God gave Moses the tablets on Mt. Sinai with instructions to take the laws written on them to the Israelites impatiently waiting for Moses' return, copyright owners believe they can go to legislatures, get them to enact laws, and the public will simply obey the commandments. This approach didn't work for God and Moses, so why copyright owners believe a top-down approach to obeying copyright law will work for them is a mystery, especially given the rich history of the approach not working in the past.

One answer to why the Mt. Sinai mistake is repeated over and over again by copyright owners is that it meshes with their world view, which is one of control: control over those who create works, control over the distribution of those works, and control over prices and consumption by the public. Any breach in this system of control is viewed as an existential threat to making money. Under the Mt. Sinai approach, copyright = control = money. Law is therefore the necessary first step in this control equation; the coercive power provided by law is, for too many in the copyright industries, not external to their businesses, it *is* their business model.[1] This fanatical obsession with control explains why the copyright industries so consistently take anti-consumer actions: it is not that the industries hate their customers, as is commonly assumed, but rather that the industries believe the only way they can make money from their customers is to tightly control customers' access to and use of their works. The effect of this approach is a hostile relationship and bad business models. Control has nothing to do with incentives to create; efforts at absolute control have absolutely nothing to do with incentives. Indeed, control by non-creators can reduce creators' incentives to produce the very works copyright aims to encourage.

The top-down legal approach to shaping the marketplace is based on mistaken assumptions about consumer behavior. All laws have shaping behavior as their principal purpose. There are two ways behavior is assumed to be shaped: through incentives and through deterrence. Incentives encourage desired behavior by providing rewards; deterrence discourages undesirable behavior by providing penalties. Law and economics theorists regard law as a form of behavioral pricing. The objective is to price undesirable behavior high enough to cause its voluntary cessation:

> An increase in the price of engaging in an illegal activity will induce individuals to reduce or even eliminate their involvement in such activity, and what illegal activity remains will be that for which the marginal benefits to individuals continue to exceed even the higher marginal cost.[2]

Copyright laws are based on both the incentive and deterrence principles: incentives are given to copyright owners in the form of exclusive rights; deterrence is provided in the form of civil and criminal penalties supposedly set high enough to discourage infringement from occurring in the first place. But behavior-shaping tools are effective only if application of those tools produces the desired behavior. I reviewed in chapter 3 the theory that copyright is a necessary incentive to create. I concluded it largely is not. I examine here whether the deterrents provided by penalties actually stop people from infringing copyrighted works. I conclude they largely don't.

WHY PEOPLE OBEY OR DISOBEY THE LAW

Tom Tyler is a professor at New York University, with a joint appointment in the Psychology Department and the Law School. In 1990, he published a foundational book, *Why People Obey the Law*.[3] In 1997, he published an article on compliance with intellectual property laws.[4] He has published many other articles exploring the reasons people obey or disobey the law, cooperate or don't cooperate with authorities, how legal and other regimes obtain and lose legitimacy, as well as the societal implications for the loss of legitimacy. His research tells us a great deal about how to craft effective copyright laws.

The first requirement is that laws be consistent with societal values. Rather than drawing on societal values that lead to cooperation—such as the availability of lawful copies at fair prices with a fair share of the royalties going to the artists—the deterrence approach taken by our copyright laws is purely coercive. Coercion rarely succeeds in forcing compliance with laws that significantly depart from shared societal values, as our current copyright law do. Professor Tyler argues that

> a law-abiding society is one in which people are motivated
> not by fears, but rather by a desire to act in socially appro-
> priate and ethical ways.... To have a law-abiding society,
> we must have a polity in which social values lead them to

feel responsible for following rules, irrespective of the likelihood of being caught and punished for rule breaking.[5]

The belief that legislatures can force the public to obey copyright
laws the public disagrees with is a fundamental error.[6] Such laws
are not just ineffective; copyright owners mistakenly rely on them
as a substitute for responding to market demand. By violating the
law of demand, copyright owners lose their best chance to get
voluntary cooperation with copyright laws. It should not, therefore, be surprising that many have come to see copyright as a
means by which copyright owners impose, through law, bad business models, and see the legislators who pass copyright laws as
willing accomplices.[7]

Only good business models, and never law, are the solution to
bad business models. There is only one way to get people to obey
copyright laws, and that is to have copyright laws that support
good business models. Our current laws don't do this, and thus it
is not surprising that many people don't believe in them.[8] Laws
that people don't believe in lack deterrent force.

In crafting an effective deterrence strategy, the question to be answered is not the one asked by Max Weber in his 1914 book *Economy
and Society*—why people *ought* to obey the law—but rather why
people obey the law sometimes but not other times. There are two
reasons, both of which we will now analyze: First, people obey laws
they regard as fair; and, second, while the public may disagree with a
particular law, it may nevertheless obey it if the process by which the
law was enacted is regarded as fair and legitimate and if the issue is
one on which reasonable people may disagree. In pluralistic societies
it is rarely possible to get unanimity, and because of this people generally recognize that there can be honest differences in values. Where
there are such honest differences, the process by which the differences
are resolved becomes quite important.

Legitimacy of Process as a Requirement for Effective Laws

One might think people are only willing to follow laws they agree with. This is to a large extent true, but it is not entirely true: people recognize that there are "two sides to every issue" and that decision-makers have to make judgment calls. They also recognize that sometimes they will win those judgment calls and other times they won't. But so long as they feel that the arguments on all sides were close and that the process by which the decision-making occurred was fair, people are willing to follow at least some laws they disagree with. This provides lawmakers with an invaluable opportunity to lead. Regrettably, it is an opportunity that lawmakers routinely squander.

The opportunity to lead depends on being able to participate in an open, fair procedure of debate about the laws proposed. Meaningful participation in a legitimate process of decision-making results in a feeling of obligation to abide by the outcome of that process, and therefore has both practical and social value. As Professor Tyler noted:

> People are more likely to regard as fair, and to accept, decisions in which they participated. In the area of law, this suggests the importance of involving citizens in the development and implication of intellectual property laws. If people feel that they have participated in the creation of legal rules, those rules are more likely to be viewed as legitimate, and therefore obeyed.[9]

But for a feeling of legitimacy to arise, people must have the opportunity to state their case to lawmakers before decisions are made. Lawmakers must pay attention and genuinely consider the arguments being made to them. Hearings can't be what they all too often are: staged, cheerleading events, stacked with proponents of the legislators' proposals, who then praise the legislators for their "great leadership" in giving the proponents what they want, with only token sacrificial witnesses in opposition, who are usually scolded for their allegedly immoral behavior. Procedural unfairness is always in aid of substantive unfairness.[10]

In addition to a legitimate opportunity to participate, lawmakers must be neutral in the process by which they arrive at their decisions. This doesn't mean lawmakers cannot have formed any views (which would be totally unrealistic), but rather that they are open to changing their views through persuasion.[11] As Second Circuit Judge Pierre Leval once told me, the best way to know you have a mind is to change it. Unfortunately, this rarely happens. Too many times lawmakers have formed views that they blindly stick to, views that are based on one side's presentation, and likely a false representation of others' views. In such situations, those seeking to change lawmakers' minds rightly feel frustrated and regard the process as illegitimate, regardless of how open the process is, as it is not an open process but an open mind that is the most important. Faced with closed minds, citizens justifiably ignore lofty declarations of neutrality and a professed desire to "balance" all interests.

Here is an example that I experienced first hand. In the late 1980s, there were a series of opinions from the U.S. Court of Appeals for the Second Circuit in Manhattan, involving when biographers could use unpublished letters in their books. There was an initial opinion (involving J.D. Salinger) that had some troubling language.[12] There were extreme reactions to this language from some book publishers and their lawyers, leading to a hyperbolic concern by one Senator who declared in a newspaper Op-Ed that we were facing "The End of History" (or, more accurately, at least of its telling). Quickly, legislation was introduced. A rare joint hearing of the Senate and House intellectual property subcommittees was held. I was the lead witness, testifying on behalf of my then-current employer, the U.S. Copyright Office. As the lead witness, Senator DeConcini, chair of the Senate subcommittee and chair of the hearing, expected me to be a cheerleader for the bill. I demurred, infuriating him. My view was that there were many witnesses coming after me, including three Second Circuit judges, authors, publishers, and others. I, and hopefully the members of Congress, should want to listen to their testimony before deciding whether legislation accomplished its goals. If it did then we would support it. I didn't dodge questions, and instead gave straightforward answers. Senator DeConcini would have none of that—he only wanted one answer: yes, we supported the bill as drafted without hearing any witnesses who would have to live with the bill if passed. When I refused to give him that answer, he sarcastically asked me in his very last question why I had bothered to show up. I returned the sarcasm. Here is the relevant passage from the hearing transcript:

SENATOR DECONCINI. Mr. Patry, I take it from your statement that the [Copyright] Office does not take a position in favor or opposed to this bill; is that accurate?

MR. PATRY. We believe that the legislative process has to identify, clearly, what the goal of the legislation is. Is the goal of the legislation to reverse some of the language in the Supreme Court's decision in *Harper & Row* saying that the unpublished nature of a work is a key but not determinative factor? Probably not.

I think from the floor statements [introducing the bills], it is evident that the approach is to try and eliminate what is viewed as a virtually per se rule in the second circuit, which is that normally unpublished works enjoy complete protection [according to] the Copyright Act.

If it is believed that a legislative solution is appropriate—and here, I believe the Copyright Office does not have an institutional interest in the legislation. In our normal course of work, we don't make fair use determinations. We view our role here as being an advisory role to you in drafting legislation. I think the key is to find out from the authors and publishers and from the judges whom you have here today, will this bill help them do what you want [it] to do, will it give them more guidance?

SENATOR DECONCINI. I take it from your statement—correct me please, if I am inaccurate—that if a standard could be written, that is what we should do, or at least consider.

MR. PATRY. Yes. And it may be that the bills, as drafted, will accomplish that. Interestingly, there are two different views, I think on the drafting of the statute. Some people believe that it doesn't accomplish anything because fair use already applies to unpublished works, so why are you going to amend the statute to do what it already does?

Other people believe that is the beauty of the drafting, that it does not attempt to overreach. I think the important thing is to find out from the judges whether or not this particular language will accomplish your goals. If it does, we support it.

SENATOR DECONCINI. So, for the record, the Copyright Office has no position on this bill?

MR. PATRY. On the drafting. If it is believed that the drafting, as it is, is appropriate to the goals, we will support it.

SENATOR DECONCINI. And you don't know. You are here for this hearing also?

Mr. Patry. Yes, I am. That's right. I think that is why I came at 9:30.[13]

Currently, significant numbers of the public question the way our copyright laws are enacted, and as a result do not feel bound by laws they regard as illegitimate. Once lost, legitimacy, like trust, is very difficult to regain. In a survey released in July 2010, the U.S. Congress had a favorable approval rating of only 11 percent, lower than any other institution, and below even car salesmen.[14] More than half of the population said they have "very little" or "no" confidence in Congress, the highest low-confidence vote for any institution since the Gallup polling company first asked the question in 1973.[15] Even "big business" and health mainte-nance organizations scored 8 points higher than Congress.

An Example of Failure—The 1999 Work for Hire Amendment

In the field of copyright, it is possible Congress's approval rating is even lower. Few members of the public, especially those opposing proposals, have a chance to have their voices heard by lawmakers.[16] Sometimes no one gets a chance to speak in opposition. Here is one example: On November 29, 1999, Congress amended section 101 of the Copyright Act to include sound recordings (a recorded performance) as a new, tenth category of specially ordered or com-missioned work for hire.[17] Under the work for hire doctrine, the employer or commissioning party is considered to be the author and owner of all rights. The actual creator has no copyright interest in the work, receiving instead whatever benefits are provided for in the employment contract or commissioning agreement.

The purpose of the 1999 amendment was to deny perform-ers and their estates the right to terminate old contracts. This denial would occur because if performers were considered to be employees of the record label, they would not have any copyright interest at all: the right to terminate old contracts is limited to authors. The seriousness of this effort to strip performers of status as authors is seen in a recent court decision holding that classic albums by Bob Marley were works for hire of Island Records and thus owned 100 percent by the label.[18] According to the court, Marley was a mere employee of Island Records, acting under the label's supervision and direction, and possessing no authorship interest at all. To believe this is to believe pigs can fly.

The 1999 take-away provision was snuck through at the request of the Recording Industry Association of America (RIAA). It was placed in an unrelated bill on satellite retransmissions of copyrighted works, at the very end of the Congress, without a bill having been introduced, and without hearings. The House Judiciary Committee staffer who snuck the provision in was shortly thereafter hired by RIAA for a very well-paying position. He remains in that position today.

Composers and performers understandably went ballistic. Recording artist Sheryl Crow complained, "To let the looming presence of large organized special interest groups, working on behalf of film and recording companies, control the fate of the artist community is alarming."[19] Representative John Conyers agreed: "There were no hearings, no markups, no consideration of any kind by the Members. . . . I contend, Mr. Chairman, that is not how this committee and this Congress should be writing our intellectual property matters. The normal process is too important."[20] The normal process is important because it conveys legitimacy and respect. In this case, Congress chose not to use the normal process because doing so would have given performing artists the chance to successfully block the bill.[21]

The Deterrence Model and Copyright Laws

There are people who will disobey laws no matter how fair or fairly enacted,[22] but properly drafted laws can be useful in affecting how often the general level of misbehavior occurs.[23] A law is effective if most citizens obey it most of the time, either for the social reasons cited above or because effective penalties are provided for those who don't. The issue is not whether to have deterrence provisions in our copyright laws, but rather, what type of deterrence provisions are effective?

Unfortunately, governments have made no effort to determine what constitutes effective deterrence to copyright violations. Professor Ian Hargreaves, in a report for the British government, undertook a thorough review of enforcement efforts and data, yet he concluded: "At this moment, no-one in the UK could make an informed assessment of what is the right level of resource for online enforcement in the UK."[24] But instead of taking the time to get things right, the punitive provisions of copyright laws have been on a mindless upward curve, defying both gravity and any relationship to need or purpose. One reason for this is that increasing penalties is an easy political win for legislators. With respect to criminal laws, few potential criminals testify at Congressional or parliamentary hearings. Even for increased civil penalties, those who oppose such unnecessary proposals are put in an awkward position: since the penalties are assessed only after one is found guilty of infringement, coming out against such proposals is construed as trying to get off the hook for bad behavior.

Lost in all of this is the only question that should be asked: what level of deterrence works? Increasing the prison sentence for copyright infringement from five to ten years without knowing that doing so will result in fewer acts of infringement doesn't make policymakers tough on crime and it doesn't mean they are looking out for the interests of creators. It merely means they have substituted show for substance. Here is why: Just because a law works well at one level doesn't mean that stronger laws are more effective. The assumption that more of a good thing is always better is as false as the assumption that less is always better. Laws, like medicines, need to be tailored to achieve the desired result. Medicines that can save lives in one dose can be fatal in other doses. There is an old medical adage that "It is the dose that makes the poison," which stems from a belief that all medicines are "poisons in one form or another, merely diluted to an appropriate dose."[25] Even drugs in non-fatal doses can have bad effects. Taking one aspirin a day is recommended by many doctors to prevent heart attacks, but more than one per day can cause bleeding ulcers, kidney, or liver damage. Modern draconian copyright laws are a disease masquerading as their own cure.

At the same time, calls for abolishing copyright laws ignore that there is a need to prevent unauthorized, non-socially useful conduct that is individually beneficial to members of the public in the short term (in the sense of not paying), but which is harmful to society in the long term (by killing the goose that lays the golden eggs).[26] But how to effectively stop such harmful conduct? While I am critical of the copyright industries' wildly exaggerated figures, there is, nevertheless, a significant amount of unauthorized behavior, some of which harms copyright owners' legitimate economic interests. Regrettably, the approach taken by policymakers to the problem has been reflexively and repeatedly to increase punishments without regard for whether this approach is effective, and without regard to the waste of government resources involved in enforcing ineffective laws.

Copyright owners seem convinced that if the public is constantly threatened with being caught and punished, their problems will go away, and they can go back to ignoring con-

sumer demand. But studies in diverse areas show that individuals' judgment about the certainty of punishment, have, at
best a minor influence on their behavior, unless a high threshold of probability is met.[27] A comprehensive study of unauthorized copying by the Social Science Research Council
notes the global rebellion against current approaches, a rebellion that is impervious to what are falsely cast as educational
campaigns:

> [C]onsumer attitudes are, for the most part, not unformed—
> not awaiting definition by a clear antipiracy message. On
> the contrary, we consistently found strong views. The con-
> sumer surplus generated by piracy in middle-income coun-
> tries is not just popular but also widely understood in
> economic justice terms, mapped to perceptions of greedy
> United States of America and multinational corporations
> and to the broader structural inequalities of globalization in
> which most developing-world consumers live. Enforce-
> ment efforts, in turn, are widely associated with the United
> States of America pressure on national governments, and
> are met with indifference or hostility by large majorities of
> respondents.[28]

Even public institutions are forced to violate the law to fulfill their
missions. The National Recording Preservation Board of the
Library of Congress noted:

> In the perception of the public, copyright law has a reputa-
> tion for being overly restrictive. This perception fosters a
> dismissive attitude toward the law in communities that can
> hardly be characterized as rogue elements of society. An
> individual representing one institution has noted that, unless
> or until instructed to cease and desist certain practices, his

organization was compelled to "fly under the radar" to support its mission.[29]

As a result, the Board concluded that:

> Were copyright law followed to the letter, little audio preservation would be undertaken. Were the law strictly enforced, it would brand virtually all-audio preservation as illegal. Copyright laws related to preservation are neither strictly followed nor strictly enforced....
>
> Libraries, archives, and other public and privately funded institutions are finding it virtually impossible to reconcile their responsibility for preserving and making accessible culturally important sound recordings with their obligation to adhere to copyright laws.[30]

Laws that are out of step with the needs of society must be changed. When we don't change them—as we have not with our copyright laws—there is massive disobedience. Characterizing wide segments of the populations as thieves and criminals is a sure sign a system of laws has failed.

SEVEN

Abandoning Exclusivity and Getting Paid Instead

The central element in copyright ideology is exclusivity. Copyright owners are said to be granted "exclusive rights,"[1] the essence of which is the ability to exclude, to be able to say no to anyone who wants to use your work, the ability to say no for a good reason, for a bad reason, or for no reason; the ability to attempt to command any price you want; the ability to impose any conditions you wish on the use of your work; and in many countries, the ability to withdraw the work from circulation.[2]

When people refer to copyright as a property right, this is what they mean[3]: It's mine and I can do what I want with it. The characterization of property as the exclusive dominion of its owner may be traced back to the single most quoted remark in Anglo-American law about property, that of Sir William Blackstone in his "Chronicles on the Laws of England," published in four volumes between 1765 and 1769. Blackstone remarked: "There is nothing which so generally strikes the imagination, and engages the affections of mankind, as the right of property. . . . That sole and despotic dominion which one man claims and exercises over the external things of the world in total exclusion of the right of any other individual in the universe."

Regrettably, much of copyright ideology is still mired in that time period, as if technological and market conditions have remained unchanged in the intervening 235 years, as if rhetorical views expressed about English landed estates at a time when England passed the first stamp tax against the American colonies can resolve the question of whether an Internet video hosting service should be liable for making Danger Mouse's *Grey Album* mash-up of the Beatles *White Album* and Jay-Z's *Black Album* available for viewing.

Leaving aside the absurdity of resolving such questions by reference to Blackstone, no form of property has ever been exclusive in the "sole and despotic" sense, even in Blackstone's time. Private property rights do provide an important underpinning for the successful functioning of capitalism. Private property rights constrain the power of the State; they provide an incentive to work and take risks. But private property rights are not and have never been absolute: their reach depends on the specific circumstances—the nature of the property, the presence or absence of what economists call externalities (a cost or a benefit that is not captured in prices),[4] and the character of the market in which the property is traded. If I own my car, I will be protected in that ownership against theft, but the State can still tell me what speeds to drive, to wear a seatbelt, to have insurance, and to register the car with the motor vehicle department and pay fees for that registration. I may own my house, but I still have to pay real estate taxes, grant easements, and be restrained from polluting my neighbors' property. The creator of a copyrighted work is given certain statutory rights, but those rights are similarly limited in order to further the public interest, including precluding the exercise of those rights in ways that impede the advance of knowledge, creativity, and innovation.

At their inception, Anglo-American copyright statutes were sketched skeletally by legislatures; legislatures left common law judges to fill in the many substantive details. In filling in those details, common law judges were guided by their perception of the purposes of copyright law: to further knowledge and to have authors paid for rights deemed to be within their legitimate market. The concept of a legitimate market has changed over time, and rightly so as economic conditions change.

Regrettably, currently both authors and the public are ill served by our current laws: authors go unpaid for many legally compensable uses, while many uses that should not be compensated for are the subject of claims by copyright owners. What are the reasons for this unhappy state of affairs?

In the case of uncompensated uses where income should flow to authors, there are two reasons why things have broken down. The first reason is the sheer volume of unauthorized activity made possible by digital formats. There is no effective way to control most of this activity, so the solution is to figure out how to compensate for it. Doing so entails giving up the ideology of copyright = control = money. The new equation must be simply copyright = compensation.[5] The RIAA's lawsuits against 30,000 individuals ended in failure, with failure defined by the lack of new monies being put in artists' pockets, by the lack of a decrease in unauthorized file sharing, and by the terrible public relations black eye RIAA, the record labels, and copyright law in general got from the controversial campaign. As discussed above,[6] copyright owners *can* compete with "free." Insisting on control, insisting on the ability to always say no, insisting that "it's my property and everyone who uses my work without my permission is a thief," may make one feel self-righteous, but it won't pay the bills. A right of remuneration, not the ability to say no to things you can't control anyway, must be the new focus.

There are four principal ways to get paid: (1) rely on one-to-one negotiations by exercising an exclusive right; (2) mandatory statutory licenses for particular works and uses, (3) levies on recording media; and (4) collective licensing. With statutory licenses, the legislature determines that copyright owners have a right to get paid but do not have the ability to block uses. The amount of the license is usually set out in the statute the first time and then adjusted at future, periodical dates by some form of governmental body. The money is paid directly to the copyright owner. The oldest of such licenses is the mechanical compulsory license in the United States, established in 1909. Under this license, once the copyright owner of a non-dramatic musical work authorizes a recording of his or her composition, anyone else can make another recording of that composition (a "cover version") upon paying a prescribed fee.

With levies, the government sets rates on recording media: in the old days, tapes or computer discs, as well as printers and photocopiers; now: USB flash drives, iPods, Mp3 players, and mobile phones. Different media are covered or exempt from levies in different countries; their rates vary wildly among countries, and even with common markets, such as the European Union. Hewlett Packard has stated it pays €12 for printers in Germany, but €178.84 in Belgium. According to a study by the Free University of Brussels, it costs the IT hardware industry €1.88 billion annually in administrative costs to comply with the different levy schemes. Even if the actual amount spent is a quarter of that amount, the amount wasted due to an unharmonized regime is quite significant. The European Commission recently gave up a 16-year effort to harmonize its laws on levies and punted to a mediator. There is no lack of studies on the economics of levies.[7] The problem is not a lack of data but a lack of political will. Turning the issue over to a mediator may help discussions, but since the mediator, no matter how skilled, lacks the ability to impose a final solution, the can is kicked down the road: the warring parties know they can always argue their case again before sympathetic national legislators who desire, understandably, to protect domestic industries, e.g., in Finland, Nokia. As an important source of income and clarity for device makers, a solution to the levy problem is critical.

With collective licensing, copyright owners pool their copyrights together with a private organization, which then licenses use of the entire repertoire to others, takes an administrative cut of license fees received, and pays the amount left over to the copyright owners.[8] There are numerous benefits to this, especially reducing transaction costs and enabling copyright owners to receive income for many small uses that would otherwise be economically impossible to negotiate one-to-one. Licensees can have available a vast repertoire without the high costs of clearing individual uses, as well as, usually, protection in the form of a government appeal over license fees. But there are also significant downsides: collecting societies can become monopolies and can block any innovation that is seen to threaten the interests of the society's managers, who may enjoy healthy salaries and benefits. Collecting societies can exercise disproportionate leverage against smaller licensees; they can be administratively inefficient and sometimes even corrupt; they can favor national right holders over foreign ones; they can retain royalties for a long time in order to "float" interest payments;[9] and they can make very bad investments.[10] For example, control over the Italian collecting society, Società Italiana degli Autori ed Editori (SIAE), was taken over by the Italian government in 1999 for four years after it reported losses of US $53 million (at 1999 exchange rates) even though collections were up. In 2008, SIAE was reported to have lost US $52.3 million in investments in Lehman Brothers, when the latter went bankrupt.[11]

By the time this book is set in print, the European Union will have submitted proposals for reform of the societies. Hopefully, those proposals will be bold ones, and will take the form of enabling legislation mandating efficient licensing. Here are a few of my proposals: First, the number and duties of societies must be dramatically reduced per country, with no more than one per right, per type of work, and preferably with one per type of work: e.g., for music, one society that can license the performance right, the making available right, neighboring rights, and all mechanical rights, including downloads. The current regime, which continues a multiplicity of rights, each licensed by a different organization, does not reflect the way current markets and technologies work. For example, it does little good to have licensing solutions only for musical compositions. To be effective, licensing must include sound recordings and, importantly, information that can track a particular composition to a particular sound recording.

I also recommend the following: There should be worldwide exhaustion of digital rights once a work has been licensed in one country. National or regional exhaustion is a relic of the analog world. Societies should be required to maintain free, publicly accessible online databases of which works they claim the right to administer, as well as contact information for the rights holders sufficient to permit users to contact the rights holders directly. There should be legally required fixed time periods to distribute monies, especially for foreign rights holders. If foreign money is not distributed within the requisite time period, the foreign rights holder or the home society of the rights holders may bring suit and are entitled to attorney's fees and penalties.

Collecting societies should be required to use ISO-standard rights management systems, in order to lower the administrative costs of obtaining information about rights held and payments due. Identification numbers for works, performers, and recordings must be standard and uniformly used. It is highly ironic that as a result of the 1996 WIPO Copyright and Phonograms treaties, countries have made it a crime to delete copyright management information, while not requiring that the information be standardized and actually used by rights holders. The compensation for the executives of the societies should be publicly posted annually, and their term of office should be limited to four years. Governance of the societies should be representative of those whose rights are being administered.

One-to-one negotiations will always be necessary for situations where we want copyright owners to control the individual use of their work, such as licensing the use of a novel or musical composition in a movie for "grand rights" (theater), or for use in advertisements. Statutory licensing is appropriate where we do not want users to bargain over the licensee fee (usually because the transaction costs are high relative to the license fee) but we do want them to pay. Collective administration is appropriate where, due to large transaction costs and the potential inequality of bargaining leverage by individual copyright owners, we want users to have to negotiate fees.

The usual theoretical model today remains the exclusive rights. This model is becoming less useful given the large-scale, global nature of the Internet. But as much attention as unauthorized uses on the Internet receive, the largest problems facing authors today are not unauthorized uses but the obstacles put in the way of buyers willing to pay for access to or copies of the work. These obstacles have caused a huge loss of income for composers, performers, and photographers (given the sheer volume of works they create). For these creators, the costs of enforcing rights are substantial, and involve search costs for identifying infringers, enforcement costs for suing infringers, transaction costs for negotiating licenses with users, and collection costs for obtaining payment from licensees. Innovative services that wish to offer the public authorized, paid access, or copies have been impeded or shut down by licensing difficulties. Prospective licensees must negotiate directly with numerous groups or companies that frequently have competing claims, and they must negotiate anew in each country.

The best illustration of this is the music industry, which we can think of as a potentially very profitable restaurant owned by an extended family that is always feuding, and has from time immemorial. They are loudly arguing out on the sidewalk in front of the restaurant. Inside the restaurant are customers lined up, all of whom love the food and have wallets full of money, ready to pay. The owners are, however, outside fighting about who gets paid: how much and for which meals. As a result of their fighting, the customers eventually leave, and everyone starves, including the chefs, the waiters, and those who grew the food and supplied it to the restaurant. The owners then blame the customers for the owners' terrible fate. The music industry family is fatally dysfunctional; policymakers have to step in and lead. Leading means making decisions that some people or even many people don't like, but which are necessary for the good of all. You can't consider yourself a leader if you don't lead in this most basic of meanings.

Here is a technical explanation of why the music industry faces these problems. Copyright consists of a bundle of different rights, including a right to authorize the reproduction of copies of the work, the right to publicly distribute copies of the work, the right to publicly perform the work, and more recently, the making available right (really a combination of the distribution and public performance rights). These rights can be, and usually are, separately assigned. This means there are multiple different owners of rights in the same piece of music. A composer can assign the right to make and distribute copies of the work to a music publisher; the music publisher then licenses the right to make and distribute recorded versions of the composition to a record company. The composer can assign the right to authorize public performances of the composition to a performing rights society, in the United States, ASCAP, or BMI.[12] There may also be a public performance right for the sound recording, and in many countries, there are collecting societies that license more than one right. The administration of all these rights entails separate administrative fees—which come out of authors' and performers' royalties; the payout rates to authors and performers varies depending upon the right that is licensed.

In order to have a music service offered to the public, all possible rights holders must sign off. It does no good to get the right to stream performances of sound recordings unless you have the right to also stream the underlying musical composition. Unless you get both rights, you can't offer the service. Given that you want to offer as wide a service as possible, you have to obtain licenses from everyone. If a single important licensor says no, you're sunk.

But it is even worse than that. There are disputes within the music industry about whether a stream requires both a public performance license as well as a reproduction and distribution license, and whether a download requires both a reproduction and distribution license as well as a public performance license.[13] There are music publishers who demand a separate license for uploading your own CD to a locker service and for then listening to it. Multiple claims are thus often made for the same conduct, with one group claiming the conduct constitutes a public performance and another group claiming the conduct constitutes a reproduction, and both demanding payment.

Those who wish to offer music services—like the restaurant customers—are happy to pay, but they should not pay multiple times to different groups for the same conduct.[14] As the U.S. Copyright Office observed, "licensors have rarely turned down the opportunity in the digital age to seek royalties, even when the basis for their requests is weak at best. Online music companies rightly complain that they need certainty over what rights are implicated and what royalties are payable so that they can operate without fear of being sued for copyright infringement."[15] Greed is not good, as Michael Douglas's character Gordon Gekko once argued in the movie *Wall Street*. Obstructionists in the music industry would do well to follow the advice of another movie character: actor Alec Baldwin's character's Blake in David Mamet's 1992 film *Glengarry Glen Ross*. Sent in by corporate headquarters to motivate real estate salesmen, he harangues them about going after prospective buyers: "They're sitting out there waiting to give you their money. Are you gonna take it?" To date, the answer has been "no."

The problem is international: many tens of millions of dollars are left on the table in Europe alone because of the inability to get pan-European licenses. Instead, licensees have to negotiate on a country-by-country basis with national collecting societies, music publishers, and record labels (to name only the top three groups), to say nothing of countries where there are no collecting societies. Authors lose because deals aren't done; the public loses because there is a dearth of authorized, complete services; copyright law as a system loses for both these reasons. The European Commission has observed:

> Consumers expect, rightly, that they can access content online at least as effectively as in the offline world. Europe lacks a unified market in the content sector. For instance, to set-up a pan-European service an online music store would have to negotiate with numerous rights management soci-

eties based in 27 countries. Consumers can buy CDs in every shop but are often unable to buy music from online platforms across the EU because rights are licensed on a national basis.[16]

It is impossible to overstate how severe the rights clearance problem is.[17] Here is one example, from just one country, the United Kingdom. Figure 7.1 explains from whom potential licensees must clear rights.

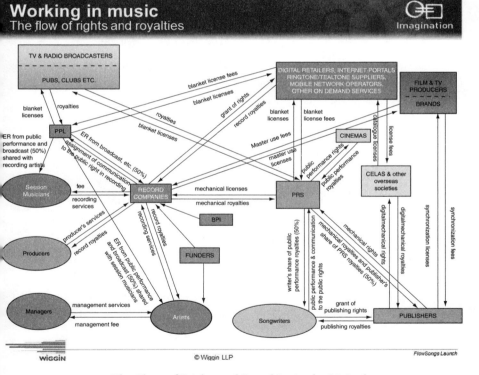

FIGURE 7.1   The Flow of Rights and Royalties in the United Kingdom. Modeled on a diagram included in the slide presentation *FlowSongs Launch*, © Wiggins LLP.

Now multiply this times almost 200 countries and you can see why there is no worldwide music service and will never be unless rights holders cooperate first with a global rights registry, and then a way is developed for global licensing. Global licensing can only be accomplished by legislative and treaty action. Time spent on this effort and on resolving fundamental questions about the nature of rights that need to be cleared, rather than suing consumers or online services, will reap authors vastly greater amounts of money in both the short and long term.

In order to accomplish this, policymakers must make bold political decisions to radically break with the past. There is reason to be skeptical that this will occur. Twenty-four years after the creation of a single European market, a service wishing to offer a lawful, one-stop paying music service cannot do so. The European Commission's May 2010 "Digital Agenda" document makes the usual noises about the need for pan-European licensing and the need to improve collective rights management. In the usual grand rhetoric, such improvements will, it is said, "stimulate creativity and help the content producers and broadcasters, to the benefit of European citizens."[18] Yet, the Commission proposes to prevent these goals from ever being accomplished by adding, "such solutions should preserve the contractual freedom of right holders. Right holders would not be obliged to license for all European territories, but would remain free to restrict their licenses to certain territories and to contractually set the level of license fees."[19] This statement is precisely why we are in the mess we are in: The problems and solutions are well-known, but a failure of political will to disturb the powerful interests that maintain the very business models causing the problems renders meaningful progress impossible.

Rights registries, in which there are easily accessible, transparent repositories of information about who owns what, where, and for how long, are critical to such progress.

EIGHT

The Length of Copyright Is Damaging Our Cultural Heritage

Providing the public with access to copyrighted works is a central tenet of copyright in all systems (hence this chapter draws examples from around the world). In order to promote culture and learning, culture and learning must be shared with others, preferably as widely as possible. It does society no good to grant copyright in a work that stays locked in a desk drawer. In the United States, such access is the sole ground for having copyright. But even in Europe and other countries where the focus is more on authors, encouraging the creation and dissemination of cultural works is also critical.

The evidence is overwhelming that the current, excessive length of copyright (life of the author plus seventy years in many countries) denies access to vast troves of culture and not only thwarts the preservation of old works, but does not incentivize the creation of new ones.[1] (I review some of that evidence below and provide copious notes to other sources.) The longer the term, the more difficult it is to track down who owns rights in the work: authors move or die, their estates close, companies to whom rights are transferred go out of business or sell those rights, sometimes many times over. On top of this, there is frequently bad data inputted at the beginning: songwriters, musical publishers, and record labels who don't register their data correctly the first time will cause endless problems for those who wish to license works where the basic data on ownership is wrong.

If you can't track down who owns rights in the work, you can't use it no matter how socially beneficial your use may be and no matter how likely it is that the copyright owner has lost all interest in exploiting the work. This was not a problem when the term of protection was short: those who argued for a longer term of protection selfishly thought only of themselves, not thinking or caring that the longer the term of protection, the greater the loss to society from the inability to create new works based on old works, and an inability to preserve old works. The long term of protection is seriously damaging to our cultural heritage.

Here are a few examples. The BBC has 1 million hours of programming in its archives that are unusable because the rights holders are unknown and there is no way to get clearance.[2] Costs for clearance of those works where rights holders can be identified are estimated to be 72 million pounds in staff time alone.[3] British museums hold 17 million photographs, of which 90 percent lack rights holder identification.[4] The problem also exists for very small projects. Karl Miller, who owns a very small nonprofit company specializing in historical performances of music gave these illustrations to the U.S. Copyright Office:

> I have had to scrap several recording projects due to "orphaned" works....

Example 1

My former teacher, a composer named Spencer Norton, wrote several works I wanted to record on CD. The disc would have been a tribute to his memory. He died in the 1970s. He copyrighted his music, yet he did not have a publisher. He had no heirs and I have had no luck tracking down the estate. As it stands now, it will be impossible to release recordings of any of his music during my own lifetime.

We also wanted to include some broadcast performances of his music. These broadcasts were done by the Oklahoma City Symphony. The Orchestra was dissolved many years ago and, as required by law, any of its remaining assets being distributed to other non-profits. The current orchestra in Oklahoma City has stated that they got nothing from the old orchestra, nor do they know of any individual owning whatever rights might exist to those broadcast performances. At this point in time, IRMA will not allow us to publish any of these recordings, even though the ownership of the broadcasts, assuming they were copyrighted, cannot be determined. Similarly, all attempts to contact the Oklahoma City local of the musician's union have turned up nothing.

Example 2

We are featuring a disc of the recordings of two of the great Italian musicians of the 20th Century, Ottorino Respighi and Alfredo Casella. Respighi made some recordings of solo songs accompanying his wife at the piano. They were released on the Parlophone label back in the 1920s. These recordings are now Public Domain in the country of origin, but not in the US. Parlophone has been out of business for many years. Therefore, due to the current copyrights, these historic performances cannot be made available to the US public through the normal means of publishing and distribution.[5]

The problem extends even more critically into the inability to make available valuable scientific and medical journals, the articles in which are often supported by public funds. The Mahidol University-Oxford Tropical Medicine Research program, based in Thailand, focuses on malaria and melioidosis. According to the World Health Organization, every year, there are about 250 million malaria cases and nearly one million deaths. In order to develop current methods for malaria prevention, the program wished to make available 1,000 journal articles from the first half of the 20th century that described a unique, unrepeatable experiment that had been done. As Professor Ian Hargreaves reports, the malaria papers remain unavailable to researchers because of rights clearance requirements, adding that "87% of the material housed in UK's main medical research database . . . is unavailable for legal text and data mining."[6] In addition to the loss of access to valuable scientific and medical information, important parts of our cultural heritage are quickly slipping away, forever. How we can profess to be deeply concerned about culture but allow it to die due to an extremely long term of copyright is a mystery. I am unaware of a single legislative proposal that comes close to addressing the problem. The orphan works proposals to date are extremely limited.[7] The problem grows every year and will be inflicted on future generations, as more and more works are created and protected for well over 100 years.

WE HAVE NO ORPHAN WORKS PROBLEM: WE HAVE A TERM OF PROTECTION PROBLEM

The question of how long copyright protection should last has existed from the inception of copyright protection[8]: Those seeking rights want protection to last as long as possible, preferably forever. Jack Valenti once quipped that given the prohibition in the U.S. Constitution on perpetual rights, he wanted rights to last forever minus a day, an event only he might be able to determine.[9] Fixing the duration of copyright poses problems for easily identifiable reasons: granting too short a term of copyright might prevent rights holders from recovering their investment and earning a reasonable profit; this is particularly the case if it takes awhile for the public to accept the work or if the investment is substantial. But too long a period of protection leads to serious problems, including the inability to use the work without the permission of or payment to those who own rights long after the author has died. Where the rights have been transferred to companies that go out of existence, or have been transferred numerous times, identifying who owns the work or where to locate the proper rights holder is prohibitively expensive, and often impossible.

Although this is often referred to as an orphan works problem,[10] the description is inaccurate: there is no orphan works problem, but rather problems that arise from too long a term of protection. Under the 1909 U.S. Copyright Act, there was no appreciable orphan works problem because the failure to renew resulted in a term of only twenty-eight years, a term that was long enough for the vast majority of works. Failure to affix a mandatory copyright notice knocked out other works where no protection was desired.

The decision to switch to a term of life of the author plus fifty years in 1978 (now life plus seventy years) and to abandon the notice and renewal requirements were bad decisions that destroyed the ability of copyright to function effectively. Short of contacting each author about each work, there is no longer a way to determine which works the author desires to protect and which works he, she, or it (in the case of companies) doesn't wish to protect: All works must be treated as under protection, requiring permission before use. While there have been calls for a compulsory license or limitations on remedies after a diligent but unsuccessful search is undertaken for the owner of an orphan work, the suggestions so far are ridiculously limited in scope. They are nibbling at the edges without solving the real problem: There is no way to fix the orphan works problem, or the larger system of copyright, without reversing the unduly long term of protection and without restoring formalities that prevent the creation of orphan works in the first place. An overly long term of copyright and the lack of formalities are the real problem, and unless we deal with them, we are doing nothing of consequence.

The Costs of Clearing Rights

Leaving intact the current regime is not feasible. Aside from the general impossibility of finding the rights owner, the costs of clearing rights are enormous even for unsuccessful efforts. The European Union Directorate for Information Society and Media gave two examples. First, as part of a major digitization project of audio-visual material in the Netherlands, the cost of handling rights clearance for 500,000 photographs and 5,000 films was estimated to be €625,000 with three people clearing rights for four years in this project. This doesn't include any license fees that might be demanded.[11] Second, in another Dutch project dealing with the digitization of 1,000 Dutch history handbooks, only fifty books were cleared in a period of five months. At this rate, clearing the rights for the whole set of handbooks would take more than eight years.[12]

The EU report noted that in the case of books, the transaction costs for out-of-print books are normally higher than the cost of digitization, which is not inexpensive either.[13] The Carnegie Mellon Library estimated that the total cost for clearing a book is $200 per book,[14] a prohibitively high cost for a meaningful project of any size. Moreover, after spending such fees, the end result is usually an inability to clear enough books to make the project live up to its goals.

Other types of works fare just as badly: In the United Kingdom, an effort was made to digitize 2,900 posters. Only 270 posters were cleared, which was 19 percent. This 19 percent had transaction costs of 70,000 Euros (not including license fees) and took 88 working days.[15] Where visual works are included within a book, finding the owners of those works is a nightmare.[16]

Funding for projects requires legal certainty; legal certainty requires considerable copyright expertise; considerable copyright expertise requires hiring lawyers; hiring lawyers requires paying lawyers. Clearance thus requires that a large chunk of funding for culturally important projects be devoted to legal fees, leaving less for the actual work of making works available.[17] Sometimes funding is refused, as was the case with the refusal of the EU to fund the MOVIE digitization project.[18]

SOME DATA ON THE NEGATIVE EFFECT OF TOO LONG A TERM OF COPYRIGHT

Professor Rufus Pollock has done an admirable job of quantifying the general, negative effect of the unnecessarily long term of copyright. Had the term of copyright remained constant at the maximum of twenty-eight years established in the 1710 UK Statute of Anne, 52 percent of the books available today would be in the public domain, instead of the 19 percent that actually are in the public domain. In the United Kingdom alone, this difference amounts to 600,000 books.[19] By contrast, in 1795 in the United Kingdom, 78 percent of all available books were in the public domain. A chart Professor Pollock created to see the effects on the public domain with a twenty-eight-year term is shown in Figure 8.1.

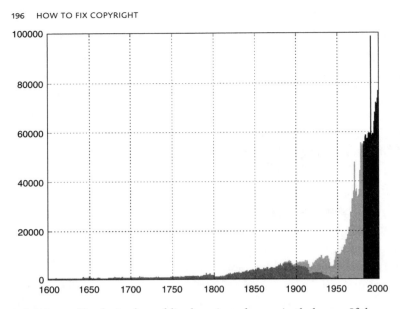

FIGURE 8.1   Books in the public domain today are in dark gray. If there was a 14+14-year regime those in the public domain would be in light gray. The total published output is in black. *Source*: http://rufuspollock. org/tags/copyright/

With a term of copyright that continues after the death of the author, dealing with heirs or estates introduces a new dynamic, one that is rarely positive. One example is what Second Circuit Judge Pierre Leval called the "widow censor,"[20] the widow who wishes to suppress information about her dead husband (or in the case of the widower censor, dead wife). Children of dead authors are notorious for making extravagant claims. Remote heirs are just as bad, as evidenced in Victor Hugo's great-great-grandson's effort to suppress a theatrical sequel to Hugo's 1862 novel *Les Miserables*.[21]

INHIBITING THE CREATION OF NEW WORKS

Too long a term of protection hurts living authors because they are prohibited from using predecessors' works unless they can track the copyright owner down and pay whatever licensing fees are demanded. As a result, we have either fewer works or sterile creations, as authors are generally required to leave out all material that not has been cleared.[22] For biographies, histories, documentaries, and other works that need to rely on numerous previous works, this represents a significant problem.

This problem has become particularly acute with retroactive grants of copyright, as they prevent large number of older works that should have gone into the public domain from doing so. Retroactive grants of protection can never incentivize the creation of new works: The authors of many works whose copyright terms have been extended are dead, and the rights retroactively granted are usually enjoyed by corporate assignees.

How Long Should Copyright Last?

So how long is long enough? If one approaches the question ideologically, the only answers are ideological and as such can never provide a satisfactory answer to those who do not share the ideology. There are a very large number of independent, empirical studies of the issue, in many languages, from many countries.[23] Unfortunately, lawmakers don't rely on these studies, relying exclusively on those clamoring for ever greater rights.

Here is one example of the type of ideological rhetoric typical of "debates" about the proper length of copyright. In the 1960s, Congress began the process of replacing the 1909 Copyright Act by requesting the Copyright Office to conduct a series of studies and roundtable discussions with experts. One recommendation

was for a term of copyright of life of the author plus twenty-five
years. Another suggestion was life of the author plus fifty years.
Herman Finkelstein, the general counsel of ASCAP, strongly objected to the life plus twenty-five proposal:

> It somewhat bothers me, because, if we view this in the
> abstract, we'd have to examine communism.
>
> Now, this isn't just dragging into this room a red her-
> ring, or one of those clichés of communism. This is serious.
> This is serious because, when Scrutton wrote his book on
> copyright back in the last century, he said, "Beware those
> who talk about a short term of copyright may be leading
> us into communism." This was long before Stalin and
> Lenin.[24]

What Mr. Finkelstein omits is that when Scrutton wrote his treatise, the term of copyright in the United States lasted only twenty-
eight years from first publication, with a possible renewal term of
fourteen years, for a possible total of only forty-two years. At the
time of Mr. Finkelstein's remarks, the term in the 1909 Act was a
twenty-eight-year original term with a renewal term of twenty-
eight years, for a total possible term of fifty-six years from first
publication. Proposing a term of life of the author of plus twenty-
five years was hardly proposing shorter term than either forty-two
or fifty-six years from first publication unless the author died at
thirty-one years of age or younger.

AN ECONOMICS-BASED APPROACH
TO COPYRIGHT TERM

We need to discuss the question of the proper term of copyright
free of ideology. The only way to do that is to undertake an eco-
nomics-based analysis,[25] grounded on the present and future value

of compensation to authors from different terms of protection. Future value is the amount that money will be worth at a future date. One dollar with an interest rate of 7 percent, received one year later, will have a value of $1.07. Present value is the value of money received today: At the same interest rate, one dollar received today has a present value of $0.93. The further into the future that money is received, the less that money is worth in present value. This is critical because whether the incentive of an expected payoff is effective is determined *at the time the work is created*.

The argument always made by proponents of extending the duration of copyright is that doing so will cause authors to create more works *today* based upon a judgment that they will receive more money later (that is, during the period of the lengthened term). Put concretely, the assertion is this: an author in 2011 thinking about whether to create another work in 2011 will base that decision on whether it is valuable to do so in 2011. Assume that an author in 2011 figures he or she will live another forty years. (There is no magic here, pick your own number.) Those who argue for a longer term of copyright argue that such an author will create more works in 2011 only if the term of copyright for those works is 110 years, not ninety years: life of the author plus fifty years, plus forty equals ninety years, versus life of the author plus seventy years equals 110 years. The argument is that the author will calculate in 2011 that a copyright that lasts until 2101 is not a sufficient incentive to create, and that only if copyright lasts until 2121 will he or she create in 2011. No one should believe that.

If the value from adding another twenty years of copyright on to the existing term of copyright is worth nothing today—and it is, in practical terms, worth nothing—adding that twenty years cannot create an incentive to create more works. The evidence shows extending the term of copyright has no present practical value. The economists' brief in the *Eldred* case before the United States Supreme Court (which challenged the constitutionality of the U.S. term extension) concluded that:

> The twenty years of copyright term added...provide a flow of additional benefits that is very far into the future, and hence very small in present value. To illustrate, suppose that an author writes a book and lives for thirty more years. In this case, under the pre-[extension] regime, the author or his assignee would receive royalties for eighty years. If the interest rate is 7%, each dollar of royalties from year eighty has a present value of $0.0045. Under the [extension], this same author will receive royalties for one hundred years. Each dollar of royalties from year one hundred has a present value of $0.0012.[26]

In the whole period of the extension, assuming very generously that the work has a constant stream of revenue, those revenues will be 0.33 percent of the present value of revenues received from years one to eighty.[27] Making copyright perpetual would increase authors' compensation by at most 0.12 percent, and these figures are unrealistically high, since the vast majority of works lose value after a short period of time.

Our current regime is a perpetual regime in all but name, giving rights holders 99.88 percent of the value of a perpetual regime, with no social benefit whatsoever and with serious social costs. The social *costs* are easy to identify: consumers paying monopoly prices to corporations for 100 years,[28] with restrictions on access and use, and a large class of unusable orphan works.[29] Term extension is a social disaster.

An empirical approach to the proper term of copyright would result in different terms for different works.[30] Some works, such as letters, e-mails, government works, and business documents would be created without copyright and need no term. How can we develop the data for each type of work? In the case of books, we could look at books in print. Jason Schultz did a study of books in print in 2002 published during the period of 1927–1946 (the period covered then by term extension), and found that of the 187,280 books published during that period, only 4,267 were available in 2002, which is 2.3 percent. Thus, term extension kept under copyright 97.7 percent of works that were no longer in print, but which could nevertheless not be used.[31]

The length of copyright has to be dramatically cut back and tailored to each type of work. The failure to do so will continue to be devastating to the creation of new works and to the preservation of our culture heritage. The time to act is now.

NINE

Reimposing Some Formalities

Reader discretion advised: This chapter contains a lot of technical copy-right stuff. There is no way around this; some things are just technical.

For most of the history of copyright, governments imposed for-malities on the existence or exercise of copyright. Unlike the popular expression, "it's just a formality," meaning it is a require-ment that doesn't really mean anything, formalities in copyright laws had real bite. In some periods of time, you didn't get a copy-right unless you complied with the formality, and there were more than one. At other times, you were granted a copyright but could lose it later if you didn't comply with the formality. Failure to comply with formalities definitely weeded out many works for which copyright wasn't desired, as well as putting into the public domain some works for which copyright was desired but whose owners inadvertently failed to dot all their i's and cross all their t's.

Examples of formalities are filing a registration claim with a government agency, providing copies of the work to government agencies or libraries, and affixing a notice of copyright on each publicly distributed copy of the work. Not all countries imposed all these requirements. The requirements have been greatly liberalized over time and largely abolished. Their wholesale abolition occurred at a late date in a number of countries[1]—for example, not until 1989 in the United States—just as the spread of digital technologies vastly expanded the number of people who created and distributed works globally, as well as the number of people who were at risk for innocent infringement for accessing and copying those works. In the past, a short term of copyright coupled with formalities and the natural restraints that arose in the hard copy world—significant costs in production and distribution—limited the public's innocent exposure to copyright infringement. With a functionally perpetual copyright duration, no formalities, and instant global distribution, matters have greatly changed. Those changes dictate the re-imposition of some formalities as a way of ensuring that copyright owners may protect their investment for a reasonable period of time, but that the public is not inadvertently subject to infringement and to enormous financial damages. I begin with the renewal requirement.

THE RENEWAL REQUIREMENT

The renewal records of the United States Copyright Office, discussed in chapter 3, show that most copyright owners, when required, twenty-eight years from the original grant of copyright, to take minimal steps to declare their continued interest in owning right to their works, failed to take those steps. I believe this occurred not out of laziness or because the requirement was onerous, but rather because few works retain any market value after twenty-eight years; most lose all value quite a bit before then.

The failure to renew was an empirical, market signal about the value copyright owners themselves placed on copyright. The renewal rates also showed a consistent difference in renewal rates for classes of works. The lowest renewal rates (0.4 percent) were for technical drawings, lectures, sermons, and other oral works. The highest renewal rate was for motion pictures (74 percent). Music was 48 percent and books only 7 percent. Our current one-size-fits-all approach ignores this significant data about how copyright owners have themselves valued copyright. Based on this evidence, the correct term of copyright should vary depending on the type of material being protected, with books getting a shorter term than motion pictures.

There are, though, variations within subject matter groups: Some books have a longer commercial life than others, and this is also true for all works. While there should be different terms of protection for each subject matter group, it is not possible to legislate the term of copyright that is appropriate for individual works within that group: some need a longer or shorter term. The way to resolve this problem is through mandatory use of formalities that require copyright owners to take steps to affirm their continued desire to claim their rights, principally the requirement that the copyright owner file a document with a government agency expressing a continued interest in the work.

Historically, formalities have been opposed by those who favor expansive copyright protection, but the tide has turned. In October 2010, Cary Sherman, President of the Recording Industry Association of America, stated, "my opinion is that . . . requiring some sort of registration, makes more sense today. We need better ways to distinguish when copyright is a beneficial property right, and when copyright is a meaningless and unwanted right." Mr.

Sherman was later asked what he meant by this, and he responded that "it may be time for creators to affirmatively assert copyright, rather than have it automatically granted to them whether they want it or not."[2] The European Union's "Committee of Sages," in its January 2011 report on preserving Europe's culture, also recommended that "some form of registration should be considered as a precondition for a full exercise of rights," even though this would require a change in the Berne Convention.[3]

Such formalities are not as one commentator erroneously called them "confiscatory,"[4] a word that refers to government seizure of private property. When the government sets conditions, including term limits and renewal requirements, on the exercise of any right and those conditions are not fulfilled, the government is not seizing the right for itself, but is instead declaring that the rights no longer exist. All copyright regimes in the world, whether common law or civil law, are confiscatory in this erroneous use of the word since all copyright regimes place a time limit on economic rights. Would one say that because there are limits on the length of copyright, the limitation is confiscatory? Hardly: the government has merely declared the rights no longer exist after a set period of time. Formalities that require copyright owners to affirmatively declare their desire to continue exercising their rights for the statutorily prescribed term of protection are no different.

The theocracy of formality-free copyright belongs to the Romantic ideal of artists starving in their Parisian garret. Copyright doesn't want to be free any more than information does. Neither want to be anything; they are not sentient. The reaction against formalities in the Romantic era was, though, understandable, since in that era, authors were often required to fulfill formalities in all countries in which they asserted rights, an onerous task indeed.[5] Nevertheless, the 1886 Berne Convention for the Protection of Literary and Artist Works did not prohibit the imposition of formalities, dealing a fatal blow to those who argue that copyright, especially in civil law *droit d'auteur* systems, is inherently inconsistent with formalities. As Dr. Stef van Gompel has written in his comprehensive review of the history of formalities in Europe:

> [T]he proceedings from the various conferences that modeled the Berne Convention do not reveal any philosophical, ideological or dogmatic arguments for their abolition. Thus, the rationale behind the proscription of formalities at the international level seems to be practical rather than idealistic.[6]

Formalities that interfere with the enjoyment and exercise of rights guaranteed by the Convention were not precluded until the 1908 Berlin revision. In almost identical terms, the preclusion is found in the first clause of current Article 5(2) of the Convention: "The enjoyment and exercise of these rights shall not be subject to any formality." Article 5(3) adds, though, that "Protection in the country of origin is governed by domestic law." The meaning of these two articles together is that countries are free to impose any formalities they wish on works by their own authors or those works whose country of origin is that country.[7] If all countries did so, formalities could be imposed without violating any treaty obligations.[8]

The United States has a rich history of formalities from the date of its first act in 1790. Until 1978, formalities such as registration and renewal and affixing a copyright notice to all published copies of the work were conditions on the existence of the right, although the precise nature of those conditions changed over time. Beginning in 1978, copyright became automatic (meaning rights vest merely upon creation), and although there was still a notice requirement, curative steps could be taken where notice had been omitted. On March 1, 1989, in order to comply with Article 5(2) of the Berne Convention, the United States implemented legislation abolishing the requirement. The renewal requirement was repealed in 1992 for pre-1978 works. (The requirement had been repealed in 1978 for post–December 31, 1977 works.)

In order for copyright to function effectively, some measure of formalities must be imposed.[9] Those formalities must be effective and not onerous. There were many problems with formalities under the 1909 Copyright Act, but those problems were interpretive, a result of the way the courts and the Copyright Office applied a bare bones statute. Their extreme interpretations of a simple statutory requirement are not inherent in formalities.

New formalities can avoid the excesses of the past. The goal of the new regime of formalities is to make copyright laws work effectively by ensuring that those who claim rights inform the public of their claim, and value those rights sufficiently to claim them. The above data show that the renewal requirement served admirably to exclude from protection large numbers of works in which the owners of the works had no commercial interest after a very short period of time. Imposing a renewal requirement is an excellent idea. The time period for renewal will be dependent on how long the term of copyright is. If the term of copyright is short, say twenty-eight years, there is no need for a renewal requirement. But the longer the term of protection is, the greater the need for renewal.

Beyond the historical record of effectiveness for the renewal requirement in separating those works in which copyright is still desired from those in which it is not, three other recent changes require that some formalities be imposed. First, the vast expansion in the material covered by copyright has resulted in ordinary citizens being subject to liability for copying or retransmitting e-mails, business documents, and in many countries, government works. Second, the technological functioning of the Internet results in the making of billions of unauthorized copies a day, by search engines acting as ordinary search engines; by Internet service providers acting as ordinary Internet service providers; and by citizens receiving e-mails from others, viewing websites, listening to streamed music or audiovisual works; indeed, by engaging in almost any activity on the Internet. Third, the global nature of the Internet has made available works from around the world, the rights to which are extremely difficult to determine. Things have changed dramatically since formalities were abolished in national laws and through treaties. Reestablishing formalities is not a complete solution to the changes in the world of producing creative works, but it would at least significantly winnow down the number of problems.

Policymakers have a responsibility to ensure that ordinary users do not inadvertently run afoul of the law. One way to do that is to make those claiming rights declare their intention to claim their rights and to periodically affirm their continued interest in the work by filing a document with a government agency. These documents must be made publicly available, including via online searching. Affixation of copyright notice is also an effective way of making the public aware of the assertion of copyright. There are also no prohibitions on countries imposing formalities such as registration as a condition to special remedies such as statutory damages. The United States has such a requirement for both domestic and foreign works.[10]

While there are things individual countries can and should do on their own, a comprehensive approach to formalities requires a revision to treaties, including the Berne Convention.

TEN

The Moral Panic over Fair Use

The term "moral panic" comes from sociology. It was made popular in the early 1970s in describing wildly exaggerated reactions to
changing mores.[1] Examples of moral panics include the Salem
Witch trials, marijuana during the "Reefer Madness" period of
the 1930s,[2] the comic book Congressional hearings in the 1950s,[3]
McCarthyism, and the events that gave rise to the coining of the
term: the Mods and Rockers battles, in the UK during the mid-
to late-1960s.

I use moral panic here to refer to the trumped-up creation of
an alien threat. I do not exaggerate by using "alien": in 2005, the
then-Attorney General of Australia, Philip Ruddock, referred to
fair use as alien to the Australian legal tradition,[4] apparently unaware that the fair use factors were already contained in the
Australian copyright act.[5]

The rhetorical device of turning fair use into a moral panic is
made by those who oppose adapting copyright to the digital era.

Fair use thus serves as a classic moral panic: an effort by vested interests to preserve the status quo through creating a false enemy whom, we are told, must be vanquished for the alleged good of society as a whole. What is this evil fair use? I will discuss below the technical details of the doctrine, but at its heart, fair use is a way to ensure that the goal of furthering creativity is not impeded by an overly restrictive view of exclusive rights. Far from being an alien concept, fair use arises out of fundamental purpose of copyright: encouraging the creation of new works or providing new insights into old ones.

THE PRACTICAL EXPERIENCE WITH FAIR USE

Throughout his thirty-four years as a member of the federal judiciary—sixteen years as a trial judge in the Southern District of New York, and eighteen years as an appellate judge on the U.S. Court of Appeals for the Second Circuit in Manhattan, Pierre Leval has gained a great deal of practical experience in deciding fair use cases. He has repeatedly emphasized the need to treat transformative, unlicensed fair uses as critical to furthering the goals of creativity: "Fair use should not be considered a bizarre, occasionally tolerated departure from the grand conception of the copyright monopoly. To the contrary, it is a necessary part of the overall design."[6] Judge Leval's over three decades of experience in applying fair use has led him to a greater, not a lesser appreciation of the doctrine's importance in furthering creativity.

It is important to point out that those who regard fair use as a moral panic or as inappropriate for other countries' copyright laws lack any practical experience in applying the doctrine. In the U.S., everyday corporate lawyers make fair use determinations with substantial consequences. Many companies are both copyright owners and users. Viacom, Inc., a very large, litigious media company that has regularly spoken in favor of strong copyright rights, relies heavily on fair use for its popular "Daily Show with Jon Stewart" and "The Colbert Report." Fritz Attaway, Executive Vice President and Washington General Counsel for the Motion Picture Association of America—hardly a copy-left organization, stated: "The beauty of fair use is that it is a living thing...like our Constitution...that can adapt to new technology."[7] The idea that fair use reduces copyright owners' rights is belied by the regular practice of large U.S. media companies applying fair use in their every day commercial decisions.

The existence of a fair use defense does not mean all claims or any particular claim of fair use will succeed. I have argued cases in court in favor of fair use applying.[8] I have argued cases in court against fair use applying.[9] In all cases, the assessment is driven by whether the claimed fair use furthers the goals of copyright.

CREATIVITY ARISES FROM BOTH AUTHORIZED AND UNAUTHORIZED USES

One would be hard-pressed to see fair use or any other unauthorized use being regarded by many policymakers as a necessary part of the overall design of copyright: to the contrary. The European Union's 2001 Information Society Directive is designed to severely limit EU member countries' ability to craft socially beneficial uses, for now, and for the future. The Directive sets out broad, mandatory rights, and narrow, optional unauthorized uses, uses that are further circumscribed by the so-called three-step test.[10] A 2009 opinion by the European Court of Justice, *Infopaq International A/S v. Danske Dagblades*[11] tightened the vise-grip further through its (undemocratic) creation of a general principle that even legally permissible unauthorized uses in national laws must be narrowly construed. They must be narrowly construed, according to the court, for ideological reasons: the mere grant of exclusive rights means that creativity exists almost entirely through authorized uses. In the European Union, creativity seems to be limited to authorized creativity.

The purpose of copyright is to encourage *all* forms of creativity, not just authorized creativity. If we lived in a world with only authorized creativity, we would live in a very sterile world, as few government figures and few copyright owners are fond of others satirizing them. While productive, collaborative efforts between copyright owners and licensees are not hard to find and should be praised, it is also true that few businesses are willing to let competitors thrive rather than try to eliminate them through any means possible, including through misuse of the copyright laws.

In order to make possible the broad, social goals of copyright, we need laws that give courts guiding principles to decide disputes, rather than statutory straitjackets. Straitjackets consist of narrow lists (such as those contained in the EU's Information Society Directive),[12] drawn up by government officials, of the few types of unlicensed creativity that are permitted. The idea that government officials can effectively formulate and execute a creativity centralized command system in which all permitted uses can be carefully spelled out in advance is to believe that the Soviet-planned economies were a rousing success.

A top-down copyright regime in which creative acts are limited to those few acts the government has by regulation permitted is a road to cultural serfdom.[13] It is a regime that inhibits, rather than maximizes, cultural democracy.

THE ORIGINS OF FAIR USE AND ITS PURPOSE

The fair use privilege was developed in the eighteenth century by English common law judges in interpreting the 1710 Statute of Anne.[14] The goal of that act was to encourage learning. The English judges held that learning should also be encouraged through unauthorized uses that were not mere efforts to supplant sales of the original. Such uses included abridgments where "the invention, learning, and judgment of the [abridger] is shown in them," as well as book reviews, reviews of scientific works that included portions of the original, corrections to maps, parody and satire, criticism, and comment.[15]

Fair use now has its most well-known home in Section 107 of the U.S. Copyright Act,[16] but it too was developed by common law judges in order to further the goal of promoting learning. Fair use's DNA is mapped from the heart of copyright. Fair use consists of principles, not rules, and its goal is to ensure that creativity flourishes in the face of overly exuberant exclusive rights. Fair use is not a blank ticket for all unauthorized uses; it is instead, a tool to further socially beneficial behavior. Sometimes this means that a plaintiff bringing an infringement claim against an unauthorized user wins and gets to stop that use because fair use is rejected. Sometimes this means that the unauthorized user wins and gets to continue his or her use without permission and without payment because fair use is found. The public always wins.

THE FAIR USE FACTORS

Fair use determinations are always made on a case-by-case basis because creativity does not come in cookie-cutter forms; creativity is messy and unless the law takes that messiness into account, the law will stifle creativity. Over the centuries, four factors have come to be seen as important to the fair use analysis, but not exclusively so and not all four are always important in every case. The first fair use factor is the nature and purpose of defendant's use. This factor examines how and why the copyrighted work was used. This inquiry goes beyond the mere fact that a use is unauthorized, and instead drills down into the reasons for the use.

The second factor examines the nature of the copyrighted work. Is the plaintiff's work a factual work and a type from which it is typical to quote from or to adapt? This factor is relatively unimportant because it is common for factual works to quote from other factual works and for non-factual works (like musical works) to copy from other non-factual works. It is uncommon for a song to copy scientific descriptions from a journal article, but it is common for one musical composition to copy from another musical composition.

The third factor looks at how much of the copyrighted work was copied. Did the defendant take only enough of the work to suit his or her legitimate purpose, or did the defendant pig out and take as much as he or she wanted out of laziness?

The fourth fair use factor is concerned with the effect of defendant's work on plaintiff's market for its work. This factor attempts to evaluate whether the use is of a type we wish copyright owners to control. Parody, satire, book reviews, and many educational uses fall outside of areas we want copyright owners to control. Verbatim copying that acts as a substitute for the original is the type of use we want copyright owners to be able to stop, if they choose.

FAIR USE IS ESSENTIAL FOR INNOVATION

Fair use, with its ability to flexibly adapt to changes in technologies and markets, permits innovative companies to offer products and services that are not possible with inflexible regimes. Those who speak of encouraging innovation and job creation but who insist on "strong" intellectual property laws miss this obvious reality: It is not strong intellectual property laws that have made possible these innovative services, but the opposite—fair use and other legal doctrines (such as implied license) that have been flexibly applied in order to allow search engines and other Internet services to operate effectively. In 2010, Silicon Valley, California companies were responsible for almost 20 percent of all new employees in the State of California, despite the Valley's relatively small population (about 5 percent of the state). By contrast, according to the U.S. Bureau of Labor statistics, in the period of 1999 to 2010, the motion pictures and record industries shed 9,000 jobs.[17] If policymakers are genuine in their desire to increase innovation, they should look to those industries that are successful and find out why they are successful. The answer will not be that they were successful because they asserted copyright rights; rather they were successful by constantly bringing out new products and refining old ones.

THE OPEN-ENDED VERSUS CLOSED CANARD

Critics of the U.S. fair use doctrine point to the alleged "open-ended" nature of fair use and argue that it lacks certainty. The term open-ended is used as a derogatory synonym to mean without boundaries or without any guidance; the term open-ended is used to conjure up fears that one simply never knows what a U.S. court might do. Those who take this position do not point to any particular decisions of U.S. courts as going "off the deep-end," as having come to a decision that was reached only because U.S. courts allegedly have the unfettered ability to do whatever they want. Instead, the claims are theoretical: "a U.S. court *could* go crazy," a claim that could apply to all courts in all areas.

Describing the U.S. fair use regime as open-ended in the sense of "anything goes," is inaccurate. As an initial matter, the description ignores that the essentials of copyright infringement actions in all countries are equally open-ended: whether something is an unprotectable fact or protectable expression is open-ended in this same sense. Whether one movie or novel infringes another is based on whether the two works are substantially similar, also an open-ended inquiry. Whether the two works are substantially similar in expression depends on how much copyrighted expression was taken. How much copyrighted expression was taken involves open-ended quantitative and qualitative assessments. Whether an artist's honor or reputation has been harmed by an unauthorized use is as open-ended an inquiry as exists in copyright law, yet European policymakers and copyright owners passionately argue in favor of such inquiries. What is sauce for the moral rights goose is sauce for the fair use gander.

All of these questions involve a continuum, rather than an absolute, and are decided by a jury (where requested)[18] because it is recognized that the questions are ones of judgment, not legal interpretation. Whether one work infringes another, or whether one's moral rights have been violated cannot be known in advance and must await a trial. So much for certainty. Fair use inquiries are of the exact same nature and usually involve the same questions as the open-ended inquiries that routinely take place under European copyright laws.

The third fair use factor examines how much of the copyrighted work was taken. This is the exact same inquiry undertaken in the basic infringement analysis. The fourth fair use factor examines the impact of the use on the market for the copyright owner's work. This is the same inquiry undertaken at the damages phase of an infringement analysis. The first fair use factor examines the purpose of the use, which is also relevant for defenses such as parody or satire, uses commonly found in closed list systems too: a parody or satire defense when considered under fair use is the same when considered under a closed list. The second fair use factor examines the nature of the copyrighted work, which is also relevant in the infringement analysis for determining what is protectable expression and what is not. The differences between the basic infringement analysis and fair use analysis, where they exist at all, are a matter of degree and not kind.

Nor are judges free to do whatever they wish in making fair use determinations. The fair use analysis in Section 107 of the U.S. Copyright Act merely recognizes in the statute the common law fair use doctrine. The common law of fair use has developed over two centuries of case law. That case law has developed a coherent set of principles that are found in a number of other national statutes, including other countries' fair dealing provisions.[19] In practice, U.S. courts, like all common law courts, are governed by precedent. Hierarchically, decisions of the U.S. Supreme Court govern all lower courts, and decisions of the circuit courts of appeal govern all decisions of trial courts within that circuit. The U.S. Supreme Court has heard a number of fair use cases. I am unaware of a single complaint about how the *results* reached in those cases would be incompatible with international law.[20] The same holds true for decisions of the lower courts.

Criticizing a legal doctrine because, in some dispute in the future, some court *might* reach a result that some *might* disagree with misapprehends the rule of law both nationally and internationally, and is equally a problem in countries that have closed lists; i.e., enumerated lists of permitted uses. After all, a court in France is equally as likely or unlikely to correctly decide a parody defense as a U.S. court.

Closed lists are defended in part by claiming they provide certainty. The claim of certainty is a myth. Having a closed list is no guarantee that a correct decision will be reached in construing whether a particular enumerated use qualifies or not. There is no guarantee that a court in Australia, Canada, or the United Kingdom will not adopt an interpretation that is too restrictive or too liberal from the standpoint of the legislators who enacted the provision.

There are a number of other problems with closed lists of permitted uses. First is the inherent problem of legal indeterminancy: Lists of enumerated uses require words to specify which uses are permitted. It is very difficult to select words that have the necessary precision so that courts and potential litigants can easily determine their meaning *before* engaging in desired conduct. Here is an example. There is a law that says "No vehicles permitted in parks."[21] We will assume that all places considered to be parks have a sign that says "Park" to make the example simple. What about "vehicles" though? Does the term include a military truck in perfect working order installed as part of a war memorial? Does the term include golf carts, baby carriages, or children's cars that can be operated by pedals? Does it include bicycles? Does it include two-wheeled scooters, does it include two-wheeled scooters that are motorized? The answers to these questions are likely to be resolved by reference to the perceived purpose of the law, and not by its words. That's what fair use is too, an expression of purpose. Fair use is no more vague than "no vehicles permitted in park."

Here is an example of a permitted use from a closed list that is ambiguous: "research." Does "research" encompass both commercial and non-commercial research? Does it permit the previewing of thirty seconds of a sound recording by a consumer? Does it permit the copying of entire works or only parts, and if the latter how do you know how much you can copy? Does the exemption apply when the copyright owner has established a market for the work in question, or only when there is no such market? Does the existence of a potential license constitute such a market, regardless of the terms of the license? Can a party who is entitled to the research privilege hire a third party to do the copying for them? These are only a few of the ambiguities.

The answers to those ambiguities cannot be answered merely by pointing to the presence of "research" on a closed, exhaustive list of privileges. The answers will be given according to other principles, principles not found in the list, but which animate all copyright laws: is the use in the broad, social interest? The alleged sharp divide between the approach found the European Union and in the United States does not exist when it comes to the type of inquiry judges in all countries are required to undertake.

There is, however, a very sharp divide between the flexibility found in the United States and the top-down straitjacket imposed by European Union directives. That divide greatly inhibits creativity and innovation in the EU and therefore gives U.S. companies a distinct advantage. As British Prime Minister David Cameron observed in November 2010, in calling for a review of English copyright law: "Over there, they have what are called 'fair-use' provisions, which some people believe gives companies more breathing space to create new products and service.... I want to encourage the sort of creative innovation that exists in America."[22] The irony of course is that fair use was a British invention.

Fair use is not, even in the United States, viewed as the answer to all problems, as a magic legal elixir that will automatically lead countries to the Promise Land of increased creativity and innovation. Fair use is part of a much broader legal scheme, including safe harbors and implied licenses, while creativity and innovation are more often the result of non-legal factors, including attitudes toward risk-taking and failure, a venture capital system, and clustering of other inventive companies and people. Adopting fair use by itself will not cause the very different European cultural and business environment to transform itself to Silicon Valley on the Thames, Rhein, or Seine. But without flexible provisions (regardless of the name given to them), it is difficult to see how innovation and creativity can thrive regardless of the country and regardless of the legal regime.

IT'S NOT THE LABEL THAT MATTERS BUT THE CONDUCT

Those who oppose fair use have turned it into a moral panic by claiming that wholesale adoption of fair use will destroy creativity and innovation. The fact that the United States is quite creative and innovative under a fair use regime should be enough to refute such silly statements. The UK Hargreaves report also noted that UK companies operate successfully in the United States, thereby refuting the idea that companies fare better under closed list regimes.[23] What matters is not a label but the functional effect of a law: Does it permit conduct we wish to stop as well as conduct we wish to permit? We must decide what conduct we want and then draft laws that enable that conduct: whether we call such laws fair use, fair dealing, or fish-bait is irrelevant.[24] The European Union stated in its May 2010 Green Paper "Unlocking the Potential of Cultural and Creative Industries" that "in order to be able to fully unleash their dual and economic potential, the cultural and creative industries need an increased capacity for experimenting and innovating." Yet, Europe continues to insist on the use of closed lists and use of the three-step test to throttle any meaningful changes to copyright laws that would in actual practice permit experimenting and innovating. You can't have it both ways.

Dynamism Requires Flexibility

One thing we should want all laws to do is to be capable of adapting to new circumstances that match our past and present expectations of what the law should be. If we have been able to make a copy of an audio tape cassette or a VHS tape for personal use, we are likely to think we should be able to do the same for a CD or a DVD. The ability of fair use to reach such common sense results is fair use's greatest strength. The inability of closed lists to reach the same result without amendment is closed lists' greatest weakness. The question is not therefore whether to have fair use or closed lists, but whether we have laws that can respond in a common sense, flexible way.

Closed lists must be regularly updated on the penalty of crushing technological or market innovations: no legislature, no matter how careful or insightful, can think of all current uses, much less think of uses, technologies, or markets that are not yet existence. In the past, technologies and therefore business models changed slowly. This is no longer the case. The rapid pace of technological innovation brought about by the Internet and digital tools has radically collapsed the time lines for businesses to adapt and therefore for laws that seek to regulate business issues arising from the Internet. Static laws that attempt to establish for all time the rules governing technological and market innovation will impede that innovation. This doesn't mean the Internet should be without regulation as John Perry Barlow argued in his 1996 "Declaration of Independence of Cyberspace."[25] But it does mean that the nature of the Internet must be taken into account: policymakers cannot pass stronger versions of laws founded on the early eighteenth-century London book industry and expect them to be effective for twenty-first-century markets and technology.

A principal attribute of the Internet is its unplanned, distributed nature, with distributed here meaning multiple autonomous computers and software interacting without a central command. The lack of a central plan and command has made the spectacular growth of the Internet possible, and it is what makes the creativity on the Internet so exciting too: creativity is now something we all can engage in, without regard to borders and without having to go through gatekeepers. Creativity is no longer a central command activity; it is dynamic. If we want to encourage the new creativity, we need dynamic, flexible laws.

The flexibility of fair use is particularly suited for inherently dynamic situations. Closed lists are particularly suited for static situations. We should not choose between these two approaches since they address very different fact situations. We need fair use or functional equivalents because there are many situations that are dynamic. You cannot legislate detailed rules to decide dynamic situations; you can only set forth guiding principles. Fair use is precisely such a set of principles, principles that have been tested in the forge of thousands of court cases and opinions. Fair use works in dynamic situations because dynamic situations require dynamic legal principles.

Culture is usually dynamic; we may have canonical works, but at one time they weren't canonical, they were the new works on the block. All new works either build on works of the past or are understood in context with the present and the past in a dynamic relationship. If we want to further culture, we need dynamic laws. Dynamic laws tailored to the dynamic nature of creativity do not mean an absence of guidelines. First of all, there are some fairly static situations, situations with identifiable fact patterns. For example, where a consumer buys a lawfully made hard copy of a book, the consumer should be able to subsequently give away or sell that copy. Or, where a newspaper is reviewing a book, the reviewer should be able to quote from the book to explain points made in the review. In these type of situations, concrete exemptions, whether contained on a list or otherwise, are desirable. Where we can identify static, recurring problems, we should provide specific guidance.

But static fact patterns are not the norm in copyright because of the dynamic nature of creativity, technology, and markets. At the same time that copyright is touted as leading to innovation—which is inherently dynamic—the uses necessary to allow such innovation are foreclosed by static, closed lists of permitted uses. It is not at all coincidental that vested rights holder interests favor closed lists while innovative companies favor fair use or other flexible, functional equivalents. As Dr. Francis Gurry, the Director General of the World Intellectual Property Organization cautioned, "Copyright should be about promoting cultural dynamism, not preserving or promoting vested business interests."[26]

Innovation Requires a Dynamic Legal System

Innovation is by its nature dynamic. Innovation's power lies in what economist Joseph Schumpeter termed "creative destruction": the introduction of innovative products and business models that displace old ones.[27] If an innovative product or service does not provide competition to existing products or services, it is not innovative. Competition is inextricably linked to innovation. Laws are not.

The Internet and information technologies are key drivers of the twenty-first-century economy and cultural development, but such development is possible only if copyright laws do not inhibit their growth. Internet search engines provide one example of how copyright laws have to adapt to permit conduct we should all agree is desirable. The ability to search for lawfully made images, video, music, and textual content involves making a copy of that content for search purposes. Search engines crawl the web constantly and make copies of the entire web (unless individual sites are password protected or blocked through the use of simple, readily available software code such as robots.txt.). Web pages are then analyzed and ranked; links are provided to a user in response to a query. Search engines often provide a snippet from relevant websites so that users can decide which sites to access. These snippets are similar to library card catalogues and should be exempt under fair use, fair dealing, code-based exemption provisions, or doctrines such as implied consent. The back-end copying of the web must be exempt too in order for consumers to be able to see the snippets in response to their queries. Without that back-end copying, search is impossible.

When you view a Web page, your browser needs to make a local copy of the page on your computer. In order to transfer data across the Internet, data "packets" are sent between Internet service providers' routers. In effect, this means that the router makes and sends a copy of the "packet" to the next router in the chain, and so on until it reaches its recipient. E-mail servers must make copies of messages in order to transfer them from sender to recipient. Video streaming sites must temporarily store—"cache"—and buffer copies or portions of the audiovisual works being streamed in order to present an uninterrupted viewing experience.

These are all socially desirable uses that not only do not harm the market for copyrighted works, but increase their market by connecting potential purchasers to rights holders. It doesn't matter whether one calls such uses fair uses, fair dealing, or anything else; what matters is that we identify the behavior we wish to encourage and then enact laws that enable that behavior. Everything else is a distraction—whether the reproduction right, the making available right, the performance right, or any other right is "implicated" is meaningless. Whether this technology or that technology is used is also meaningless. Law is a means to an end, not an objective in itself, and copyright laws are no different. Copyright laws are not an end in themselves, but rather a means to socially desirable behavior. Focusing on behavior rather than on who has a right or an entitlement will go a long way toward making our copyright laws effective. Adopting dynamic, flexible legal principles that can quickly respond to changes in behavior, rather than waiting for governments to legislate permitted innovation is critical.

Flexible Rights Require Flexible Uses

A hallmark of modern copyright laws is the grant of flexible, open-ended rights. Artists are always finding new ways to express themselves, including in new media. Any copyright law that rigidly limited protection to those forms of expression in existence at the time the legislation was enacted would most assuredly stifle creativity. The last omnibus revision of the U.S. Copyright Act was in 1976, and many of those provisions were not changed after agreement on them in the 1960s, but flexible drafting protected them. Many forms of current creativity did not exist in the 1960s.

The need for flexibility exists for exclusive rights: if a sound recording is counterfeited, it shouldn't matter whether the medium of the piracy is vinyl records, tape cassettes, CDs, or mp3s. Requiring amendments to prohibit each of these new forms reproduction of as they came along would insufferably deprive copyright owners of the right to stop harmful behavior.

These same principles also apply to transformative, unauthorized uses: those who seek to avail themselves of fair use, fair dealing, or whatever label one applies, are, after all, authors too. Why one would ever think that one group of authors requires flexibility but another group of authors doesn't, is a complete mystery. Flexible rights and flexible uses are part of a single creative process. It's time our laws reflect this simple truth.

The Misnomer "Limitations and Exceptions"

Words matter. We choose particular words because we want to convince others of the thoughts those words convey. The phrase "limitations and exceptions"—referring to socially beneficial but unauthorized uses—captures nicely the point being made. Limitations and exceptions will be allowed, it is argued, by those who oppose them, if "there is a public interest . . . that justifies overriding the private rights of authors in their works in . . . particular circumstances."[28] By phrasing the discussion as one in which the "private" rights of authors are deemed the default rule, the public's interest is cast as an unnatural and unwelcome "limit" on or "exception" to the desired natural state of affairs. Copyright owners are alleged to have unfettered rights in their works, even if by copyright owners we mean large, multinational corporations who have bought rights, on the cheap, from the actual creators. The language "limitations and exceptions" is consciously employed to make an entirely political, rather than a descriptive, point. That point is that copyright owners are good and those who use copyrighted works without permission are bad. We see this in a recent statement by an intergovernmental figure that "limitations and exceptions" are part of a "negative" agenda.

We must recognize that the phrase "limitations and exceptions" is a moral panic, of which fair use is just one part. As with all moral panics, "limitations and exceptions" is a semantic device employed to preserve the status quo through creating a false enemy, in this case a threat to natural or property rights. Copyright is not and has never been a property right. Copyright laws are regulations created by governments to further broad societal goals. Those goals are pragmatic, not ideological, and as pragmatic, they accord certain privileges given to copyright owners, and certain privileges given to the public. There is no basis to regard any privilege as more important than another because they all work toward the common good. Cultural works arise out of society-at-large, and therefore everyone has a stake in the resolution of issues involving their creation and use. To date, copyright debates have mostly focused on rights: who has them, and who has, supposedly, violated them. We must accept that no one has rights, but that everyone has obligations, to each other, and to the common good. Framing debates in terms of entitlements is the source of the them-versus-us mentality—"I have rights and you don't." Dropping the divisive and unhelpful rhetoric of entitlements and limitations and exceptions to entitlement is an important first step forward to pragmatically fixing copyright. It is not the label that matters, but how we achieve a result that is in the overall interest of society. Sometimes that means giving one set of authors the right to stop other authors from doing unauthorized acts with copyrighted works. Sometimes that means giving the latter group of authors the right to do things with copyrighted works without permission or payment to the first set of authors. When this latter event occurs, it is not through a limitation or exception, it is instead through the ordinary operation of copyright law acting in the public's interest. Authors—all of them—do not stand in opposition to the public interest, but solidly within it. "Limitations and exceptions" insultingly and inaccurately suggest they don't.

ELEVEN

"The Answer to the Machine Is in the Machine" Is a Really Bad Metaphor

The Answer to the Machine Is in the Machine
Title to a 1995 article by Charles Clark,
a British publishing lawyer

I love language and metaphors. My last book discussed the effect of metaphoric language on the debates over copyright.[1] That effect can be positive or negative, but most often it is negative. It is negative because emotionally charged, inaccurate metaphors are chosen as a way to demonize opponents, usually as a predicate to getting new laws passed. Bad people must be punished, by putting them in jail or by making them pay steep fines. We know these people are bad because they are called bad, metaphoric names. There is much in a name.

Despite the pervasive misuse of language in copyright discourse, if, as many linguists believe, we process thought through metaphors,[2] there is no way to avoid using metaphors, nor should we: metaphors are wonderfully expressive vehicles. Some metaphors are figurative, such as "Juliet is the Sun." Shakespeare's metaphor conjures up in the reader warm, positive thoughts about

Juliet through transferring the warm, positive thoughts we have about the sun. Some metaphors are conceptual, such as "Life Is a Road." This metaphor is frequently employed in reference to choices we have to make and the difficulties of relationships. Paul McCartney's song, "The Long and Winding Road," uses this metaphor. Conceptual metaphors must be apt if we are to correctly understand the thought being conveyed. President George W. Bush was famous for his confused metaphors, such as: "We ought to make the pie higher;" "The senator has got to understand he can't have it both ways. He can't take the high horse and then claim the low road;" "Free societies will be allies against these hateful few who have no conscience, who kill at the whim of a hat." When metaphors are inapt, we either don't get the desired meaning, or worse, we form false conclusions, conclusions that are hard to shake because of the staying power of metaphors. (Much like a terrible advertising jingle we can't get out of our heads.)

Conceptual metaphors create new meanings by taking one concept and automatically associating with another: "Lawyers are sharks," or "John is a pig." Unlike similes ("John eats like a pig"), metaphors make direct associations and thus deliver an emotional wallop along with their intended associations: Saying John eats like a pig is a negative comment on his table manners, but it doesn't make broader statements about his character. The metaphor "John is a pig," does. Metaphors result in an instantaneous, unconscious opinion about a person or subject. Once this opinion is made, it is very hard to change it: We think we have reached the opinion ourselves, but we haven't—the opinion has been automatically created within us by the metaphor. Untangling the automatic opinions made by a metaphor takes a great deal of effort. If someone says John is a pig, it will be hard for us not to forget that, even if we disagree about John. Like "John is a pig," the metaphor, "the answer to the machine is in the machine" makes a powerful metaphoric association between two concepts, even though one of those concepts is itself a metaphor (machine) and the other concept isn't articulated (the problem for which the answer is in the machine). As we shall see, this powerful metaphor has no real meaning, but dangerously purports to present a solution to a complex but never stated problem. Compounding this danger is the fact that we don't realize it is a metaphor; instead, we mistakenly think the phrase is meant as a literal prescription. Colin Turbayne noted this problem in his book *The Myth of Metaphor*:

> There is a difference between using a metaphor and taking it literally.... The one is to make believe that something is the case; the other is to believe that it is. The one is to use a disguise or mask for illustrative or explanatory purposes; the other is to mistake the mask for the face.... After the disguise or mask has been worn for a considerable period of time it tends to blend with the face, and it becomes extremely difficult to "see through it."[3]

Instead of realizing that "The answer to the machine is in the machine" is a metaphor, we take it as a practical guide to action. Indeed, the origin of the saying was in lobbying (successfully) for powerful new laws. The actual purpose of the metaphor turns out to be, "The answer to the machine is to use laws against the machine."

WHY "THE ANSWER TO THE MACHINE IS IN THE MACHINE" IS A REALLY BAD METAPHOR AND SHOULDN'T BE USED

Metaphors are often used in law, usually to convey abstract principles. In the area of the First Amendment, we have "a marketplace of ideas" and "the wall of separation between church and state." These metaphors are employed to help us understand factors that judges will use to decide legal disputes about issues that are hard to tangibly capture. "The answer to the machine is in the machine" is similarly offered to help us understand how to decide disputes about copyright and new technologies, but unfortunately it fails miserably in that purpose. The metaphor is unhelpful because it begs all the issues raised, while pretending to provide a solution to them. The metaphor is, moreover, tautological. It is as if it said, "The answer to nuclear power is in nuclear power," or "The answer to global warming is in global warming." Mr. Clark's metaphor is actually worse than these two examples, because while we know what nuclear power is and what global warming is said to be, we have no idea of what the problem with machines is, how machines caused the unidentified problem, or how machines can provide the answer to that problem. In fact, we don't even know what a machine is, since "machine" is itself a metaphor within the larger metaphor.

If you don't believe the metaphor is confusing, ask ten of your colleagues what they think the metaphor means. I did. Here are the responses, in the order received, all from people involved in copyright and technology issues:

1. The answer to problems of technology will be found in different technologies.
2. Technological solutions can solve technological problems.
3. Human and social solutions are inadequate to solve technological problems.
4. Problems created by technology can't be solved by laws.
5. To make copyright work on a technical system (like the Internet) you'd need to look at the system itself for the means to implement the law.
6. I have no idea.
7. Advances in technologies create problems that can only be solved by further advances in those same technologies.
8. The answer to beating a machine (say, at chess) is understanding how it works.

9. The semantic web is the answer to all potential problems of access, control, and copying online. In other words, the proliferation of metadata standards will solve the "problem" of the existing behavior of computers, and in particular, search engines.

10. The challenge to copyright that the machine has always posed historically—shifting production cost and thus power—can be met by building a response into the same machine.

Any metaphor that can generate so many different meanings among educated, involved readers has failed its proper purpose—helping us understand. "The answer to the machine is in the machine" is not only internally a bad metaphor, it is also deeply misleading in its effect. At its most progressive reading, the metaphor might be said to express a belief that whatever the problems are faced by copyright owners from new technologies, the answer to those problems must be found in developing new, constructive ways to engage with those technologies to your advantage. For example, if digital technology reduces sales of analog compact discs, you should switch to sales of digital singles, maybe bundled with other value added material, such as online interviews with the band or streamed live performances. You figure out what natural advantages the new medium has, and then capitalize on those advantages. This is what is some people believe the "in the machine" part of the metaphor means. This progressive reading is, though, completely at odds with the way Mr. Clark himself used the metaphor.

It turns out Mr. Clark had a very specific purpose in using the metaphor, one not evident from the language. His purpose was to get legislatures to pass new laws that would dramatically change the way we access and use the Internet. The answer to the machine was to use laws against it. To understand this, we have to understand the history of the metaphor's formulation.

THE ORIGINS OF THE METAPHOR

The metaphor was first used as the title of an article submitted in conjunction with a colloquium held in July 1995 in Amsterdam, called "The Future of Copyright in a Digital Environment." Mr. Clark participated in that colloquium. Given that the article was written in 1995, the ideas in it are, not surprisingly, seriously dated, as they are from a very early stage of the development of the World Wide Web, a period three years before Google was founded, and ten years before YouTube was founded. In this period, copyright owners had their first glimpse of a world that they would no longer be able to control, as they had for the past 300 or so years. That glimpse was frightening. When copyright owners are frightened by new technologies, they seek new laws to stop them. Mr. Clark was no different, which is not a criticism. He was very much a man of his times, as all of us are. The time in question was one where copyright owners saw law as critical to protecting them from a new world they didn't like because they couldn't control it and because it upset existing long-established business models. In the classic copyright owner's equation, copyright = control = money.

It is unlikely many people have read Mr. Clark's article. The article is not available online or in digital form,[4] even though online licensing is the very subject of the article. There are only two, very obscure, hard copy versions of the article available, both in books, and both books are out of print. The proceedings of colloquium to which the article was submitted are available only via print on demand, for the steep price of $137 for a 248-page paperback book that looks barely typeset.[5] The article is also contained in a second book, this one co-edited by the German copyright scholar Dr. Thomas Dreier. Dr. Dreier's book contains a great deal of Mr. Clark's writings, but it was published by the Norwegian

Center for Computers and Law. I found one used copy available from Amazon.com in the United Kingdom.

Many law review articles cite the metaphor, but no one ever quotes from Mr. Clark's article, which is another reason why I think few people have ever read it. I have read it, and here is the final sentence of the article: "The answer to the machine may turn out to be not only in the machine, but the machine will certainly be an important part of the answer." This view retreats considerably from the snappy metaphor, but even in this slightly expanded form, it never helps us understand what the machine is, what the question is, or what the answer is. Other than the title, this sentence is the only named reference to machines in the entire article. If we want to know what the metaphor meant to Mr. Clark, we will have to understand it in the context of the article to which it was attached as the title.

THE POLITICAL CONTEXT OF THE METAPHOR'S FORMULATION: THE BATTLE FOR DIGITAL LOCKS

Context is always critical to understanding metaphors. The context to Mr. Clark's metaphor was a successful effort in 1996 to have the World Intellectual Property Organization in Geneva adopt treaties mandating civil and criminal penalties for circumventing digital locks. These treaties lead to the Digital Millennium Copyright Act in the United States and to the European Union's Information Society Directive. Mr. Clark was involved in the negotiations for the treaties, and according to those present in Geneva at the time, he employed the metaphor in those negotiations. The article provided background support for the lobbying.

Mr. Clark's article probably wasn't intended as a traditional article. It appears to be an outline submitted for the colloquium proceedings, much like continuing legal education classes require some type of written materials in order to vest attendees with the desired class credit. Mr. Clark was an excellent writer (as seen in the metaphor); had he really wanted to express himself on complicated issues, he was more than able to do so. He did not do so in this case. The article is only seven pages long, consisting almost entirely of summaries of various projects, with many long block quotations.

There are only two themes sketched out. The first concerns what he called closed circuit systems. The second concerns what he calls open access systems. By closed circuit systems, Mr. Clark meant adoption of the digital lock (anti-circumvention) provisions then being proposed before WIPO by the United States. Those provisions shortly became part of the DMCA and the EU's Information Society Directive. Mr. Clark favored both civil and criminal penalties for circumventing those locks, and quoted favorably from the then-current proposals. This is the closed circuit system he spoke of. That system was, and remains, a way to negate the nature of digital technologies by subjecting them to whatever restrictions copyright owners decide to place on them. In an irresponsible delegation of power, governments throughout the world have vested in large, multinational media companies and their trade associations, the ability to determine when and how new services may be offered to the public, including the features contained in consumer electronic goods. This delegation occurs through legislation that makes it a civil offense and a crime to circumvent digital locks that companies create without any governmental supervision. It is as if the police were paid from the tickets they hand out and got to make up the rules for when violations of law occur.

Those who quote Mr. Clark's metaphor as being progressive are not aware that his advocacy of new digital locks laws underpinned the metaphor, and wrongly assume that Mr. Clark was proposing to use rights management data to facilitate online licensing, outside of that legal underpinning. There is no question that more data about copyrighted works and potential licensed uses of them will be a win-win: a win for the public because they will have access to more works, and a win for authors and publishers because they will make money. This is the progressive vision of what the answer to being "in the machine" means. It is not what Mr. Clark meant, though.

Mr. Clark's open access systems can only be understood by reference to his closed circuit systems. Mr. Clark made clear that open access systems were entirely dependent on the closed circuit system of digital locks being in place first. "Open access" is thus controlled by closed, digital locks. How would open access systems work in conjunction with digital locks? It is not possible to tell because Mr. Clark never defined "open access." Instead, he spoke of an "identifying system." For such a system, he distinguishes between "intelligent" and "dumb" identifiers. An intelligent identifier is one that "would encompass all the information relevant to the copyright[ed] work, its various rightsholders, the terms on which the work can be licensed for various uses, etc." There is a great deal of work currently being done on this issue, for books, music, audiovisual works, and photographs. It is important work, and when done well, has the potential to greatly assist licensors, licensees, and the public. A dumb identifier would "simply identify the work, and refer to a repository for further information." The repositories he mentioned were the traditional collecting societies, such as performing rights societies.

Mr. Clark also referred to the various identifiers as being employed to "record and reward" uses. Whether identifiers would be employed to require licensing for all uses, even those not traditionally licensed, is impossible to know. But whatever he meant by open access systems, it wasn't open access in the sense of without digital locks controlling access and without restrictions on use after access. For all of the definitiveness of the metaphor (the answer *is* in the machine), Mr. Clark was far more realistic about practical applications, concluding "The answer to the machine may turn out to be not only in the machine, but the machine will certainly be an important part of the answer." This is, of course, equally vague; the only thing we may be certain of is that laws, in the form of digital locks, were the most important.

Entirely left unaddressed in either form of the metaphor is the critical question: identifying the problem. The entire metaphoric construct is built around there being a problem to which we must find an answer, whether in the machine or outside of the machine. Obviously, we can't find an effective answer to a problem we don't understand. Nowhere does Mr. Clark tell us what he thinks the problem is. There is a loose sense that the problem must be with the machine, but since the machine is itself a metaphor, it's a dead-end to simply say the problem is with the machine. Beyond this, we must also ask, are all machines a problem? If not all machines, which machines? Which problems are caused by machines, all problems or only some? If only some, which ones? How do those machines cause problems? We are given no guidance at all on these questions.

This context and the text of the article show that the answer to the machine for Mr. Clark was not the machine, but law, law to be used against the Internet. The problem of the machine turns out to be the ordinary problem of incumbents attempting to preserve existing business models. The machine is the old moral panic of technologies. In short, Mr. Clark's metaphor is merely a reformulation of the centuries-old approach of copyright owners that law is the solution to business problems, through either banning new technologies or gutting them so that they are safe. I reject this argument in chapter 5. In that chapter, I argued instead that technology creates opportunities, opportunities to respond to new market demand, new customers, and to keep existing ones. Those opportunities can only be capitalized on, however, by taking advantage of the new technologies, not by remaking them into the old technologies. Mr. Clark would disagree.

CURRENT USES OF THE METAPHOR BY PUBLISHERS

Given Mr. Clark's long and illustrious history as a European book publishing lawyer, it shouldn't be surprising that the European Publishers Council (EPC) has recently adopted his metaphor as their "Big Idea" for the European Commission's "Big Idea" project for its Digital Agenda. It is odd, though, that a failed metaphor created in 1995 for a very different world should be thought to be an idea at all, big or not, for 2011 and the world beyond. In 1995, people accessed the world through phone dial-up. The World Wide Web had just been launched. Napster hadn't been invented. The first downloadable ringtones to mobile telephones did not occur until 1998, and in Finland. There were no iTunes, no Google, no YouTube, no Facebook, no Twitter. Despite the fact that the digital world has radically changed since 1995, the metaphor is put forth as a timeless, boundless, universally applicable practical tool. In truth, the metaphor was wrong at the time and it is wrong now.

The EPC's approach to the metaphor at first seems unusual. For Mr. Clark, digital locks were preeminent, coming first. Without them, nothing else would occur. For the EPC, they are at the end of an (undefined) process, perhaps because digital lock laws now exist, whereas for Mr. Clark, the metaphor was a lobbying tool to get those laws passed. The EPC's use of the metaphor is, however, merely an updating of Mr. Clark's closed circuit system through the creation of a new form of control, one which, if backed by a new set of laws, will change the Internet into a platform for the haves over the have-nots. Those who can't pay will live in a digital ghetto.

The EPC's emphasis is on what it calls technical infrastructure, another metaphor, or if you like, a euphemism. It is a euphemism for what the EPC calls a new era, the era of a "machine-mediated process" for online licensing of copyrighted works. Examples are given of such processes. Some of these examples are very progressive and should be encouraged; they include Creative Commons, books registries, and the Arrow project for facilitating the licensing the digitization of library collections. Others are extremely regressive. They are regressive because they are dependent upon the development and acceptance (likely mandatory) of what are called "licensing standards." Examples include the news industry's ACAP protocol and UltraViolet project to deliver interoperable digital locks for home networks. These are standards not in the sense most people think of standards: agreement among a wide-swath of experts, intended to be applied broadly and not to benefit one group alone. ACAP is not a standard in this sense: it is a narrow industry developed system intended to benefit that industry alone. It is a bad solution in search of a non-existent problem.

By lumping unrelated and very different projects together under the rubric of a single (failed, old) metaphor, publishers demonstrate that they have yet to figure out how to operate in a digital economy. The Big Idea that machine-dictated terms developed by media companies will solve problems of rights management is a false idea: None of the problems with rights management have been created by technology, nor by users. These are entirely self-inflicted wounds created by rights holders. The problems of accurate data and how to license copyrighted works existed in the analog world, and from the time of the very first rights register, that of the London "Worshipful Company of Stationers and Newspaper Makers, " which received a royal monopoly over the publishing and printing business in 1557, and which set up a register to record which of its members owned which rights.

Whatever utility the metaphor "the answer to the machine is in the machine" has (I think none), it definitely has no relevance to rights information. Technology, in the form of transparent, accurate, complete online rights registries, such as that proposed by WIPO's International Music Registry, can help greatly in discovering where the problems are and in giving people access to rights information, but the universal principal of Garbage In, Garbage Out applies online too: Rights registries will only be so good as the information inputted is good, and that is a manual problem caused by humans, not machines, metaphoric or not.

Nor can the presence alone of rights management information address behavioral problems, whether by machines or people. The answer to behavioral problems is figuring out why the behavior is occurring and then addressing the root cause in a constructive way. As discussed in earlier chapters, if there is significant unauthorized copying of works online, we have to ask why? Is it because there are few lawful alternatives? If so, the answer is to flood the market with lawful alternatives. A significant problem with Mr. Clark's metaphor is that it writes out of the equation why human behavior on the Internet is occurring, and falsely suggests that machines can solve human behavioral problems. Machines, like laws, are created and controlled by humans. The answer to human problems must be solved by humans.

THE END OF THE PUBLIC INTEREST IN COPYRIGHT

I believe Mr. Clark's and the EPC's failure to address the human behavioral issue are not accidental. The logical conclusion to their approach is that each and every piece of content and each and every use of that content online is to be controlled through digital locks and restrictive licensing. In this world, consumers will have two choices: accept the conditions imposed on them or not. Behavior is reduced to this simple binary choice. The machine—in the form of Internet Service Providers (ISPs)—will be commanded by governments to punish those who find ways to beat the system. Rene Summer, the Director of Government and Industry Relations for the Swedish Ericsson Group, wrote in June 2011 that these days are already upon us:

> ISPs are being forced to act as digital security agents on behalf of economic rights holders by listening in, screening, surveying and filtering the exchange of information between consumers. Such strict enforcement further damages the prospects of legal digital alternatives by introducing the principle of innovation by permission. It also carries unwelcome echoes of the old Eastern-bloc surveillance societies that modern Europe has decisively rejected.[6]

Under this Big Brother approach, we needn't worry about fair use, fair dealing, or any public interest provision. Media-company-developed standards for infrastructures backed up by digital locks and possibly new laws, as well digital rights management laws, have the very real potential to eliminate all "limitations and exceptions." Such provisions, as a derogation from property rights and the European natural right theory of the supremacy of authors, will be seen as outmoded. The answer to consumers is apparently to turn them into passive, consuming machines. The answer of consumers must be to convince policymakers to reject failed, dangerous metaphors.

TWELVE

Effective Global Copyright Laws

The universal nature of music, art, and literature explains their enduring appeal and presents their creators with the opportunity to reach a global audience. The ability of copyright owners to be paid for exploitation of their works beyond their own national boundaries has been important since at least the late eighteenth and early nineteenth centuries. Famous composers, including Haydn, Mozart, and Beethoven sought to prevent unauthorized printing of their works by publishers in other countries by entering into simultaneous publication agreements.[1] (A well-known 1795 painting by Francisco Goya of the Spanish Duke of Alba shows the Duke examining an unauthorized copy of one of Haydn's works.) A number of bilateral agreements were signed in the period 1837–1850. Efforts at concluding an international agreement began in earnest in the late 1870s, culminating in the Berne Convention for the Protection of Literary and Artistic Works in 1886. Today, the Berne Convention is administered by the World Intellectual Property Organization (WIPO) in Geneva, a UN agency. WIPO has 184 Member Countries, from Afghanistan to Zambia.

Some important countries initially stayed outside of the Convention, principally the United States, which did not join until March 1, 1989. Bilateral agreements remained important for many decades after the formation of the Berne Union, and have enjoyed a renaissance recently in the form of free trade agreements. Regional trade agreements, among a select group of countries who then seek to impose their will on countries who were not at the bargaining table, is the latest trend, witnessed in ACTA, the misnamed Anti-Counterfeiting Trade Agreement. I say misnamed because ACTA is not much concerned with counterfeiting nor with trade; instead, it seeks to create new, substantive legal rights. The Trans Pacific Partnership (TPP) agreement currently being negotiated among nine countries is another example.[2]

These types of agreements are designed to sidestep established multilateral forums such as the WIPO and the World Trade Organization where developing countries have a voice; they are designed to take away the discretion of legislatures to amend their own laws; they are designed to prevent countries from cutting back on the excessive rights contained in those agreements. If, for example, a country decided that life of the author plus seventy years is too long, that country would have to abrogate all agreements it has entered into containing the obligation, thereby risking benefits obtained for other sectors of the economy.[3]

Developed countries negotiating the agreements candidly admit the pitfalls of their approach. A leaked cable from the U.S. Embassy in Rome discusses Italian complaints about ACTA:

> The level of confidentiality in these ACTA negotiations has been set at a higher level than is customary for non-security

agreements. According to [the Italian government], it is impossible for member states to conduct necessary consultations with IPR stakeholders and legislatures under this level of confidentiality.[4]

A leaked cable from the U.S. Embassy in Sweden a year later notes:

> [T]he secrecy issue has been very damaging to the negotiating climate in Sweden. All political parties have vocal minorities challenging the steps the government has taken to step up its IPR enforcement. For those groups, the refusal to make ACTA documents public has been an excellent political tool around which to build speculation about the political intent behind the negotiations. If the instrument for example had been negotiated within the World Intellectual Property Organization (WIPO) critics say, WIPO's Secretariat would have made public initial draft proposals.... [T]he secrecy around the negotiations has led to that the legitimacy of the whole process being questioned.[5]

Including intellectual property within trade agreements is a strategy that was originally developed by the United States in the early 1980s; it reached the big-time in the 1994 Trade-Related Aspects of Intellectual Property Rights (TRIPS) section, which formed part of the outcome of the Uruguay Round negotiations under the General Agreement on Tariffs and Trade. In such agreements, intellectual property issues are subsumed within a larger trade agenda. For large, intellectual property (IP)-exporting countries such as the United States, obtaining ever-stronger rights is seen as obtaining ever-stronger control over foreign markets. But what are the benefits for IP net-importing countries? Few if any; on the contrary, there is a net loss. Behind the scenes, developed countries admit this. In the leaked December 2010 document, New Zealand trade negotiators wrote to colleagues from other countries negotiating the proposed Trans Pacific Partnership agreement:

> Analysis of the costs and benefits of IP protection shows that there is a tendency towards overprotection of IP in all our societies, particularly in the areas of copyright and patents. . . .
>
> The problems of overprotection are particularly acute for technology importing countries, including developing countries. The analysis shows that for these countries, IP rights that are too strong will detract from innovation rather than promote it.[6]

Then why do such developing countries agree to ever-higher levels of protection that are not in their best interest? There are many answers, perhaps as many as there are net-importing countries. For smaller countries, the reason is lack of bargaining position. For other countries, it is the hope of obtaining benefits for other domestically important sectors; after all, if you are an IP net-importing country, there are other segments of your economy that you wish to expand through trade. In order to benefit these other segments, good policy in intellectual property is sacrificed. One example is Brazil, where after repeated pressure and threats from the United States of retaliation against the importation of Brazilian goods, non-IP domestic industries began to pressure the government to agree to the United States' IP demands: "Shoe exporters . . . panicked. People in Rio Grande do Sul [an agricultural area] went nuts. 'I, a shoemaker, who makes shoes for the U.S. . . . I'm going to lose my benefits because there's DVD piracy? What do I have to do with that?"[7]

A RISING TIDE LIFTS ALL BOATS, OR DOES IT?

Not surprisingly, developed countries argue in favor of global uniformity of intellectual property laws at levels of protection that favor the multinational corporations that dominate their domestic industries.[8] Bare expressions of naked self-interest are uncommon, and are instead usually clothed in expressions of alleged mutual benefit between developed and developing countries: high levels of IP protection benefit all countries, we are told.

One of the most common linguistic tools used to disguise the self-interest of developed countries and their industries is the metaphor "a rising tide lifts all boats." The metaphor is a powerful one because it promises equality for all, and offers hope for developing countries that aspire to the level of economic well-being found in developed countries. The rising tide metaphor purports simultaneously to lift everyone "up" on the same tide, regardless of where they start from before the tide starts to rise. Who can complain about the rising tide egalitarian approach of providing the same benefits to everyone? What small boat owner doesn't aspire to buy a yacht? If the rules are the same for everyone, then dinghies are lifted up just like the yachts. And if the yachts are lifted up a bit more than dinghies, the dinghies might not complain so long as they are lifted up too.[9] It is also argued that rules protecting dinghies against yachts will prevent dinghies'"upward" mobility, to the detriment of ambitious dinghies and ultimately to the detriment of the whole fleet, which will be dragged "down" by slackers.

The metaphor works visually; when you hear it, you picture an ocean scene with a number of boats gently floating, some fancy, some ordinary. This image is then transferred to the very different, abstract concept of the appropriate level of protection to be provided by intellectual property laws. We are to believe, through transferring the associations of the rising tide metaphor, that stronger intellectual property laws are good (like a rising tide) because they benefit everyone, and benefit everyone the same way. Yes, it is acknowledged, stronger intellectual property laws are good for the developed countries, but such laws are also asserted to be good for developing countries to whom the metaphor is being offered. Rising tide laws are, moreover, process and facially neutral: nothing in the way they were enacted or written expressly favors developed countries. Certainly no unfairness can occur under such circumstances, we are told.

The metaphor contains the implied promise that if the protections afforded by intellectual property laws are increased, developing countries will become developed countries, or will at least enjoy a level of benefits comparable to those in developed countries: the same access to pharmaceutical drugs, the same works of authorship. China may be an example of a country where the domestic industry ultimately benefits from intellectual property laws, but that country is exceptional in many ways.

The implied promise of developing countries becoming developed countries is important because it papers over the obvious fact that, in practice, and at least in the short and medium term, stronger intellectual property laws in importing countries result in losses for importing countries and benefits to exporting countries. Even at the most optimistic, any alleged benefits to developing countries are far off in the future.[10] While countries may make the rational decision to endure short-term losses in order to achieve greater long-term gains, long-term growth in developing countries may be threatened due to the entrenchment of foreign companies in some local markets, and the lack of a necessary infrastructure for local entrepreneurs who might take advantage of IP rights.

Occasionally, immediate losses from increased protection are acknowledged, but developing countries are reassured that the inequality is temporary: Magically, increasing losses now will later be turned into increased benefits, allegedly because domestic industries will later be able to extract revenues from other countries lower on the food chain, and maybe even from developed countries. The then-Director General of the World Intellectual Property Organization, Árpád Bogsch,[11] in discussing the purported benefits of two treaties it concluded in 1996, blithely stated with no basis in fact:

> Adherence and implementation of the treaties offer a number of benefits for countries regardless of their stage of development. It provides important economic incentives to creative individuals and companies in the new digital environment. The treaties provide a substantial legal basis for healthy electronic commerce. They sustain the national copyright industries, attract investment, and protect local creativity.[12]

Archbishop Tomasi, the permanent representative of the Vatican to the United Nations, challenged these assumptions:

> The adoption of stronger IPRs in developing countries is often defended by claims that this reform will attract significant new inflows of technology, a blossoming of local innovation and cultural industries, and a faster closing of the technology gap between developed and developing countries. It must be recognized, however, that improved IPRs by [themselves are] highly unlikely to produce such results.[13]

In 2006, the UK Gowers report had reached the same conclusion:

> The economic evidence and, in particular, the history of currently developed countries suggest that a single

one–size–fits–all approach is inappropriate. Stronger IP protection can ultimately reap rewards in terms of greater domestic innovation in developing countries and in developing countries with sufficient capacity to innovate. However, it has little impact on innovation in developing countries without the capacity to innovate, and it may impose additional costs. Given that different IP regimes are more appropriate at different stages of development, it would make sense to allow individual nations to choose when to strengthen their IP regimes, rather than to seek to enforce a certain perspective.[14]

Without an educated citizenry, adequate domestic research and development firms, meaningful participation in financial markets, and effective means to bring domestic innovations to market, the purported benefits to developing countries will not occur. Yet, lawmakers in developing countries are wrongly led to believe that a failure to enact stronger intellectual property laws without such preconditions will cut off a bright future. What lawmaker wants to be accused of disadvantaging his or her own business owners?

Tellingly, the rising tide metaphor is not employed within developed countries: the United States, for example, does not claim that U.S. copyright laws benefit all equally within the United States; such a claim would be absurd, but it is no less absurd to argue that the metaphor works for developing countries. Indeed, when the United States was itself a developing country it rejected the pleas of developed countries such as Britain to protect foreign authors. From 1790 to 1891, it was deliberate U.S. policy to deny protection to the works of foreign published works, a policy that greatly benefitted U.S. economic development.[15] If there is to be an effective global copyright law, it has to work well for all countries, at all stages of development.

Looking behind the rising-tide metaphor, it is readily apparent there are significant problems with it, the same ones found with trickle-down economics: both assume that helping the rich now will help the poor later. But not all boats are made alike and not all are in the same shape. A rising tide will certainly help the stronger boats, but the same cannot necessarily be said of the weaker ones, which might sink instead. The metaphor assumes rising tides are the only way for everyone to advance, that everyone's interest is always in stronger laws. There may, however, be low-tide economic markets, markets that exist only when there are low tides. An example of a low-tide market is a small domestic record industry that caters to local markets. Raising the tide and opening the flood gates to foreign record companies will eliminate these markets. A number of developed countries around the world have content quotas for this reason, yet nevertheless employ the rising tide metaphor for developing countries.

The rising-tide metaphor can also be thought of in conventional economic terms. Adam Smith claimed, in the eighteenth century, that an increase in the size of markets leads to increases in the diversity of offerings.[16] Trade among countries increases this diversity by introducing people in one country to the goods, services, and cultures of others.[17] Most of the early great powers, beginning with the Ancient Greeks, were sea powers. The Greeks spread their culture wherever they went, whether that spread was voluntary or forced as part of a conquest. France, Great Britain, Holland, Spain, and Portugal did the same. The trade routes to the Far East transmitted more than spices.

From the Industrial Revolution forward, increased literacy rates and mass production led to an expansion of culture so that it was no longer the province of the upper classes. Walt Whitman remarked, "To have great poets, there must be great audiences."[18] Whitman believed that poetry could be appreciated by the working class and later regretted that he had not toured the country and given readings to the working class.[19] Alexis de Tocqueville, in studying the United States, took a different view, concluding that "market growth serves as a magnet, pulling creators towards mass production and away from serving niches," resulting in "a culture of the least common denominator...."[20] De Tocqueville's rather than Smith's views seems to have prevailed. Is bad taste a necessary result of large markets, though? There is considerable evidence that our current fare—those works that are the biggest sellers are indeed dumbed down. Here are some of the movies for 2011: *Scary Movie 5*, *Spider-Man 4*, *Mission Impossible 4*, *Spy Kids 4*, *Pirates of the Caribbean 4*, *Terminator 3*, *Transformers 3*, *Happy Feet 2*, *Alvin and the Chipmunks 3*, *Cars 2*, *Kung Fu Panda 2*, *Get Smart 2*. The top grossing film in the United States in 2010 was *Toy Story 3*.

At the same time, large markets, like those in New York City, do provide opportunities for diverse, niche offerings. The growth of Internet platforms like YouTube and blogs has led to fantastic offerings of specialty tastes from around the world. Professor Taylor Cowen had it right when he said "markets bring more homogeneity *and* more diversity. This dual trend characterizes consumer taste as well as cultural products generally."[21] This duality is a consequence of trade, and results in countries becoming "commonly diverse,"[22] as citizens throughout the world can meet without national boundaries on Internet social networks and share information about their cultural likes and dislikes (and sometimes copies of cultural works themselves).

Dominance of U.S. cultural works leads to a dominance of U.S. culture, and it is easy to see why. No country can foster the creativity of its own citizens if the financing, production, and distribution of works is controlled by foreign corporations, especially when, as in the case of the U.S., the size of the U.S. market and the comparative wealth of its companies results in vast comparative advantages to the creation and marketing of U.S. works.

India provides an interesting example of how a country has dealt with these problems. Backyard Indian companies were "energetically recording and marketing all manner" of regional musical works that previously had been ignored by the dominant British record company. Rather than targeting the same broad national audience served by the large companies, the backyard companies were aiming at "a bewildering variety" of audiences, some quite narrow, such as Punjabi truck drivers. Local ownership of the means of production is "incomparably more diverse.... As a result, the average non–elite Indian is now, as never before, offered the voices of his community..."[23]

These passages are not about the present or about digital technology, but rather about the 1980s and the introduction of audio-cassette tapes and players.

Fast-forwarding to the present, India has a very strong domestic film market: half of the world's tickets are sold in India, but Hollywood accounts for only 8 percent of the domestic market. Bollywood distributors price their products at $US2.12 for DVDs. This pricing has resulted in large sales: The DVD of the film *Jab We Met* (a Hindi romantic comedy)[24] by the Indian company Moser Baer sold six million DVDs five weeks after its theatrical release.[25] By contrast, Warner Brothers' movie *The Dark Knight* was sold for the equivalent of $US663.00. There is no substitute for strong local companies competing for local consumers. If governments wish to encourage their own cultural industries, they must stop making criminals out of their own citizens for the benefit of foreign (mostly U.S.) companies, and spend money on building their own cultural industries, without which local industries can't arise. Famous *tropicalismo* musician Gilberto Gil took such steps during his service as Brazil's Minister of Culture, in his

Cultural Points program.[26] The program consisted of grants to install recording and video studios in community centers in Brazil's poorest neighborhoods and teaching residents how to use them. Platforms like YouTube enable such people to reach a worldwide audience, bypassing the traditional gatekeepers.

THE FALLACY OF ENFORCEMENT

In chapter 5, I reviewed the fallacy of stronger laws being an effective form of deterrence against unauthorized conduct. The best way to prevent the sale of unauthorized goods is to flood the market with authorized goods.[27] Creating demand for copyrighted works, but then not meeting that demand leads to the creation of unauthorized markets. This process is replicated on the global level: the existence of vast unauthorized markets across the world is not a sign of the moral shortcomings among the citizens in those countries, but rather is the result of copyright owners clinging to failed business models. Multinational corporations make the vast bulk of their profits in developed country markets, and thus have little interest in serving other markets, especially when doing so means that they would have to compete in those markets on those markets' terms, principally in terms of price.

The Social Science Research Council, in a comprehensive study of global consumption of media presented to WIPO stated: "Media piracy has been called 'a global scourge,' 'an international plague,' and 'nirvana for criminals,' but it is probably better described as a global pricing problem."[28] Where goods owned by multinational corporations are offered at all in developing countries, they are offered at the same prices as in developed countries, or at comparative prices that place the goods far out of reach of all but the most wealthy in developing countries. The centrality of pricing and distribution problems in developing countries is obvious, yet strikingly absent from most policy discussions.[29] The stark differences on pricing and distribution in developing countries reveal why the enforcement efforts of multinational corporations have been a failure. That it is a failure isn't disputed. The Social Sciences Research Council reported, "we have seen no evidence—*and indeed no claims*—that enforcement efforts to date have had any impact on the overall supply of pirated goods. Our work suggests, rather, that piracy has grown dramatically by most measures in the past decade, driven by...high media prices, low local incomes, technological diffusion, and fast-changing consumer and cultural practices."[30] The table below shows why; it exhibits the absolute and relative prices for one album that had an international market, the musical group Cold Play's *Viva La Vida*, which sold over nine million copies and led the charts for digital downloads.

Coldplay: *Viva la Vida* (CD)

	Legal Price (US$)	CPP Price	Pirate Price	Pirate CPP
United States of America	17	---------	NA	---------
Russia	11	59	5	26
Brazil	14	80	2.5	14
South Africa	20.5	164	2.7	22
India	8.5	385	1.2	54
Mexico	13.7	75	(.4) 1	5.75

(CPP = Consumer Purchasing Power)
Report of the Social Science Research Council, "Media Piracy in Emerging Economies: Price, Market Structure and Consumer Behavior" at paragraph 35. December 1, 2010, submitted to the Advisory Committee on Enforcement, Sixth Session ("ACE Report").

In South Africa—a country where one-third of the population earns less than US$1 a day—the absolute (non-comparative) legal price exceeded that of the United States, but in none of the countries was the comparative price—the price that reflects cost of living differences—the same as in the United States. Pirate CDs were, however, priced closer to the comparative cost of living, but still not equivalent. Where an Indian consumer was presented with the choice of buying the CD at the equivalent of US$385 (CPP) for the authorized copy, or US$54 for the unauthorized CD, the choice was clear.

Below is another example, in which Warner Brothers' movie *The Dark Knight*, which had over US$1 billion in box office receipts, broke all records for DVD sales.

The Dark Knight (DVD)

	Legal Price (US$)	CPP Price	Pirate Price	Pirate CPP
United States of America	24	---------	5	---------
Russia	15	79	5	26
Brazil	15	85	3.5	20
South Africa	14	129	(.4) 2.8	22
India	14	635	(.3) 1.2	54
Mexico	27	154	(.4) .75	4

Parentheses indicate lowest observed price

Parentheses indicate lowest observed price

(CPP = Consumer Purchasing Power)

Report of the Social Science Research Council, "Media Piracy in Emerging Economies: Price, Market Structure and Consumer Behavior" at paragraph 35. December 1, 2010, submitted to the Advisory Committee on Enforcement, Sixth Session ("ACE Report").

Here, the absolute price of the authorized DVD in Mexico exceeds that in the United States. And again, in none of the countries was the comparative price—the price that reflects cost of living differences—the same as in the United States. Pirate DVDs were, however, priced closer to the comparative cost of living, but still not equivalent.

Here is a third example, which presents an even more striking illustration of why enforcement efforts without reform of pricing are doomed, that of Microsoft's Office 2007:

Microsoft Office 2007 (Home and Student Edition, 2009 prices)

(CPP = Consumer Purchasing Power)

	Legal Price (US$)	CPP Price	Pirate Price	Pirate CPP
United States of America	149	---------	NA	---------
Russia	150	795	NA	26
Brazil	109	879	NA	20
South Africa	114	985	NA	22
India	155	849	.75	54
Mexico	100	5400	2	4

Parentheses indicate lowest observed price

Report of the Social Science Research Council, "Media Piracy in Emerging Economies: Price, Market Structure and Consumer Behavior" at paragraph 49. December 1, 2010, submitted to the Advisory Committee on Enforcement, Sixth Session ("ACE Report").

In what rational market would a software product be priced at US$149 in the United States and at the consumer purchasing power adjusted price of US$5,400? Here is another way to think of what such prices mean. In 2004, Marcelo D'Elia Branco, Brazil's liaison between the open source community and the government estimated that one license for Microsoft's Office suite meant Brazil had to export sixty sacks of soybeans. As then-President Lula da Silva observed, "For the right to use one copy of Office plus Windows for one year or a year and a half, until the next upgrade, we have to till the earth, plant, harvest, and export to international markets that much soy. When I explain this to the farmers, they go nuts."[31]

The only approach to such situations is obvious and has been known for centuries: offering the same goods at different prices to different audiences based on their ability to pay. In the late 1840s, Giovanni Ricordi, Giuseppe Verdi's music publisher and agent, began an effort to force opera houses throughout Europe to pay a fee for each performance. This effort led to a rebellion by smaller opera houses, who refused to pay anything and sought to obtain unauthorized copies for their performances of Verdi's operas. Rather than fight them, Ricordi suggested to Verdi that "It is more advantageous to provide access to these scores for all theatres, adapting the price to their special means, because I obtain much more from many small theatres at the price of 300 or 250 Lire, than from ten or twelve at the price of a thousand."[32] Verdi agreed, and as a result enjoyed unprecedented wealth.

In other cases, no effort is made to offer legitimate product. In such cases, the Social Research Council found:

> Where there is no meaningful legal distribution, the pirate market cannot be said to compete with legal sales, or generate losses for industry. At the low end of the socio-economic ladder where such distribution gaps are common, piracy is often simply the market. The notion of the moral choice between pirated and licit—the basis of antipiracy campaigns—is simply inoperative in such contexts, an impractical narrative of self-denial. . . .[33]

This denial was seen within the United States, when the music industry succeeded in having the courts shut down Napster and then failed to offer any legitimate alternatives. Moreover, as the Hargreaves review in the UK observed in May 2011, research has found "no evidence that changes since the launch of the original Napster file sharing in 1999/2000 have affected the quantity of new recorded music or artists coming to market."[34] In too many cases, then, the problem arises from copyright owners' lack of interest in fulfilling market demand. No law can cure this failure. But there is hope for the future. In a 2009 interview, MPAA Director of Special Projects Robert Bauer was quoted as saying, "Our job is to isolate the forms of piracy that compete with legitimate sales, treat those as a proxy for unmet consumer demand, and find a way to meet that demand."[35] One way was recently suggested by Ben Karakunnel, director of business intelligence at Warner Brothers' antipiracy unit, as reported in the paidContent.org website:

> In the international markets, illegal WB content in which pirates dub or subtitle themselves is increasingly popular. For one unspecified program Karakunnel used as an example, it wasn't until the third day after its initial airdate that one such pirate-created translated version accounted for 23 percent of pirated files of that particular program. By day 10, it accounted for 74 percent. Said Karakunnel, "If we can get dubbed or subtitled language versions in the first two days, we can beat them to the punch."
>
> Typical pirates steal in addition to making legitimate entertainment purchases like box office, DVD and even online transactions. Even the most diehard pirates spend some money, though less than more casual infringers. "One of the main things we're doing is looking at why they do things legitimately on certain products and not on others," said Karakunnel.
>
> With thinking like that, WB just might find it will do more to curtail piracy by letting it read the marketplace's needs rather than playing defense.[36]

This is a refreshing approach. There will still be those who cause damage to copyright owners through massive unauthorized copying, and who have no interest in purchasing legitimate works. But the number of such people is small, far smaller than we have been led to believe. A recent study by a group of international scholars on who are the publishers of unauthorized content on the peer-to-peer file network BitTorrent revealed that many of them are copyright owners themselves seeding false files: 30 percent of the content and 25 percent of the downloads are attributable to copyright owners' own guerilla actions.[37] Those who make available unauthorized content and who make money off of doing so are responsible for 30 percent of the content and 40 percent of the downloads. The top 100 of those who make content available, a number that includes both copyright owners and non-copyright owners, account for 66 2/3 percent of all content and 75 percent of all downloads. Going after the very small number of those who are doing most of the harm is entirely justified. What is unjustified are heavy-handed techniques against the mass of the population, whether through three-strikes-and-you're-out approaches, or threats of lawsuits with crippling penalties. Copyright owners have all the tools they need to go after the bad guys, and we should support them in those efforts. However, copyright owners should also support the good guys by providing reasonably priced, convenient authorized goods. If they don't, no copyright law can help them.

Notes

Introduction

1. In Zen and the Art of Motorcycle Maintenance, Robert Pirsig observed, "The real purpose of the scientific method is to make sure nature hasn't misled you into thinking you know something you actually don't know." I thank Dr. Ben Goldacre for the reference.
2. Plato Apology 38a.
3. Digital Opportunity: A Review of Intellectual Property Growth, Foreword (May 2011).
4. See Ian Hargreaves, Digital Opportunity: A Review of Intellectual Property and Growth, Foreword (May 2011): "We urge Government to ensure that in future, policy on Intellectual Property issues is constructed on the basis of evidence, rather than the weight of lobbying...."
5. Paul A. David, The Evolution of Intellectual Property Institutions and the Panda's Thumb, paper prepared for presentation at the Meetings of the International Economic Association in Moscow, August 24–28, 1992.
6. See remarks of Maria Martin-Pratt, head of the copyright unit, European Union Internal Market Directorate, at CISAC'S June 8, 2011, World Copyright Summit, Brussels, Belgium.

Chapter 1

1. See www.bookstats.org.
2. See Mira Rajan's excellent new book, Moral Rights: Principles, Practice and New Technologies (2011, Oxford University Press).

3. For example, in 2010 the band OK GO left its label, EMI, over a dispute involving the embedding of YouTube videos. See http://www.okgo.net/2010/03/10/onwards-and-upwards/.

4. See David Kusek, "Attention Music Manager and Artists; you may be owned BILLIONS in unpaid royalties," March 31, 2011, Future of Music Coalition website, available at: http://www.futureofmusic-book.com/2011/03/music-managers-and-artists-could-collect-over-2-billion-in-unpaid-royalties/; http://www.musicweek.com/story.asp?sectioncode=1&storycode=1045428&c=1.

5. See Ben Sisario, Eminem Lawsuit May Raise Pay for Older Artists, New York Times, March 27, 2011, available at: http://www.nytimes.com/2011/03/28/business/media/28eminem.html. In the original, the order of 35 cents and a nickel is reversed, I think by mistake, hence my correction.

6. See Evelyn Rusli, A Force Behind Lady Gaga Inc., New York Times, June 5, 2011, available at: http://dealbook.nytimes.com/2011/06/05/a-force-behind-the-gaga-effect/.

7. These are admittedly broad statements that have important exceptions: Radiohead has pioneered new business models, such as giving fans the ability to set a price for buying albums. Increasingly, established artists and bands are seeing the advantage of platforms such as YouTube for hosting and monetizing against authorized versions of live shows, although this sometimes puts them into conflict with their record labels.

8. See Roy Blount, Jr., The Kindle Swindle?, New York Times, February 14, 2009, available at: http://www.nytimes.com/2009/02/25/opinion/25blount.html.

9. This is not the case generally with collecting societies, who wish to have as wide a repertoire as possible in order to be an attractive clearing house and to increase revenues through increased licensing.

10. See http://torrentfreak.com/mpaa-democratizing-culture-is-not-in-our-interest-110420/.

11. Frederick Hayek expressed concern about media companies' dominance over the channels for reporting about their own commercial endeavors, writing in "The Intellectuals and Socialism" (originally published in 1949 in the University of Chicago Law Review, available at: http://aetds.hnuc.edu.cn/uploadfile/20080316211019875.pdf):

It would be interesting to discover how far a seriously critical view of the benefits to society of the law of copyright, or the expression of doubts about the public interest in the existence of a class which makes its living from the writing of books, would have a chance of being publicly stated in a society in which the channels of expression are so largely controlled by people who have a vested interest on the existing situation.

12. Frank Smith, To Think, 62, 64 (1990).

13. See Creative Content in a European Digital Single Market: Challenges for the Future, A Reflection Document of DG INFOSO and DG MARKT page 2, October 22, 2009: "Copyright is the basis for creativity. It is one of the cornerstones of Europe's cultural heritage and of a culturally diverse and economically vibrant content sector."

14. See Ruth Towse, Creativity, Copyright and the Creative Industries, 63 Kyklos 461 (2010). Professor Towse is Professor of Economics of Creative Industries at Erasmus University Rotterdam, The Netherlands. She specializes in cultural economics and the economics of copyright. I have learned a great deal from her outstanding scholarship.

15. See Bruno Frey, Not Just for the Money: An Economic Theory of Personal Motivation (1998, Beacon Press).

16. George Orwell, Why I Write 1 (1946) (Penguin Great Ideas edition). I thank Irwin Stelzer for this wonderful little collection of essays.

17. See William and Hilda Baumol, On the Economics of Musical Compositions in Mozart's Vienna, 18 Journal of Cultural Economics 171 (1994).

18. See McCartney + Lennon Wrote Swimming Pool Song, Contactmusic.com, August 23, 2005, available at: http://www.contactmusic.com/new/xmlfeed.nsf/story/mccartney-+-lennon-wrote-swimming-pool-song.

19. Bleistein v. Donaldson Lithographing Co., 188 U.S. 239, 251–252 (1903).

20. See 17 United States Code Section 102(a): "Copyright protection subsists. . . .in original works of authorship. . . ."

21. EMI is owned by CitiCorp. Warner Music Group is owned by Access Industries, Inc., a private industrial group run by Len Blavatnik, a Russian businessman.

22. Hearing Before the Subcommittee on Courts and Intellectual Property of the Committee on the Judiciary, U.S. House of Representatives,106th Congress, 2d Session, page 120 (May 25, 2000). Serial No. 145. Available at: http://commdocs.house.gov/committees/judiciary/hju65223.000/hju65223_0f.htm.

23. See http://en.wikipedia.org/wiki/Studio_system.

24. See http://en.wikipedia.org/wiki/Cinema_of_the_United_States#Golden_Age_of_Hollywood.

25. 334 U.S. 131 (1948).

26. Edward Jay Epstein, The Big Picture: Money and Power in Hollywood 112 (2006, Random House). See also Schuyler Moore, The Biz: The Basic Business, Legal and Financial Aspects of the Film Industry (2007, 3d edition, Silman-James Press).

27. http://thehollywoodeconomist.blogspot.com. The $12 million figure at the end does not represent the studio's net outlay (which was $8.7 million), but rather a fee received that permitted it to reduce the outlay ultimately to $8.7 million.

28. See http://www.nakedcapitalism.com/2010/05/guest-post-where-there%E2%80%99s-smoke-there%E2%80%99s-a-smoke-machine-a-case-for-movie-futures.html.

29. See Mark Harris, The Day the Movies Died, GQ Magazine, February 2011, available at: http://www.gq.com/entertainment/movies-and-tv/201102/the-day-the-movies-died-mark-harris?currentPage=al.

30. See http://www.nytimes.com/2011/06/14/movies/laura-ziskin-behind-spider-man-films-dies-at-61.html?_r=1&hpw.

31. See Matthew Phenix, Does Product Placement in the Movies Sell Cars?, Wired Magazine, May 6, 2008, available at: http://www.wired.com/autopia/2008/05/does-product-pl/.

32. See http://en.wikipedia.org/wiki/Romance_novel.

33. Her website notes: "In 2002, Ms. Steel was decorated by the French government as an 'Officier' of the distinguished Order of Arts and Letters, for her lifetime contribution to world culture. She was awarded the second highest rank of the Order." http://www.randomhouse.com/features/steel/meet_about.html. J.K. Rowling's Harry Potter series has sold half as many copies, around 400 million. Ms. Steele's award, as well as a 2006 Legion of Honor award for

comedian Jerry Lewis, proves France's perverse delight in praising mediocre American talent while at the same time publicly criticizing the culture that spawned such lamentable efforts. See Ruth Beth Gordon, Why the French Love Jerry Lewis: From Cabaret to Early Cinema (2001, Stanford University Press).

34. See http://blogs.forbes.com/dorothypomerantz/2011/06/09/the-best-paid-celebrities-under-30/.

35. Ruth Towse, Creativity, Incentive and Reward: An Economic Analysis of Copyright in the Information Age 5 (2001, Edward Elgar Publishing).

36. I speak here only of economic rights. *Droit moral*, non-economic rights that give authors the ability to control the contexts in which their works are used, is an important right.

37. See William Osborne, Marketplace of Ideas: But First the Bill?, published in ArtsJournal.com, March 2004, available at: http://www.osborne-conant.org/arts_funding.htm; Gunther Schulze and Anselm Rose, Public Orchestra Funding in Germany – An Empirical Investigation, 22 Journal of Cultural Economics 227 (1998), available at: http://sdsu795.tripod.com/tai03.pdf.

My point in the text is not to advocate specifically for increased funding for symphony orchestras, but rather to use them as a type of generally recognized culture that cannot compete well in the marketplace. For a recent book about the role of classical music in general culture, see Julian Johnson, Who Needs Classical Music? Cultural Choice and Musical Value (2011, Oxford University Press).

38. The National Endowment for the Arts does make spot grants, and in May 2011 assisted the financially strapped Baltimore Symphony Orchestra with a $100,000 grant for touring. See http://www.prweb.com/releases/2011/5/prweb8460323.htm. In Fiscal Year 2010, the NEA made grants totaling $139 million to all the arts. See http://www.nea.gov/about/Facts/AtAGlance.html.

39. See Robert Flanagan, Report to Andrew W. Mellon Foundation, The Economic Environment of American Symphony Orchestras, March 2008, available at: http://www.gsb.stanford.edu/news/packages/pdf/Flanagan.pdf.

40. Information about the collective may be found here: http://www. clarinetcoco.com/. The collective is part of a larger collective effort, the Fractured Atlas, which helps artists and arts organizations function more effectively as businesses by providing access to funding, healthcare, and education. See http://www.fracturedatlas.org/site/about.

41. See www.kickstarter.com.

42. The European Union, for example, launched 2009 as a year of creativity and innovation. See http://create2009.europa.eu/.

43. This publisher is not Oxford University Press.

44. See Robert Caves, Creative Industries: Contracts Between Art and Commerce (2000, Harvard University Press).

45. Reproduced in Copyright Law Revision Part 3: Preliminary Draft for Revised U.S. Copyright Law and Discussions and Comments on the Draft 286 (September 1964).

46. Thucydides, Book Five, History of the Peloponnesian Wars, reproduced in The Landmark Thucydides: A Comprehensive Guide to the Peloponnesian War 352 (Robert Strassler ed., The Free Press 1996). The Athenians made good on this realpolitik by killing the Melian men, enslaving the Melian women and children, and then repopulating it as an Athenian state. See http://en.wikipedia.org/wiki/Melian_dialogue, and A.B., Bosworth. "The Humanitarian Aspect of the Melian Dialogue." The Journal of Hellenic Studies 113 (1993): 31, http://www.jstor.org/stable/632396; W. Liebeschuetz. "The Structure and Function of the Melian Dialogue." The Journal of Hellenic Studies 88 (1968): 75, http://www.jstor.org/stable/628672.

47. See http://en.wikipedia.org/wiki/Melian_dialogue.

48. Available at: http://news.bbc.co.uk/2/hi/8681410. See http://www.michaelgeist.ca/content/view/5563/125/.

49. See http://business.financialpost.com/2011/05/30/judge-approves-settlement-in-music-royalties-class-action/.

50. See http://www.michaelgeist.ca/content/view/5563/125/.

51. See Statement of Charlie McCreevy, EU Commissioner for the Internal Market, November 21, 2006, at the European Parliament's Committee on Legal Affairs, quoted in chapter 2.

52. Single Market Communication at 3.

53. Single Market Communication at 34.

54. See Chapter 2.

55. Cf. Herbert Hovenkamp et al., IP and Antitrust: An Analysis of Antitrust Principles Applied to Intellectual Property Law (2d ed. 2010); Christina Bohannan and Herbert Hovenkamp, IP and Antitrust: Reformation and Harm, 51 Boston College Law Review 905 (2010).

56. See Baumol's Cost Disease: The Arts and Other Victims (Ruth Towse, editor, 1997, Edward Elgar Publishing).

57. See Ruth Towse, Creativity, Copyright and the Creative Industries Paradigm, 63 Kyklos 461 (August 2010).

58. Id. at 463.

59. Princeton University Press, 2004.

60. Scherer at 178.

61. Scherer at 179–180.

62. Scherer at 181.

63. Scherer at 195.

64. For example, after the success of James Fennimore Cooper's *Last of the Mohicans*, his publisher paid Cooper for the copyright in his previous five books. But see Grantland Rice, The Transformation of Authorship in America, Chapter 4 (University of Chicago Press 1997), for a discussion of what Professor Rice regards as Irving's conflicted views on copyright and the profession of authorship, particularly as expressed in the Sketch Book.

65. Either as the principal purpose or instrumentally for the production of works.

66. See Stephen Sondheim, A Little Night Music (1973).

67. Ludwig von Mises, Bureaucracy 17 (1944, 2007 edition, Liberty Fund, Inc.).

68. Id.

69. Dr. Francis Gurry, The Future of Copyright, Sydney Australia, February 25, 2011.

70. See The Technium, "Better Than Free," January 31, 2008, available at: http://www.kk.org/thetechnium/archives/2008/01/better_than_fre.php.

71. Digital Opportunity: A Review of Intellectual Property and Growth, Foreword (May 2011).

72. In the United States, recorded performances are embodied in "phonorecords" rather than "copies," but this is a semantic not substantive difference, having to do with international issues.

73. Technically, many of these laws are placed in statutes that also contain the copyright laws, but are in a different part of that statute.

74. Digital Video Recorders were introduced in 1999 at the Consumer Electronics Show. They have a long and complicated history, involving copy protection schemes, a successful effort by the movie studios to get the Federal Communications Commission to amend its regulations to give the studios control over copying (the broadcast flag), as well as lawsuits.

75. See Hal Varian and Richard Roehl's prescient article, "Circulating Libraries and Video Rental Stores," December 1996, revised March 9, 2000, available at: http://citeseerx.ist.psu.edu/viewdoc/summary?doi=10.1.1.46.6846.

76. See Address of Dr. Francis Gurry, Director General of the World Intellectual Property Organization, November 26, 2010, Beijing, China.

77. See Chapter 6.

Chapter 2

1. Ludwig von Mises, Bureaucracy 36 (1944, 2007 edition, Liberty Fund, Inc.).

2. There are exceptions to the exclusive rights regime, principally compulsory licenses. Collective management of rights also generally involves takes a non-exclusive rights approach.

3. See Sami Valkonen and Lawrence White, An Economic Model for the Incentive/Access Paradigm of Propertization, 29 Hastings Communications and Entertainment Law Journal, 359, 363 (Spring 2007).

4. See http://blogs.telegraph.co.uk/news/tobyharnden/100059061/christopher-hitchens-on-george-w-bush-and-the-stupidest-thing-any-president-has-ever-said.

5. See http://blogs.telegraph.co.uk/news/tobyharnden/100059061/christopher-hitchens-on-george-w-bush-and-the-stupidest-thing-any-president-has-ever-said.

6. Property and Growth, Foreword (May 2011).

7. Digital Opportunity, Chapter 8, paragraph 8.9.

8. See chapter 11.

9. See discussion below about impact statements done for the European Commission's 2008 recommendations on extending the term of protection for sound recordings.

10. See ec.europa.eu/internal_market/copyright/docs/term/ia_term_en.pdf -.

11. See http://rufuspollock.org/tags/copyright/.

12. Such review should be mandated legislatively to avoid separation of powers or authorization issues.

13. See http://www.slightlyrightofcentre.com/2011/01/exclusive-ec-raised-concerns-on-uk.html.

14. Id., Response 8.

15. A May 2011 report of the Special Rapporteur to the United Nations on the promotion and protection of the right to freedom of opinion and expression decried the increasing digital divide between the poor and other members of society, and condemned efforts like those in the UK, France, and New Zealand to cut off Internet access for alleged copyright violations as an outright violation of human rights under the International Covenant on Civil and Political Rights. See United National General Assembly, document A/HRC/17/27, May 16, 2011, paragraphs 61 and 78, available at: http://www2.ohchr.org/english/bodies/hrcouncil/docs/17session/A.HRC.17.27_en.pdf.

16. The Queen (on the Application of) British Telecommunications PLC v. Secretary of State for Business, Innovation and Skills, paragraph 249 [2011] EWHC 1021 (Admin)(April 20, 2011).

17. White, An Economic Model for the Incentive/Access Paradigm of Propertization, 29 Hastings Communications and Entertainment Law Journal, 359, 363 (Spring 2007).

18. See, e.g., MGE UPS Systems, Inc. v. GE Consumer & Industrial, Inc., 2010 Westlaw 3769210, 96 United States Patent Quarterly 1123 (5th Cir. 2010); R.C. Olmstead, Inc. v. CU Interface, 606 F.3d 262 (6th Cir. 2010); Multimatic Inc. v. Faurecia Interior Systems USA, 358 Fed. Appx. 643 (6th Cir. 2009); Cartel Asset Management v. Ocwen Financial Corp., 249 Fed. Appx. 63 (10th Cir. 2007);

Champagne Metals v. Ken-Mac Metals, Inc., 458 F.3d 1073 (10th Cir. 2006); Bucklew v. Hawkins, Ash, Baptie & Co., LLP., 329 F.3d 923, 933 (7th Cir. 2003) (Posner, J.) ("The testimony by an expert witness for plaintiff that 10 percent of the profits on HAB's sales of HMS for Windows were due to the buyers' being able to buy the infringing forms from HAB had no factual basis whatsoever, and we repeat previous reminders to the bench and bar of this circuit that proof of damages requires proof."); Interplan Architects, Inc. v. C.L. Thomas, Inc., 2010 WL 4065465 (S.D. Tex. 2010); Design Ideas Ltd. v. Things Remembered, Inc., 2009 WL 12590035 (C.D. Ill. 2009); Lamoureux v. Anazahealth Corp., 2009 WL 1162875 D. Conn. 2009); Faulkner v. National Geographic Society, 576 F. Supp. 2d 609 (S.D.N.Y. 2008).

19. 471 F.3d 1293, 1309 (Fed. Cir. 2006).
20. These are actual examples quoted in the Hargreaves Review, Chapter 8, paragraph 8.3.
21. See Richard Watt, Copyright and Economic Theory: Friends or Foes? (2000, Edward Elgar Publishing).
22. James Boyle, The Public Domain, Chapter 9 (2008, Yale University Press).
23. See further discussion in Chapter 5.
24. For works created on or after January 1, 1978. For works first published before that date, a more complicated regime was in place, based on a fixed number of years measured from the date of first publication.
25. Copyright Law and the Supply of Creative Work: Evidence from the Movies, available at: http://serci.org/documents.html.
26. In the European Union, works that had been in the public domain in some countries had protection restored.
27. See Chapter 3.
28. Edward Rappaport, Copyright Term Extension: Estimating Economic Value, CRS Report to Congress, May 11, 1998.
29. Gowers Review of Intellectual Property, available at http://webarchive.nationalarchives.gov.uk/+/http://www.hm-treasury.gov.uk/gowers_review_index.htm. Accord: Ruth Towse, Creativity, Incentive and Reward: An Economic Analysis of Copyright and Culture in the Information Age 126 (2001, Edward Elgar).

30. This is particularly the case in the United States, with its heavy concentration of media companies. It is less true in other countries.

31. In April 2009, the European Commission voted in favor of extending the term of protection from 75 years to 95 years. See http:// ec.europa.eu/internal_market/copyright/term-protection/term-protection_en.htm.

32. The speech is available here: http://www.musicweek.com/story.asp? sectioncode=1&storycode=1036434&c=1.

33. Hargreaves Review, Chapter 10, paragraph 10.13.

34. I use the word "album" here out of convenience; the provision would apply to a recording of a single song too.

35. Some form of this approach is currently taken in Austria, Belgium, Germany, Luxemburg, Nordic countries, Portugal, and Spain. See Impact Assessment on the Legal and Economic Situation of Performers and Record Producers in the European Union, commission Staff Working Document, Commission of the European Communities, April 23, 2008, paragraph 6.3.3.

36. I use the term "album" as short-hand for any recording, which may be of a single song.

37. Report of the Social Science Research Council, "Media Piracy in Emerging Economies 4 (2011).

38. Intellectual Property: Observations on Efforts to Quantify the Economic Effects of Counterfeit and Pirated Goods, GAO 10–43, Government Accounting Offices, available at: www.gao.gov/new.items/d10423.pdf. See also Loren Yager, Director, International Affairs and Trade, Government Accountability Office (GAO), Washington, D.C., Observations on Efforts to Quantify the Economic Effects of Counterfeit and Pirated Goods, WIPO Advisory Committee on Enforcement, Sixth Session, Geneva, December 1–2, 2010.

39. Paul Furber of the Web Brainstorm blog explains:
    BSA says surveys were conducted in 28 countries representing "a mix of geographies, levels of IT sophistication, and geographic and cultural diversity." These included, among others, China, India, Pakistan, Thailand, Taiwan, Vietnam, Hungary, Poland, Russia, Germany and Italy.

[BSA] extrapolates numbers from the 28 countries to form conclusions about the 111 that appear in the final report. But even for those countries that are surveyed, the sample size is woefully small given the number of PCs there are in the world: just 6,000 consumers and 4,300 business respondents are the world's global proxy for the final results. This works out to 150 businesses per four countries.

What's the statistical error and standard deviation of this sample? The BSA in the UK told Brainstorm that the study "is not a statistical estimation or survey that lends itself to probability analysis, so there is no standard deviation."

http://www.brainstormmag.co.za/index.php?option= com_content&view=article&id=3925:lies-damn-lies-and- the-bsa&catid=70 :cover&Itemid=108.

40. See Nate Cochrane, $900m Piracy report author defends conclusions, itnews for Australian Business, March 17, 2011, available at: http://www.itnews.com.au/News/251527,900m-piracy-report- author-defends-conclusions.aspx.

41. GAO Report at 21–22.

42. Media Piracy in Emerging Economies at 17.

43. Hargreaves Review, Chapter 8, paragraph 8.48.

44. See Nate Anderson, "Only 9% (and falling) of U.S. Internet users are P2P pirates," ArsTechnica, 2011, available at: http://arstechnica.com/ tech-policy/news/2011/03/only-9-and-falling-of-us-internet-users- are-p2p-pirates.ars.

45. He made these remarks in his farewell address to the nation on January 17, 1961. See http://www.h-net.org/~hst306/documents/ indust.html. I thank Jonathan Band for the term "piracy-industrial complex."

46. Moral Panics and the Copyright Wars at 30–34.

47. Media Piracy in Emerging Economies at 16.

48. www.badscience.net. See also his 2010 book, "Bad Science: Quacks, Hacks, and Big Pharma Flacks" (Faber & Faber).

49. See Ben Goldacre, "Illegal downloads and dodgy figures," June 5, 2009, The Guardian, available at: http://www.guardian.co.uk/com- mentisfree/2009/jun/05/ben-goldacre-bad-science-music- downloads.

50. See a number highlighted by Glyn Moody in "Submission to UK Independent Review of 'IP' and Growth," February 24, 2011, available at: http://blogs.computerworlduk.com/open-enterprise/2011/02/submission-to-uk-independent-review-of-ip-and-growth/index.htm.

51. Ian Hargreaves, Digital Opportunity: A Review of Intellectual Property and Growth, Executive Summary (May 2011).

52. Id. Chapter 10, paragraph 10.7.

53. Id., paragraph 10.10.

54. Id., paragraph 10.6.

55. Media Piracy in Emerging Economies at 16. Ronald Coase similarly pointed out the proper approach is to "compare the total social product yielded by…different arrangements," Ronald Coase, The Problem of Social Cost, 3 Journal of Law and Economics 1, 34 (1960).

56. Both charts are taken from this source: http://theunderstatement.com/post/3362645556/the-real-death-of-the-music-industry.

57. Available at: http://yarchive.net/macaulay/copyright.html. He also pointed out that the rights would have been owned by a publisher who would have pocketed all the royalties anyway.

58. H.R. Rep. No. 2222, S. Rep. No. 1108, 60th Cong., 2d Sess. 7 (1909).

59. See generally Intellectual Property Protection of Fact-based Works: Copyright and Its Alternatives (Robert F. Brauneis ed., 2009, Edward Elgar).

60. 499 U.S. 340 (1991).

61. Here is the text of the article:

> 3. Not later than at the end of the third year after the date referred to in paragraph 1, and every three years thereafter, the Commission shall submit to the European Parliament, the Council and the Economic and Social Committee a report on the application of this Directive, in which, inter alia, on the basis of specific information supplied by the Member States, it shall examine in particular the application of the sui generis right, including Articles 8 and 9, and shall verify especially whether the application of this right has led to abuse of a dominant position or other interference with free competition which would justify appropriate measures being taken, including the establishment of non-voluntary

licensing arrangements. Where necessary, it shall submit proposals for adjustment of this Directive in line with developments in the area of databases.

62. DG Internal Market and Services Working Paper, First evaluation of
Directive 96/9/EC on the legal protection of databases, Commission of the European Communities, Brussels, December 12, 2005.

63. Report at 20.

64. Report at 22.

65. Report at 23.

66. Report at 5.

67. Report at 25.

68. The Max Planck Institute for Intellectual Property, Competition
and Tax Law made this point in comments on the report:

The report confirms that once legislation is enacted, getting rid of
it will be possible only in exceptional cases—turning the clock back
may be a theoretical option, but it will hardly ever materialize in
practice. As is stated in the evaluation report, in spite of its weak
foundation, the "attachment to the sui generis right has become a
political reality" (p. 25). The most important lesson to be learned
from this is therefore of a general nature: Inserting an in-built agenda
for subsequent evaluation cannot provide an efficient safeguard
against the development into permanence of legal rules which, in a
well-meant response to stakeholders' claims of a high degree of ur-
gency, have not been submitted to the necessary amount of scrutiny
during the legislative process—even when it turns out that they fail
to meet the expectations that initially motivated their acceptance.
There is no feasible alternative to the legislature doing its home-
work thoroughly before creating a fait accompli.
Position Paper at 2.

Chapter 3

1. Directive 2001/29/EC of the European Parliament and of the
Council of May 22, 2001, on the harmonization of certain aspects
of copyright and related rights in the information society, OJ L 167,
June 22, 2001, page 10, available at: http://eur-lex.europa.eu/Lex-
UriServ/LexUriServ.do?uri=CELEX:32001L0029:EN:HTML.

Canada considers that copyright laws are "an important marketplace framework and cultural policy instrument." Canadian Bill C-32, preamble.

2. See Chapter 10 for a discussion of the metaphoric use of the term "high."

3. Ruth Towse, Creativity, Copyright and the Creative Industries, 63 Kyklos 461, 463 (2010).

4. My friend Hannu Wager has cautioned me that this statement should be "we should start from the premise that one size does not fit all domestic laws" because depending on the level of detail of international agreements, a certain amount of required provisions should fit all.

5. The works of Ruth Towse and David Throsby are excellent starting places. See, e.g., Ruth Towse, A Textbook of Cultural Economics (2010, Cambridge University Press); Ruth Towse, Creativity, Incentive and Reward: An Economic Analysis of Copyright and Culture in the Information Age (2001, Edward Elgar Publishing); Ruth Towse, Cultural Economics: The Arts, the Heritage and the Media Industries (1997, two volumes, Edward Elgar Publishing); Baumol's Cost Disease: The Arts and Other Victims (Ruth Towse editor 1997, Edward Elgar Publishing); David Throsby, The Economics of Cultural Policy (2010, Cambridge University Press); David Throsby, Economics of Culture (2001, Cambridge University Press); David Galenson, Conceptual Revolutions in Twentieth Century-Art (2009, Cambridge University Press); David Galenson, Old Masters and Young Geniuses: The Two Life Cycles of Artistic Creativity (2006, Princeton University Press); Fabien Accominotti, Creativity from Interaction: Artistic Movements and the Creativity Careers of Modern Painters (May 9, 2009); Richard Caves, Creative Industries: Contracts Between Art and Commerce (2000, Harvard University Press); Teresa Amabile, Creativity In Context: Update To The Social Psychology Of Creativity (1996, Westview Press).

The Department of Economics at Macquarie University, Sydney, Australia, has undertaken five comprehensive studies of the actual working conditions of artists. The last study, published in June 2010, is called "Do You Really Want to Get Paid?" The fourth study, published in June 2003 is called, "Don't Give Up Your Day Job."

6. See The Cambridge Handbook of Creativity 8–9 (James Kaufman and Robert Sternberg editors, 2010, Cambridge University Press).

7. See Ruth Towse, Creativity, Incentive and Reward: An Economic Analysis of Copyright and Culture in the Information Age 6 (2001, Edward Elgar). Even those with talent need to learn their craft, a process that can take a lifetime.

8. But see Tyler Cowen, In Praise of Commercial Culture (2000, Harvard University Press).

9. Ruth Towse, A Textbook of Cultural Economics 363 (2010, Cambridge University Press).

10. See Carl Shapiro and Hal Varian, Information Rules 390 (1999, Harvard Business School Press).

11. http://www.billboard.biz/bbbiz/content_display/industry/e3i4a-d94ea6265fac02d4c813c0b6a93ca2. Of course, the overall sales of albums has been going down due to the prevalence of digital singles.

12. New York Times, March 15, 2008, at page A1. At the 2011 SXSW, 1,900 bands played.

13. Robert Frank and Philip Cook, "The Winner-Take-All Society: Why the Few at the Top Get So Much More than the Rest of Us" 8 (1995, Penguin Publishing).

14. See Tali Sharot, The Optimism Bias: A Tour of the Irrationally Positive Brain (2011, Pantheon Books); George Lakoff, The Political Mind 227–229 (2009, Penguin Books paperback); http://en.wikipedia.org/wiki/Optimism_bias. Some might attribute this tendency to a Greenspanian "irrational exuberance," but professors Lakoff and Sharot attribute it to innate human characteristics.

15. I am using the term "publish" here as short-hand for the distribution, in any form, of copyrighted works, including by reproducing, performing or displaying them.

16. The use of the term "bookseller," as compared to other possibilities like book publisher, printer, or stationer, is arbitrary since the lines between these various functions was not clear. See James Raven, The Business of Books: Booksellers and the English Book Trade 4–5, 136 (2007, Yale University Press).

17. Alexander at 25.

18. By the time of the 1842 Act, the focus had shifted away from authors to the public. The draft preamble of the Act referred stated: "Whereas

it is expedient...to afford greater encouragement to the Authors.... "The preamble as enacted, however, replaced the reference
to authors, reading: to afford "greater encouragement to the production of Literary Works of lasting benefit to the World." See John
James Lowndes, An Historical Sketch of the Law of Copyright 85
(1840).

19. Especially relative to the United States during the comparable
period. In 1850 90.4 percent of the population in the United States
could read and write, but in England the rate was approximately
50–60 percent. Catherine Seville, The Internationalisation of Copyright Law: Books, Buccaneers and the Black Flag in the Nineteenth
Century 147 (2006, Cambridge University Press). By one measure,
the ability to sign your name on a marriage register, the literacy rate
at the passage of the Statute of Anne was 45 percent for men and 25
percent for women in Britain, but this measure seems exceedingly
lax. See Michael Suarez, Introduction to 5 The Cambridge History
of the Book in Britain 8–9 (2009).

20. Alexander at 27. See also William St Clair, The Reading Nation in
the Romantic Period 19 (2004. Cambridge University Press) ("the
reading nation was at the time concentrated among the higher
income groups").

21. William St Clair, The Reading Nation in the Romantic Period 109
(2004, Cambridge University Press).

22. James Raven, The Business of Books: Booksellers and the English
Book Trade 222 (2007, Yale University Press).

23. James Raven, The Business of Books: Booksellers and the English
Book Trade 347 (2007, Yale University Press).

24. Available at: http://www.copyrighthistory.org/htdocs/data/com-
mentary/uk_1878/uk_1878_com_1472007103725.html.

25. Hinton v. Donaldson, available at: http://mimuspolyglottos.blogspot.
com/2009/08/lord-kamess-opinion-in-case-of-hinton-v.html. See
also the commentary available at: http://www.copyrighthistory.org/
cgi-bin/kleioc/0010/exec/ausgabeCom/%22uk_1773%22.

26. St. Clair, The Reading Nation in the Romantic Period at 113. But
see James Raven, The Business of Books: Booksellers and the English Book Trade 231–232 (2007, Yale University Press) (criticizing
St. Clair as focusing too much on certain works of fiction, and taking

the position that there were cracks in the monopoly of the London booksellers before 1774).

27. St. Clair at 116.

28. See also id. at 137. See also Andrea Immel, "Children's books and school-books," in 5 The Cambridge History of the Book in Britain 736 (2009).

29. See http://estc.bl.uk/F/?func=file&file_name=login-bl-estc.

30. Adapted from James Raven, The Business of Books: Bookseller and the English Book Trade 150 (2007, University of North Carolina Press). As with all statistical analysis, there are strengths and weaknesses. For discussions of the ESTC in this respect, see William St. Clair, The Reading Nation at 24–25; David McKitterick, " 'Not in the STC': Opportunities and Challenges in the ESTC," 6 The Library 178–194 (2005).

   While there was a large population growth at the beginning of the 19th century, the population growth in the two decades following *Donaldson* was not dramatic.

31. See generally, James Raven, Judging New Wealth: Popular Publishing and Responses to Commerce in England, 1750–1800 (1992, Oxford University Press).

32. Raven, Judging New Wealth at 117.

33. See Mira Rajan's excellent new book, Moral Rights: Principles, Practice and New Technology (2011, Oxford University Press).

34. See Ludwig von Mises, Bureaucracy 11 (1944, 2007 edition, Liberty Fund, Inc.): "A genius is always a teacher, never a pupil; he is always self-made. He does not owe anything to the favor of those in power."

35. Adam Smith, 1 The Wealth of Nations, Part 1, Chapter X, page 124, quoted in Ruth Towse, A Textbook of Cultural Economics 297 (2010, Cambridge University Press). Smith was, apparently, incensed at the exorbitant fees earned by castrati, id. at 13. See also the inappropriately named Classical Music Without Fear 31 (2003, Indiana University Press) (noting that in Italy alone at the end of the 16th century, four thousand boys were being castrated for musical careers, making a most peculiar kind of growth industry). One cannot say that the prejudice against castrati ended; rather the public's tolerance of them ended, by the mid-nineteenth century. In 1832, French

composer Hector Berlioz tells of going to a concert in Rome, filled
with what he called wretched music:

> to crown all, the solos in this strange *farrago* were sung in a
> soprano voice, proceeding from a big man with a rubicund
> face and an immense pair of black whiskers.
>
> "Good heavens," I said to my neighbor, who was choking
> with laughter, "is everything miraculous in this favored coun-
> try? Did you ever see a bearded *castrato* before?"
>
> *"Castrato!"* cried an Italian lady who was seated in front of
> us, and whose indignation was aroused by our laughter and
> our remarks—*"d'avvero non e castrato!"*
>
> "Do you know him, madam?"
>
> *"Per Bacco! non burlate. Jmparate, pezzi d'asino, che quel vir-*
> *tuoso maraviglioso e il marito mio."* They were husband and
> wife!
>
> Hector Berlioz, Autobiography 218–219 (David Cairns,
> translator and editor, 2002, Everyman's Library). The last known
> recording of a castrato was made in 1903, and was issued by the
> Vatican. See Allessandro Moreschi, The Last Castrato: Complete
> Vatican Recordings, available at Amazon.com.

36. The classic article on this point is Sherwin Rosen, The Superstar
Effect—The Economics of Superstars, 71 American Economic
Review 845, (1981), available at: http://faculty.arec.umd.edu/cm-
causland/RAKhor/RAkhor% 20Task7/Rosen81.pdf.

37. See Ruth Towse, A Handbook of Creativity 306–306 (2010, Cambridge University Press), and Jack Stillinger, Multiple Authorship
and the Myth of Solitary Genius (1991, Oxford University Press).

38. A phrase coined by Edward Bulwer-Lytton in his 1830 novel Paul
Clifford. That novel has this infamous beginning:

> It was a dark and stormy night; the rain fell in torrents—ex-
> cept at occasional intervals, when it was checked by a violent
> gust of wind which swept up the streets (for it is in London
> that our scene lies), rattling along the housetops, and fiercely
> agitating the scanty flame of the lamps that struggled against
> the darkness.

39. See Miley Cyrus Trash Talks Rebecca Black's "Friday," March 30,
2011, International Herald Tribune, available at: http://www.ibtimes.

com/articles/128771/20110330/rebecca-black-miley-cyrus-friday-trash-talk-slams.htm.

40. As I discuss in the following section, by transformative copying, I mean the ability to copy someone else's material toward the ultimate goal of creating another work. I do not refer to verbatim copying that acts as a substitute for purchase of the original.

41. John Maynard Keynes, The General Theory of Employment, Interest and Money, Chapter 24 (1936).

42. William Patry, 3 Patry on Copyright Section 9:97 (West Publishing Company, 2011 supplement).

43. See William Patry, 3 Patry on Copyright section 9:59 (West Publishing Company, 2011 supplement).

44. 4 Esp. 168, 170–171 (1803).

45. Hans-Georg Gadamer, Truth and Method 291 (Continuum Press, 2004 revised edition).

46. Available at: http://www.bartleby.com/200/sw4.html.

47. Quoted in Evan Eisenberg, The Recording Angel: The Experience of Music from Aristotle to Zappa 104 (1986).

48. This fussy phrase is from the Prescription Act of 1832, 1832 c. 71 and was intended to replace the more felicitous "time immemorial" in the first, 1275, Statute of Westminster, which limited British legal memory to July 96, 1189, the day of the ascension of Richard the Lionhearted. See http://en.wikipedia.org/wiki/Time_immemorial.

49. Bridgeport Music, Inc. v. Dimension Films, 410 F.3d 792 (6th Cir. 2005). But see Saregama India Ltd. v. Mosley, 687 F. Supp.2d 1325 (S.D. Fla. 2009), which came out differently in another sampling case. The Bridgeport Music case was not the first of these. The first was Grand Upright Music Ltd. v. Warner Bros. Records, Inc., 780 F. Supp. 182, 183 (S.D.N.Y. 1991).

50. 410 F.3d at 798.

51. The court of appeals' decision was followed by a German court in Kraftwerk v. Moses Pelham, known as a the "Metall Auf Metall" case, discussed in Simon Apel, Bridgeport Music, Inc. v. Dimension Films (USA), Metall auf Metall (Germany) and Digital Sampling—"Bright Lines Rules?," 2 Zeitschrift für GeistigesEigentum/Intellectual Property Journal (ZGE/IPJ), Issue No. 3 (2010), and Neil Conley

and Tom Braegelmann's translation of the decision, available at: http://papers.ssrn.com/sol3/papers.cfm?abstract_id=1504982.

52. I use album here as short-hand for any recorded performance, including singles.

53. See generally, Paul Edwards, How to Rap: The Art and Science of the Hip-Hop MC (2009, Chicago Review Press).

54. http://www.ibiblio.org/pub/electronic-publications/stay-free/archives/20/public_enemy.html. Other musicians have had problems getting their labels to permit sampling of their own albums: tropicalismo artist Gilberto Gil, when he was Brazil's Minister of Culture, wanted to use a Creative Commons license to permit others to take snippets from his songs to make new songs. His label refused. As he explained in a speech at New York University:

> My first idea was to license three of my greatest hits: "Refazenda," "Refavela," and "Realce." These are three songs whose titles begin with the prefix Re—to introduce the idea of the permanent transformation of everything that exists, of the uninterrupted re-making that produces culture, life, and the world. Warner Music, owner of the company that published these songs wouldn't let me go ahead. I thought Warner was making a mistake, even in capitalistic terms. With the sampler, many more people started producing good music, and therefore many more good properties are now available to be sold by recording companies.
>
> But I didn't want to argue, nor did I want to explain my standpoint. . . . I don't think recording companies are ready to understand samplers. . . . I went and found some songs of mine that belonged to my own recording company and I decided on "Oslodum," whose lyrics celebrate and encourage the appropriation of Brazilian culture by all the world's peoples. . . . If I have fed so much on the cultures of others and it has been so important for my art, why shouldn't others also propose new uses for what we create in Brazil?
>
> Available at: http://www.nyu.edu/fas/NewsEvents/Events/Minister_Gil_speech.pdf.

55. See David Owen, Copies in Seconds: Chester Carlson and the Birth of the Xerox Machine 1 (2004, Simon & Schuster).

56. See this BBC story about a father who bought his sixteen-year-old son a clarinet formerly owned and played by Artie Shaw: https://mail.google.com/mail/u/0/?shva=1#inbox/12c313b2d2ad6215.

57. The first seventeen of those years were under the baton of George Szell, who died in 1970.

58. Remarks of David Thomas, quoted in: http://en.wikipedia.org/wiki/Robert_Marcellus. Marcellus was influenced by his long and close collaboration with mouthpiece refacer Everett Matson, his long and close collaboration with reed maker Robert Marks, and his teacher, the Swiss clarinetist Daniel Bonade. Bonade was the most influential clarinetist and teacher of the first generation of American clarinetists. Bonade, a Swiss clarinetist, studied with a French clarinetist, Henri Lefevbre, who studied with Cyrille Rose, who studied with Hyacinthe Klosé. It was Klosé who, along with Louis-August Buffet, made the modern clarinet.

59. In his autobiography Life (2010, Little Brown), Keith Richards writes: of being a young boy and hearing Elvis's recording of "Heartbreak Hotel": "I'd never hear it before, or anything like it. I'd never hear of Elvis before. It was almost as if I'd been waiting for it to happen. When I woke up the next day I was a different guy." Life at 58.

60. See http://www.lettersofnote.com/2011/05/it-wasnt-rip-off-it-was-love-in.html.

61. Keith Richards, Life 236 (2010, Little Brown).

62. See Jonathan Lethem, The Ecstasy of Influence: A Plagiarism, Harper's Magazine, February 2007, available at: http://harpers.org/archive/2007/02/0081387:

> In 1941, on his front porch, Muddy Waters recorded a song for the folklorist Alan Lomax. After singing the song, which he told Lomax was entitled "Country Blues," Waters described how he came to write it. "I made it on about the eighth of October '38," Waters said. "I was fixin' a puncture on a car. I had been mistreated by a girl. I just felt blue, and the song fell into my mind and it come to me just like that and I started singing." Then Lomax, who knew of the Robert Johnson recording called "Walkin' Blues," asked Waters if there were any other songs that used the same

tune. "There's been some blues played like that," Waters replied. "This song comes from the cotton field and a boy once put a record out—Robert Johnson. He put it out as named 'Walkin' Blues.' I heard the tune before I heard it on the record. I learned it from Son House." In nearly one breath, Waters offers five accounts: his own active authorship: he "made it" on a specific date. Then the "passive" explanation: "it come to me just like that." After Lomax raises the question of influence, Waters, without shame, misgivings, or trepidation, says that he heard a version by Johnson, but that his mentor, Son House, taught it to him. In the middle of that complex genealogy, Waters declares that "this song comes from the cotton field."

Mr. Lethem in turns acknowledges that much in this paragraph came from a recital of the Lomax story from Siva Vaidhyanathan's book "Copyrights and Copywrongs." Professor Vaidhyanathan got the story from Alan Lomax, who got it from Muddy Waters.

63. Quoted in James Boyle, "Sold Out," available at: http://www.law.duke.edu/boylesite/Sold_out.htm.
64. George Orwell, Why I Write 2 (1946) (Penguin Great Ideas edition).
65. Maurice Beebe "Ulysses and the Age of Modernism." 10 James Joyce Quarterly (University of Tulsa) 172, 176 (Fall 1972).
66. Quoted in John Cipolla, "Buddy DeFranco, The Standard Bearer," in 38 The Clarinet Magazine, No. 1, December 2010, Page 52.
67. See http://en.wikipedia.org/wiki/Will_Lamartine_Thompson; James Boyle, The Public Domain 128–129 (2008, Yale University Press). I am indebted to Professor Boyle for the information about Ray Charles. Thompson could not find a musical publisher who would accept his songs, so he started his own, successful publishing company.
68. Boyle at 134.
69. See, e.g., Clarence Jones and Stuart Connelley, Behind the Dream: The Making of the Speech that Transformed a Nation (2011, Palgrave Macmillan); Eric Sundquist, King's Dream: The Legacy of Martin Luther King's "I Have a Dream" Speech (2009, Yale Univer-

sity Press); Drew Hansen, The Dream: Martin Luther King, Jr., and the Speech that Inspired a Nation (2005, Harper). King's plagiarism in his student work stands on a different footing.

70. Richard Taruskin, The Limits of Authenticity: A Discussion: The Authenticity Movement Can Become a Positivistic Purgatory, Literalistic and Dehumanizing, in 12 Early Music (February 1984), reprinted in: Text and Act: Essays on Music and Performance, 67–82 (1995, Oxford University Press).

71. Jay-Z, Decoded 254 (2010, Spiegel & Grau).

72. The best novelistic treatment of this is William Gaddis's 1955 book "The Recognitions."

73. For a fascinating discussion of the concept of authorship in Renaissance Italy and of the Venetian Council of Ten Decree of 1545, see Joanna Kostylo's Commentary on the Venetian Decree of 1545 regulating author/printer relations, on the invaluable Primary Sources in Copyright website. Professor Kostylo's commentary is available at: http://www.copyrighthistory.org/cgi-bin/kleioc/0010/exec/ausgabeCom/%22i_1545%22.

74. See Early Music Borrowing (Honey Meconi ed. 2004); http://en.wikipedia.org/wiki/Parody_mass.

75. See http://en.wikipedia.org/wiki/Josquin_des_Prez.

76. http://en.wikipedia.org/wiki/Paraphrase_mass.

77. http://en.wikipedia.org/wiki/Josquin_des_Prez.

78. K. 180.

79. For further examples and a discussion, see Charles Rosen's article, "Influence: Plagiarism and Inspiration," in 19th Century Music, Issue 2, Autumn 1980, pages 87–100.

80. See http://en.wikipedia.org/wiki/Mashup_%28web_application_hybrid%29; Matthew Rimmer, Copyright Law and Mash-Ups: A Policy Paper, Australian National University (2010); "Mashing-Up Culture: The Rise of User-Generated Content," Proceedings from the COUNTER Workshop, Uppsala University, May 13–14, 2009); James Boyle, The Public Domain, Chapter 6 ("I Got a Mashup") (2008, Yale University Press); Olufunmilayo Arewa, From J.C. Bach to Hip Hop, 84 North Carolina Law Review, 546 (2007).

81. See Aram Sinnreich, Mashed Up: Technology, and the Rise of Configurable Culture (2010, University of Massachusetts Press); Stefan

Sonvilla-Weiss, Mashup Cultures 2010. Springer); Sound Unbound: Sampling Digital Music and Culture (Paul Miller, editor, 2008, MIT Press); Robert Szymanski, Audio Pastiches: Digital Sampling, Intermediate Copying, Fair Use, 3 University of California, Los Angeles 271 (1996).

82. http://googlemapsmania.blogspot.com/.

83. His YouTube channel may be found at: http://www.youtube.com/user/kutiman.

84. See http://techcrunch.com/2009/03/11/kutiman-killed-the-video-star/. Kutiman's works prompted a blog that "deconstructed" Kutiman's works, here: http://kutimandeconstructed.blogspot.com/.

85. See http://en.wikipedia.org/wiki/Girl_Talk_(musician). See also Joseph Grobelny, Mash-Ups, Sampling, and Authorship: A Mashupsampliography, 11 Music Reference Services Quarterly 2290239 (2008).

86. See http://en.wikipedia.org/wiki/The_Grey_Album. See also the film documentary by Benjamin Franzen and Kembrew McLeod, "Copyright Criminals," IndiePix Films, 2010, http://www.copyrightcriminals.com/; and Brett Taylor's film documentary, RiP! A Remix Manifesto, Eyesteel Film and National Film Board of Canada, 2009, http://nfb.ca/rip_a_remix_manifesto/.

87. November 16, 2010, available at: http://www.npr.org/2010/11/15/131334322/the-fresh-air-interview-jay-z-decoded.

88. The Rza, The Wu-Tang Manual 192 (2005).

89. See Olufunmilayo Arewa, The Freedom to Copy: Copyright, Creation and Context, 41 University of California at Davis Law Review 477 (2007).

90. Alfonso Montouri and Ronald Purser, Deconstructing the Lone Genius Myth: Toward a Contextual View of Creativity, 35 Journal of Humanistic Psychology 69, 82 (1995).

91. The U.S. Copyright Act defines "derivative work" as:

   A "derivative work" is a work based upon one or more pre-existing works, such as a translation, musical arrangement, dramatization, fictionalization, motion picture version, sound recording, art reproduction, abridgment, condensation, or any other form in which a work may be recast, transformed, or adapted. A work consisting of editorial revisions, annotations, elaborations, or other modifications, which, as a whole, represent an original work of authorship, is a "derivative work."

92. William Landes and Richard Posner, The Economic Structure of Intellectual Property Law 109 (2003, Belknap, Harvard University Press). Their answer, alas, turned on a mistaken view of originality.

93. See William Patry, 3 Patry on Copyright.

94. See William Patry. Patry on Fair Use, Section 1:19 (2011 edition, West Publishing Company); Isabella Alexander, Copyright Law and the Public Interest in the Nineteenth Century, Chapters 6 and 7 (2010, Hart Publishing); Ronan Deazley, On the Origin of the Right to Copy 80–85, 106, 136–139 (2004, Hart Publishing).

95. There will still be exceptions, such as the right to authorize the making of a movie out of a novel, and there are also difficult issues with moral rights. My point here is that we need to thoroughly revisit the expansion of derivative rights, and keep those that protect legitimate markets, while repealing those that don't.

96. Meaning that copyright protection doesn't depend on prior, government action, or on compliance with notice requirements and the like. Although it is frequently argued that such a system is required by a natural rights approach to authors' rights, Professor Stef van Gompel has demonstrated this is incorrect. See Stef van Gompel, Formalities in Copyright Law: An Analysis of their History, Rationales and Possible Future (2011, Kluwer Law International).

97. H.R. Rep. No. 222, S. Rep. No. 1108, 60th Cong., 2d Sess. 14 (1909).

98. Id.

99. See H.R. Rep. 7083, 59th Cong., 2d Sess. 14 (1907).

100. The most comprehensive examination of these records is found in William Maher, Copyright Term, Retrospective Extension, and the Copyright Law of 1790 in Historical Perspective, Copyright Soc'ty U.S.A. 1021 (2002). Mr. Maher conducted an extensive review of the records discussed in an oft-cited study, Federal Copyright Records 1790–1800 (James Gilreath & Elizabeth Wills 1987). See also Christopher Sprigman, Reforma(aliz)ing Copyright, 57 Stan. L. Rev. 485 (2004). In an email to me, Mr. Gilreath explained about these records:

My book was a list of the records sent to the government officially claiming copyright. It was a list that had never been put together. As I mention in the introduction, some records—primarily those for Connecticut—no longer exist. I had hoped that the introduction would help locate them. It didn't, as far as I know. Charles Evans' Early American Imprints, which Mr. Maher used as a source, is a bibliography of books that were published or might have been published. Many publishers list on the front page that a book was copyrighted but didn't bother to send in a request for copyright. The book had no copyright records even though it might be listed in Evans' work. They really were not copyrighted. As you know, publishers were always claiming things that were not accurate. In any case, it is impossible to know which books published or anticipated being published in places such as Connecticut actually had copyright records since those records were never found and Evans had no access to such things.

It is a minor point. The type of books with existing copyright and those listed in Evans' bibliography were of the same kind of book subject, which was the main point of my introduction. I could not have accurately included Evans' books in Federal Copyright Records because being listed in Evans was not an actual record.

101. See H.R. 25133, Section 18, reported and discussed in H.R. Rep. No. 7083, 59th Cong., 2d Sess. 14 (1907). The life plus thirty term conditioned on the author filing a notice in the final year of the first twenty-eight years of protection that the copyright owner was still interested in protection.

102. William Landes & Richard Posner, The Economic Structure of Intellectual Property Law 237 (Harvard University Press, Belknap 2003).

103. See http://www.copyright.gov/orphan/comments/reply/OWR0116-Interaction Law.pdf.

104. Barbara Ringer, Renewal of Copyright, Copyright Office Study No. 31, at 221 (1960).

105. See https://www.eff.org/about/staff/jason-schultz.

106. CRS STUDY at 6, available at: www.policyarchive.org/handle/10207/bitstreams/510.pdf.

107. The 1909 Copyright Act Congress cited the "exceptional case of a brilliant work of literature, art, or musical composition [that] continues have a value for a long period," as the reason for extending the renewal term in that act from 14 to 28 years. H.R. Rep. No. 2222 at 14; S. Rep. No. 1108 at 14.

108. See http://en.wikipedia.org/wiki/Edward_Thurlow,_1st_Baron_Thurlow.

109. Quoted in Alexander at 36.

110. Quoted in Isabelle Alexander, Copyright Law and the Public Interest in the Nineteenth Century 259 (2010, Hart Publishing).

111. Professor Ruth Towse has pointed out, however, that copyright in practice has historically been more concerned with encouraging the activities of these entrepreneurs than with encouraging the creation of content by individuals. See Ruth Towse, Creativity, Copyright and the Creative Industries, 63 Kyklos 461, 463 (2010).

112. See Ruth Towse, Creativity, Copyright and the Creative Industries, 63 Kyklos 461, 467 (2010).

113. Quoted in John Quiggin, Zombie Economics: How Dead Ideas Still Walk Among Us 136 (2010, Princeton University Press).

114. See http://en.wikipedia.org/wiki/Jobs_created_during_U.S._presidential_terms.

115. Beginning in 2003, the top marginal rate was set at 35 percent.

116. See http://motherjones.com/politics/2011/02/income-inequality-in-america-chart-graph.

117. Robert Reich, Aftershock 21 (2010, Alfred A Knopf).

118. See http://www.epi.org/economic_snapshots/entry/webfeatures_snapshots_20060621/, which explains:

CEO pay is realized direct compensation defined as the sum of salary, bonus, value of restricted stock at grant, and other long-term incentive award payments from a Mercer Survey conducted for the Wall Street Journal and prior Wall Street Journal-sponsored surveys. Worker pay is the hourly wage of production and nonsupervisory workers, assuming the economy-wide ratio of compensation to wages and a full-time, year-round job.

119. Robert Reich, Aftershock 6 (2010, Alfred A. Knopf).

120. See ww.waynerosso.com/2011/02/23/warner-music-the-pillaging-of-a-once-great-record-company/.

121. See http://www.deadline.com/2011/04/list-media-moguls-with-out-of-whack-pay/.

122. See http://articles.latimes.com/2011/may/29/business/fi-executive-pay-media-20110529.

123. Ruth Towse, Creativity, Copyright and the Creative Industries, 63 Kyklos 461, 467 (2010).

124. See discussion immediately below.

125. It has been estimated that some 1,750 separate small collections hold unique or difficult-to-find footage. The Library of Congress holds copies to about 200,000 films; the UCLA Film & Television Archive about 50,000, and the Museum of Modern Art 15,000. Report at 4.

126. Anna Vuopala, European Commission DG Information Society and Media Unit E4 Access to Information: Assessment of the Orphan works issue and Costs for Rights Clearance at 5 (May 2010).

127. Jason Schultz, The Myth of the 1976 "Chaos" Theory (2002).

128. See Brief of George Aklerlof et al. in Eldred v. Ashcroft, No. 01–68, before the United States Supreme Court, May 20, 2002 at pages 8–10.

129. April 29, 2005, letter from Tim Brooks to Jule Sigall, Associate Register of Copyrights for Policy & International Affairs, available at: www.copyright.gov/orphan/comments/reply/OWR0037-Brooks.pdf.

130. Id.

131. National Recording Preservation Board, The State of Recorded Sound Preservation in the United States: A National Legacy at Risk in the Digital Age 116 (August 2010).

132. See Ruth Towse, Creativity, Copyright and the Creative Industries Paradigm, 63 Kyklos 461, 462 (August 2010).

133. See the excellent article by Susan Galloway and Stewart Dunlop, A Critique of the Cultural and Creative Industries in Public Policy, 13 International Journal of Cultural Policy 17 (2007).

134. See Peter Meusburger, "Milieus of Creativity: The Role of Places, Environments and Spatial Contexts," in Milieus of Creativity: An Interdisciplinary Approach to Spatiality of Creativity (2009, Peter Meusburger et al., editors, Springer-Verlag).

135. David Throsby, Economics and Culture 3 (2001, Cambridge University Press).

136. American Heritage English Dictionary definition.

137. See Robert Friedel, A Culture of Improvement: Technology and the Western Millennium (2007, MIT Press).

138. "The Dialectic of Enlightenment," final chapter, "The Culture Industry: Enlightenment as Mass Deception." A 2002 edition with a new translation by Edmund Jephcott and published by Stanford University Press is the best English language version.

139. See http://en.wikipedia.org/wiki/Bread_and_circuses.

140. "The Impact of Culture on Creativity" (June 2009), available at: http://www.keanet.eu/en/impactcreativityculture.html.

141. Report at 37.

142. Report at 51.

143. See Susan Galloway and Stewart Dunlop, A Critique of the Cultural and Creative Industries in Public Policy, 13 International Journal of Cultural Policy 17 (2007).

144. The United Nations Conference on Trade and Economic Development's 2010 "Creative Economy" report has a definition so loosey-goosey, tautological, and non-specific as to sweep in vast swaths of the economy:

The creative industries

- are the cycles of creation, production and distribution of goods and services that use creativity and intellectual capital and primary inputs;
- constitute a set of knowledge-based activities, focused on but not limited to arts, potentially generating incomes from trade and intellectual property rights;
- comprise tangible products and intangible intellectual or artistic services with creative content, economic value and market objectives;
- stand at the crossroads of the artisan, services and intellectual sectors; and
- constitute a new dynamic sector in world wide trade.

Creative Economy Report at 8. More helpfully, UNCTAD goes on to provide detailed classifications, only some of which concern traditional copyright industries.

145. See Ruth Towse, Creativity, Copyright and the Creative Industries, 63 Kyklos 461, 472 (2010). A May 2011 European Commission communication also reached a 2.7 percent figure, but excluding software and databases. See Single Market communication at 5.

146. Work Foundation's document, "Staying ahead: the economic performance of the UK's creative industries" at page 6, available at: http://www.theworkfoundation.com/research/publications/publicationdetail.aspx?oItemId=176&parentPage.

147. See SEO Economic Research, Assessing the Economic Contributions of the Copyright-Based Industries (Rob van der Noll and Joost Poort).

148. See Ray Ju, et al., Does Copyright Law Promote Creativity? An Empirical Analysis of Copyright's Bounty. 62 Vanderbilt Law Review 1669 (2009) (noting lack of empirical support); Jeanne Fromer, A Psychology of Intellectual Property, 104 N.W. U.L.R. 1441 (2010).

149. "The Impact of Culture on Creativity," A Study prepared for the European Commission, Directorate-General for Education and Culture 70 (June 2009).

150. See "From creation myth to the reality of innovation today," May 13, 2011, available at: http://blogs.parc.com/blog/2011/05/from-creation-myth-to-the-reality-of-innovation-today/.

151. "Creativity and the Economics of the Copyright Controversy," 6 Review of Economic Research on Copyright Issues 5 (2009).

152. Id. at 8.

153. Id.

154. See Jessica Sibley, Harvesting Intellectual Property: Inspired Beginnings and "Work Makes Work" Two Stages n the Creative Processes of Artists and Innovators, Notre Dame Law Review 2011.

155. Clearly, there is a wide diversity in motivations, beyond those surveyed.

156. Statement of Charlie McCreevy, EU Commissioner for the Internal Market, November 21, 2006, at the European Parliament's Committee on Legal Affairs.

157. Communication from the Commission to the European Parliament, the Council, the Economic and Social Committee and the Committee of the Regions: A Single Market for Intellectual Property Rights

Boosting creativity and innovation to provide economic growth, high quality jobs and first class products and services in Europe, Provisional Version, May 2011. ("Single Market communication").

158. This is not the only incomprehensible foundational remark made by the Commission in its Single Market communication. On page three the Commission states: IPR are property rights that protect the added value generated by Europe's knowledge economy on the strength of its creators and investors." I have no idea what this means.

159. "The Impact of Culture on Creativity" (June 2009), available at: http://www.keanet.eu/en/impactcreativityculture.html.

160. Report at 21.

161. See U.S. Copyright From Letter 122, available at: http://www.copyright.gov/fls/fl122.html.

162. See Who Owns the Korean Taco?, NY Times, July 2, 2010, available at: http://freakonomics.blogs.nytimes.com/2010/07/02/who-owns-the-korean-taco/; Tania Su Li Cheng, "Copyright protection of haute cuisine: recipe for disaster?," 30 European Intellectual Property Review 93 (2008); Christopher Buccafusco, "On the Legal Consequences of Sauces: Should Thomas Keller's Recipes Be Per Se Copyrightable?," 24 Cardozo Arts & Entertainment Law 1121 (2007); Journal Emmannuelle Fauchart and Eric von Hippel, "Norms-Based Intellectual Property Systems: The Case of French Chefs ," MIT Sloan Research Paper No. 4576-06 , January 1, 2006, available at: http://papers.ssrn.com/sol3/papers.cfm?abstract_id=881781; Nora Mout-Bouwman, "Protection of culinary recipes by copyright, trade mark and design copyright law," 10 European Intellectual Property Review 234 (1988).

163. See Susan Galloway and Stewart Dunlop, A Critique of the Cultural and Creative Industries in Public Policy, 13 International Journal of Cultural Policy 17, 25 (2007).

Chapter 4

1. See T. Guanhong, A Comparative Study of Copyright and the Public Interest in the United Kingdom and China, (2004) 1:2 SCRIPTed 272, http://www.law.ed.ac.uk/ahrc/script-ed/issue2/china.asp; Enynna

Nwauche, The Public Interest in Namibian Copyright Law, Namibia Law Journal Volume 1 Issue (January–June 2009).

2. The Federalist Papers, 270–271 (Rossiter, ed. Longman 1998).

3. There are many citations to this quote, but the attribution to Keynes is not solid.

4. See Christophe Geiger, The Future of Copyright in Europe: Striking a Fair Balance between Protection and Access to Information, Report for the Committee on Culture, Science and Education –Parliamentary Assembly, Council of Europe December 7, 2009, available at: www.130.79.225.47/pdf/actualite/Report_Future_of_Copyright_oct_2009.pdf.

5. Iowa State University Research Foundation, Inc. v. American Broadcasting Cos., 621 F.2d 57, 60 (2d Cir. 1980); Triangle Publications, Inc. v. Knight-Ridder Newspapers, Inc., 626 F.2d 1171, 1181 (11th Cir. 1980).

6. Harper & Row, Publishers, et al. v. Nation Enterprises, et al., 471 U.S. 539; 105 S. Ct. 2218; 85 L. Ed.2d 588; 53 U.S.L.W. 4562, at 558.

7. 499 U.S. 340 (1991).

8. 499 U.S. at 349–350.

9. Available at: http://www.wipo.int/treaties/en/ip/wct/trtdocs_wo033.html#preamble. The elision at the end deleted the words "as reflected in the Berne Convention," which may or may not change the sense in the text.

10. See generally, my Moral Panics and the Copyright Wars (2009, Oxford University Press).

11. Mark Johnson, The Body in the Mind 72 (1987, University of Chicago Press).

12. See the opinion of Chief Justices French and Justices Crennan and Kiefel in IceTV Pty Limited v. Nine Network Pty Limited, [2009] HCA 14 (High Court of Australia) "Copyright strikes a balance of competing interests and policy considerations."

13. Obviously, where the issue is how to read a statute or whether the defendant committed murder, the metaphor does not play this role.

14. Ruth Towse, Creativity, Incentive and Reward: An Economic Analysis of Copyright and Culture in the Information Age 140 (2001, Edward Elgar).

15. See Maffeo Pantaleoni: At the Origin of the Italian School of Economics and Finance (Mario Baldassarri, editor, St. Martin's Press in Association with Rivista di Politica Economica, Sipi, Roma, 1997).

16. Maffeo Pantaleoni, Contributions to the Theory of Distribution of Public Expenditures, translated by D. Bevan, in Classics in the Theory of Public Finance 22 (Richard Musgrave and Alan Peacock editors, Macmillan, 1994). Pantaleoni was speaking specifically of the budgetary process.

17. See http://en.wikipedia.org/wiki/Bounded_rationality.

18. Quoted in Leland Gregory, Great Government Goofs 18 (1997, Dell Books).

19. See Niva Elkin-Koren, It's All About Control: Rethinking Copyright in the New Information Landscape, in The Commodification of Information 79 (Niva Elkin-Koren & Neil W. Netanel eds., Kluwer Law International, 2002). Under one theory, invocation of the balance metaphor by those seeking ever-expanding rights works hand-in-hand with the property metaphor since the result of expansion is the creation of a property right.

20. See Neil Netanel, Why Has Copyright Expanded? Analysis and Critique, in 6 New Directions on Copyright Law (Fiona Macmillan editor, Edward Elgar 2008).

21. Augustine Birrell, Seven Lectures on the Law and History of Copyright in Books 13 (1899).

22. I am well aware copyright law attracts a number of natural law adherents. Copyright has never been a natural right in any known country. Even by the second half of the nineteenth century in France, Stef van Gompel has written that

> copyright was not consistently perceived as a right inherent in the author. The theory that the literary and artistic property rights in a work belonged to the author "naturally" because of the personal bond between the work and its creator, for example, had not entire infiltrated the French legal order. It seems that at the time, this idea was still overshadowed by the ideology that authors' rights were based on a social contract. The idea was that, upon publication, the author dispossessed himself of his work and all rights in the work, including the

exploitation rights, passed to the public. In return, the author had a private claim against

Society, which allowed him to demand remuneration for the exploitation of the work. The supporters of this theory believed that this claim took the form of a privilege granted by the legislator on behalf of the public.... [A]uthors were considered beneficiaries of the right not because they had a natural right in their intellectual creations, but because they were granted a right by virtue of the statute.

Stef van Gompel, Les formalités sont mortes, vive les formalités! Copyright Formalities and the Reasons for their Decline in Nineteenth Century Europe, in Privilege and Property 157, 173–174 (Ronan Deazley, Martin Kretschmer, and Lionel Bentley eds. 2010 Open Book Publishers).

At the practical level, beyond a baseline of automatic, formality-free copyright, the natural rights theory cannot solve any issue of significance: it cannot, for example, decide whether the proper term of protection should be life of the author plus fifty years, seventy years, or any other length; whether there should be copyright in government works; what the proper remedies should be, including whether there should be statutory damages; whether third parties should bear liability for the acts of others and if so under what circumstances; what type of technological protection measures, if any, there should be; how national collecting societies should operate in a global marketplace; whether there should be country-wide, region-wide, or world-wide exhaustion of the distribution right; what to do about orphan works; whether libraries should be able to make digital copies for archival purposes; or, whether one joint author should be able to license a work without the others' permission.

23. Jeremy Bentham, Principles of the Civil Code, 1 The Works of Jeremy Bentham, (John Bowring ed. 1843).

24. Owner as compared, say, to a bailee or trustee.

25. Susan Sell, The Globalization of Intellectual Property Rights 51 (2003, Cambridge University Press 2003).

26. For other purposes, such as transferring rights or inheritance, copyright is usually classified as personal property.

Chapter 5

1. Nick Thomas, Europeans Will Pay For Content—Why Are There So Few Compelling Options?, http://www.paidcontent.org, March 22, 2011.

2. Dr. Francis Gurry, The Future of Copyright, Sydney Australia, February 25, 2011.

3. See Washington Post, March 42, 2001, available at: http://www.washingtonpost.com/lifestyle/style/in-contrast-to-media-industrys-struggles-a-boom-for-those-who-cover-congress/2011/03/16/AB8RnzRB_story.html.

4. Losing the News (2011 reprint edition, Oxford University Press. Mr. Jones's family has owned a newspaper in Tennessee for generations; he was a reporter for the New York Times, won a Pulitzer Prize, is the director of Harvard's Shorenstein Center on the Press and Public Policy, and is a lecturer in Press and Public Policy at the Kennedy School of Government. He is a newspaper man who believes fervently in newspapers' mission.

5. Losing the News at 14.

6. Id. at 15.

7. Available at: http://www.slideshare.net/RachelSterne/googles-marissa-mayer-testimony-on-journalism.

8. Nor would people who live outside the circulation area of my local paper read that paper's website, which does have a classified section for selling cars.

9. See, e.g., remarks of James Gianopulous, Co-chairman, Twentieth Century Fox Filmed Entertainment, quoted in Michael D. Smith and Rahul Telang, Competing with Free: The Impact of Movie Broadcasts on DVD Sales and Internet Piracy, 33 MIS Quarterly 321, 321 (June 2009): "We can't compete with free. That's an economic paradigm that doesn't work."

10. See Gaiman v. McFarlane, 360 Federal Reporter 3d 644 (7th Cir. 2004), 2010 Westlaw 897364 (Western District Wisconsin March 12, 2010).

11. A video of the interview is available here: http://zine.openrightsgroup.org/features/2011/video:-an-interview-with-neil-gaiman. The experiment with American Gods was undertaken with independent bookstores.

12. See Brett Danaher, Samita Dhanasobhon, Michael D. Smith, and Rahul Telang, Converting Pirates without Cannibalizing Purchasers: The Impact of Digital Distribution on Physical Sales and Internet Piracy, June 2010, available at: http://papers.ssrn.com/sol3/papers.cfm?abstract_id=1381827.

13. August 17, 2010. See http://www.youtube.com/watch?v=Y4VsTm3TPj4. Google and WPP provided some funding for Professor Smith's research.

14. The increase for action shows was 11 percent.

Chapter 6

1. Jessica Litman, Digital Copyright, Chapter 5, Choosing Metaphors (2001, Prometheus Books): "Copyright, today, is less about incentives or compensation than it is about control."

2. Nicholas Mercuro and Steven Medema, Economics and the Law 104 (2d edition 2006, Princeton University Press).

3. Princeton University Press. A 2006 edition was published with an important afterword.

4. Compliance with Intellectual Property Law: A Psychological Perspective, 29 New York University Journal of International Law & Policy 219 (1996–1997).

5. Tom Tyler and John Darley, Building a Law-Abiding Society, Hofstra L. Rev. Spring 2000.

6. See Jessica Litman, Digital Copyright, Chapter 5, Just Say Yes to Licensing! (2001, Prometheus Books).

7. See Jessica Litman, Real Copyright Reform, 96 Iowa Law Review 1, 17 (2010): "The widespread perception of the current copyright system as illegitimate should be unsurprising. In significant part, it flows from copyright owners' assertions that, as established copyright players, they should be entitled to prescribe the rules for new entrants."

8. See Jessica Litman, Digital Copyright 113 (2001, Prometheus Books).

9. Compliance with Intellectual Property Laws at 232.

10. See remarks of Christine Varney, Assistant Attorney General Antitrust Division, U.S. Department of Justice, speech entitled "Procedural

Fairness," delivered before the 13th Annual Competition Conference of the International Bar Association Fiesole, Italy, September 12, 2009. "The two concerns—substance and process—go hand in hand. Complaints about process lead to concern that substantive results are flawed, whereas a fair, predictable, and transparent process bolsters the legitimacy of the substantive outcome." Available at: http://www. justice.gov/atr/public/speeches/249974.pdf.

Some have interpreted Ms.Varney's remarks as a dig at European antitrust investigations. See Jonathan Zuck, Procedural Fairness, in Competition Policy International, November 2009, available at: http://www.techpolicyinstitute.org/files/zuck-nov09.pdf.

11. Tom Tyler, Why People Obey the Law at 276.

12. In subsequent opinions, the court ironed things out.

13. Fair Use and Unpublished Hearings: Joint Hearing on S. 2370 and H.R. 4263 before the Subcommittee on Patents, Copyrights and Trademarks of the Senate Committee on the Judiciary and the Subcommittee on Courts, Intellectual Property, and the Administration of Justice of the House Committee on the Judiciary, 101st Cong., 1st Sess. 11–12 (1990).

14. But see Alexandra Petri, Lady Gaga or Congress? The myth of approval ratings, Washington Post, July 23, 2010, available at: http://voices. washingtonpost.com/postpartisan/2010/07/lies_damn_lies_and_approval_ra.html.

15. http://www.gallup.com/poll/141512/Congress-Ranks-Last-Confidence-Institutions.aspx. A subsequent Gallup poll in December 2010 showed 30 year historic lows on the question of whether people "approved" of Congress's actions. See http://www.sfgate. com/cgi-bin/article.cgi?f=/c/a/2010/12/16/MNFO1GR6VI. DTL.

16. Canada is an exception to this, happily.

17. Pub. L. No. 106-113, 113 Stat. 1501.

18. Fifty-Six Hope Road Music Ltd. v. UMG Recordings, Inc., 2010 WL 3564258 (S.D.N.Y. September 10, 2010).

19. United States Copyright Office and Sound Recordings as Work Made for Hire: Hearing before the Subcommittee on Courts and Intellectual Property of the Committee on the Judiciary, House of Representatives, 106th Cong., 2d Session 160 (May 25, 2000) (Serial

No. 145), available at http://commdocs.house.gov/committees/ judiciary/hju65223.000/hju65223_0f.htm.

20. 2000 Hearing at 26–27.
21. In this case, the tactic backfired, and Congress had to repeal the legislation.
22. Tom Tyler, Why People Obey the Law at 3.
23. Tom Tyler and John Darley, Building a Law-Abiding Society, 2000 Hofstra Law Review at 709.
24. Ian Hargeaves, Digital Opportunity: A Review of Intellectual Property ad Growth, Chapter 8, paragraph 8.44 (May 2011).
25. Siddhartha Mukherjee, The Emperor of All Maladies: A Biography of Cancer 143 (2010, Scribner).
26. Tom Tyler, Why People Obey the Law at 20.
27. Tom Tyler, Compliance with Intellectual Property Laws at 221.
28. Report of the Social Science Research Council, Media Piracy in Emerging Economies at 34.
29. The State of Recorded Sound Preservation in the United States: A National Legacy at Risk in the Digital Age 114 (August 2010).
30. Id. at 7.

Chapter 7

1. See, e.g., 17 U.S.C. §106.
2. I use the term European here as shorthand to refer more broadly to civil law countries that have *droit moral*.
3. The exception being that *droit moral* is based more on the author's personal connection with the work, and not a property right.
4. See http://en.wikipedia.org/wiki/Externality:

    In economics, an externality (or transaction spillover) is a cost or benefit, not transmitted through prices, incurred by a party who did not agree to the action causing the cost or benefit. A benefit in this case is called a positive externality or external benefit, while a cost is called a negative externality or external cost.

    In these cases in a competitive market, prices do not reflect the full costs or benefits of producing or consuming a product or service, producers and consumers may either not bear all of the costs or not reap all of the benefits of the economic activity, and too much or too little of the good will be produced or consumed in terms of overall costs and benefits to society. For example, manufacturing that causes air pollution imposes costs on the whole society, while fire-proofing a home improves the fire safety of neighbors. If there exist external costs such as pollution, the good will be overproduced by a competitive market, as the producer does not take into account the external costs when producing the good. If there are external benefits, such as in areas of education or public safety, too little of the good would be produced by private markets as producers and buyers do not take into account the external benefits to others.

5. Not of course for all uses; as detailed in Chapter 10, a number of socially beneficial uses should be uncompensated.

6. See Chapter 5.

7. See, e.g., José Luis Ferreira, Compensation for private copying: an economic analysis of alternative models (May 2011, Enter 2.0); Martin Kretschmer, Comparative study of copyright levies in Europe (April 2011, ESRC fellowship project at IPO); Patrick Legros and Victor Ginsburgh, The Economics of Copyright Levies on Hardware, Encore Discussion Paper 2011/34; Oxera Consulting, Ltd., Is there a case for copyright levies: An Economic Impact Analysis (April 2011); Economic analysis of private copy remuneration (EconLaw 2007).

8. A classic article on the subject is by Stan Besen, Sheila Kirby, and Steven Salop, An Economic Analysis of Copyright Collectives, 78 Virginia Law Review 383 (1992).

9. Collecting societies are hardly alone in doing this. Wall Street is notorious for such skimming.

10. There is a rich literature on the problems and potentials of collective licensing. See Collective Management of Copyright and Related Rights (Daniel Gervais editor, 2d edition, 2010 Kluwer); Teese Foged, Licensing Schemes in an On-Demand World, 32 European Intellectual Property Review 20 (2010); Christian Handke, Economics of Copyright Collecting Societies, 38 International Review of Intellectual Property and Competition Law 937 (2007); Pavel Tuma,

Pitfalls and Challenges of the EC Directive on the Collective Management of Copyright and Related Rights, 28 European Intellectual Property Review 220 (2006); Yuan Zeqing, A New Impetus for Chinese Copyright Protection: The Regulations on Collective Administration of Copyright, 28 European Intellectual Property Review 241 (2006); Peter Gyertyanfy, Why is a European Directive on Collective Management Necessary? A Perspective from a New Member State of the EU, 53 Journal of the Copyright Society of the U.S.A. 71 (Fall 2005–Winter 2006); Ariel Katz, The Potential Demise of Another Natural Monopoly: Rethinking the Collective Administration of Performing Rights, 1 Journal of Competition Law & Economics 541 (2005); Martin Kretschmer, The Aims of European Competition Policy Towards Copyright Collecting Societies, Paper for Society for Economic Research on Copyright Issues SERCIAC 2005 Montreal, 7–8 July 2005; Antonio Capobianco, Licensing of Music Rights: Media Convergence, Technological Developments and EC Competition Law, 26 European Intellectual Property Review 113 (2004); Martin Kretschmer, The Failure of Property Rules in Collective Administration of Rights: Rethinking Copyright Societies as Regulatory Instruments, [2002] European Intellectual Property Review 127; Adolf Dietz, Legal Regulation of Collective Management of Copyright (Collecting Societies Law) in Western and Eastern Europe, 49 Journal of the Copyright Society of the U.S.A. 897 (2002); Herman Jehoram, The Future of Collecting Societies, 23 European Intellectual Property Review 134 (2001); Martin Schippan, Purchase and Licensing of Digital Rights: The Verdi Project and the Clearing of Multimedia Rights in Europe, 22 European Intellectual Property Review 24 (2000); Irini Stamatoudi, The European Court's Love-Hate Relationship with Collecting Societies, 19 European Intellectual Property Review 289 (1997); Hamish Porter, European Union Competition Policy: Should the Role of Collecting Societies be Legitimised?, 18 European Intellectual Property Review 672 (1996).

11. See http://books.google.com/books?id=OLyclzAaC-4C&pg=PT1 2&lpg=PT12&dq=SIAE+Italian+collecting+society+Lehman+br-others&source=bl&ots=qPmpWPdPwV&sig=Idmz5WRQ_9-Gb3CC-2F2oJT-OMU&hl=en&ei=32TlTb3HL4bk0QGg66WzB

w&sa=X&oi=book_result&ct=result&resnum=1&sqi=2&ved=0C
B0Q6AEwAA#v=onepage&q=SIAE%20Italian%20collecting%20
society%20Lehman%20brothers&f=false.

12. SESAC is a distant third.

13. See United States v. ASCAP, 2010 WL 374292 (2d Cir. September 28, 2010) (rejecting the argument).

14. See Statement of Marybeth Peters, The Register of Copyrights Before the Subcommittee on Courts, the Internet, and Intellectual Property of the House Committee of the Judiciary, 110th Congress, 1st Session, March 22, 2007, Hearing on Reforming Section 115 of the Copyright Act for the Digital Age, at pages 6, 7:

> The Copyright Office noted this in testimony before Congress in 2007: "One of the major frustrations facing online music services today, and what I believe to be the most important policy issue that Congress must address, is the lack of clarity regarding which licenses are required for the transmission of music.... But why is this important? If both the mechanical and the performance rights are implicated and the money goes to the same copyright holders, why not make a single payment to one agent for the digital transmission of the work? The answer is that the current music licensing structure does not allow for that option."

15. Copyright Office Report at 8.

16. "A Digital Agenda for Europe," European Commission, May 19, 2010, Brussels, COM(2010) 245, Section 2.1.1.

17. For examples in the United States, see the testimony in Section 115 of the Copyright Act: In Need of an Update?: Hearing Before the Subcommittee on Courts, the Internet and Intellectual Property of the Committee on the Judiciary, U.S. House of Representatives, 108th Cong. (2004); Internet Streaming of Radio Broadcasts: Balancing the Interests of Sound Recording Copyright Owners with Those of Broadcasters, Hearing Before the Subcommittee on Courts, the Internet and Intellectual Property of the Committee on the Judiciary, U.S. House of Representatives, 108th Cong. 2004.

18. Digital Agenda at Section 2.1.1.

19. Id.

Chapter 8

1. See Hargreaves Report, Chapter 2, paragraph 2.16: "Economic evidence is clear that the likely deadweight loss to the economy exceeds any additional incentivising effect which might result from the extension of copyright term beyond present levels."

2. Digital Britain Report 2009.

3. The New Renaissance: Report of the Comite Des Sages, Reflection Group on Bringing Europe's Cultural Heritage Online at page 16, January 10, 2011.

4. Gowers Report.

5. Available at: http://www.copyright.gov/orphan/comments/OW 0036-MillerKa.pdf.

6. Hargreaves Review, Chapter 5, paragraph 5.21.

7. This includes the European Union's much-awaited proposed directive, issued in a provisional form in May 2011.

8. For a discussion of the debate in the nineteenth century about the proper length of copyright, see Lauren Pfister, La propriété littéraire est-elle une propriété? Controverses sur la nature du droit d'auteur au XIXème siècle, RIDA, no. 205, pages 116–209 (2005).

9. Cf. Rufus Pollock's response, Forever Minus a Day: Calculating Optimal Copyright Term, University of Cambridge, June 15, 2009.

10. See, e.g., Stef van Gompel and Bernt Hugenholtz, The Orphan Works Problem: The Copyright Conundrum of Digitizing Large-Scale Audiovisual Archives, and How to Solve It, IVIR, www.irir.nl; Stef van Gompel, Unlocking the Potential of Pre-Existing content: How to Address the Issue of Orphan Works in Europe?, 6 IIC 669 (2007).

11. Report at 6.

12. Report at 6.

13. Report at 21.

14. Report at 36.

15. Report at 31.

16. Report at 29:

> The copyright status of embedded illustrations needs to be established and subsequently cleared separately. This could in many cases make the already complicated rights clearance process even more challenging. In the event that the right

holders to images are not properly documented in the underlying work, analysing visual material is in many cases over-
whelmingly difficult. Right holders in the visual field have
expressed clearly that identified rights holders to visual works
embedded in written works, which themselves might be
orphan, need to be cleared if the work is to be digitised and
made accessible online.

For this reason, even if you could establish the identity of
the writer of the book itself, just one image in the book,
whose right holder is not identified and found, could potentially hinder the digitisation of the entire book.

17. In the language of welfare economics, spending large sums of money
    allocated for worthy social projects is highly inefficient.
18. EU Report at 25.
19. See http://rufuspollock.org/tags/own-work/. See also http:
    //rufuspollock.org/2009/11/26/size-of-the-public-domain-iii/.
20. Pierre Leval, Toward a Fair Use Standard, 103 Harvard Law Review
    1105, 1119 (1990).
21. See http://www.edri.org/edrigram/number5.3/les-miserables-
    sequel.
22. A brief submitted by seventeen prominent economists to the U.S.
    Supreme Court in the Eldred case wrote: "Where building-block ma-
    terials are copyrighted, new creators must pay to use those materials,
    and may incur additional costs in locating and negotiating with copy-
    right holders....By reducing the set of building-block materials freely
    available for new work, the [term extension] raises the cost of produc-
    ing new works and reduces the number created." Brief of George
    Akerlof et al. in Eldred v. Reno, No. 01-618, page 2–3. May 20, 2002.
23. See, e.g., Gowers Review of Intellectual Property, (2006), Centre for
    Intellectual Property and Information Law (CIPIL)—http://www.
    hm-treasury.gov.uk/gowers_review.htm; The Recasting of Copy-
    right & Related Rights for the Knowledge Economy (2006), Insti-
    tute for Information Law (IViR), University of Amsterdam for DG
    Internal Market;

    http://www.ivir.nl/publications/other/IViR_Recast_Final_
    Report_2006.pdf; Professor David Newbery (FBA, University of
    Cambridge), letter to Commission;

President Barroso (April 10, 2008) (Letter opposing extension from thirty-two economists including Nobel prize-winners and other persons working the field of copyright);

Bournemouth Statement, letter and statement to Commission President Barroso (June 16, 2008), academic version "Creativity stifled?" published in European Intellectual;

Property Review, September 2008, pp. 341–347 http://www.cippm.org.uk/copyright_term.html; 5. Stellungnahme des Max-Planck Instituts für Geistiges Eigentum, Wettbewerbs—und Steuerrecht zum Vorschlag der Kommission für eine Richtlinie zur Änderung der Richtlinie 2006/116 EG des Europäischen;

Parlaments und des Rates Über die Schutzdauer des Urheberrechts und bestimmter verwandter Schutzrechte (Hilty/Kur/Klass/ Geiger/Peukert/Drexl/ Katzenberger), academic version GRUR Int./2008, p. 907 [German]; European Intellectual Property Review, 2009, p. 59 [English]

http://www.ip.mpg.de/shared/data/pdf/stellungnahme-bmj-2008-09-10-def_eng.pdf (Opinion by Max-Planck Institute for Intellectual Property, Competition and Tax Law,

Munich sent to the German Federal Ministry of Justice, criticising the Commission's

approach to policy and rejecting the proposed directive (September 10, 2008)): 6;

Les artistes-interprètes pris en otage [Performers taken hostage], Professor Séverine

Dusollier, Centre de recherche informatique et droit (CRID), Universitaires Notre-Dame de la Paix de Namur, academic version: Auteurs & Media,

http://www.crid.be/pdf/public/5956.pdf (submission by Center in IT and Law (CRID), University of Namur, to Belgian government (September 2008);

Stellungnahme zum Vorschlag der Kommission für eine Richtlinie zur Änderung der Richtlinie 2006/116/EG des Europäischen Parlaments und des Rates über die;

Schutzdauer des Urheberrechts und bestimmter verwandter Schutzrechte (GRUR 2009 38)—http://www.grur.de/cms/upload/pdf/stellungnahmen/2008/2008-10-

02_GRUR_Stn_RL_2006-116_EG.pdf (Statement by German Association for the Protection of Intellectual Property (GRUR) to Federal Ministry of Justice (October 2, 2008));

Academic Joint Statement to MEPs (Kretschmer/Bently/Pollock/Hilty/Hugenholtz)—http://www.cippm.org.uk/copyright_term.html (Open Letter from leading European research centres on Intellectual Property, together with a joint statement highlighting the major flaws in the Commission's impact study and proposal (October 27, 2008);

La proposition de directive sur l'extension de la durée de certains droits voisins: une remise en cause injustifiée du domaine public [the directive proposal on term extension of neighbouring rights: an unjustified challenge of the public domain], (Assoc. Prof. Christophe Geiger, Prof. Jérôme Passa and Prof. Michel Vivant). Extracts published in: La Semaine Juridique, Edition Générale 2009, Libres propos, act. 46, full academic version forthcoming in: Propriétés intellectuelles 2009 http://www.cepi.edu (Common position signed by more than 20 French and Belgian academics criticising the proposal, sent to the European Commission, the European Parliament and the French Ministry of Culture on December 21, 2008); Presa di posizione del centro nexa su internet & societa' del politecnico di torino sulla proposta di direttiva sull'estensione dei termini di protezione dei produttori di fonogrammi e degli artisti interpreti ed esecutori (Marco Ricolfi, J.C. De Martin, Federico Morando, Alessandro Enrico Cogo, Stefano Sciacca, Carolina Cordero di Vonzo—Umberto Musone) http://nexa.polito.it/direttivafonogrammi,   https://nexa.polito.it/sites/nexa.polito.it/files/ProposedDirectivePhonograms-NEXA-

statement.pdf (Statement of the Nexa Center for Internet & Society, Politecnico Turino, Italy, calling on the Commission to withdraw the proposed directive (December 2008));

Edward Rappaport, Copyright Term Extension: Estimating the Economic Value, Congressional Research Report, May 11, 1998.

24. Copyright Law Revision Part 2: Discussion and Comments on Report of the Register of Copyrights on the General Revision of the U.S. Copyright Law, 88th Cong., 1st Sess. 96–97 (Comm. Print 1963) (November 10, 1961).

25. See Handbook of Econometrics (James Heckman and Edward Leamer, editors, 2010, Reed Elsevier).

26. Brief at 6.

27. Id.

28. With considerable understatement, the economists' brief states: "Given the redistribution from consumers to producers, the consequences for consumer welfare are more negative than [even] the consequences for efficiency." Id. at 12.

29. See Paul Heald, Property Rights and the Efficient Exploitation of Copyrighted Words: An Empirical Analysis of Public Domain and Copyrighted Fiction Bestsellers, 2nd Annual Conference on Empirical Legal Studies Paper (January 9, 2007), http://papers.ssrn.com/sol3/papers.cfm?abstract_id=955954>; and Paul Heald, Testing the Over- and Under-Exploitation Hypotheses: Bestselling Musical Compositions (1913–32) and Their Use in Cinema (1968–2007), 3rd Annual Conference on Empirical Legal Studies Paper (April 1, 2008), http://papers.ssrn.com/sol3/papers.cfm?abstract_id=1115405.

30. See Michael Yuan, Should Different Information Economies Have the Same Duration of Copyright?, 6 Review of Economic Research 13 (2009).

31. See Jason Schultz, The Myth of the 1976 Copyright "Chaos" Theory (2002); Edward Rappaport, Copyright Term Extension: Estimating the Economic Value, Congressional Research Service, May 11, 1998, at 5–6.

Chapter 9

1. See Stef van Gompel's excellent study, Formalities in Copyright Law: An Analysis of Their History, Rationales and Possible Future (2011, Kluwer).

2. Mr. Sherman's remarks were not prepared, and the above quotes are from first-hand accounts and a response given by RIAA to an inquiry about them. See http://www.techdirt.com/articles/20101015/13051411452/did-the-riaa-really-just-come-out-in-support-of-opt-in-copyright.shtml.

3. The New Renaissance: Report of the Comite Des Sages, Reflection Group on Bringing Europe's Cultural Heritage Online at 9, January 10, 2011.

4. Jane Ginsburg, The U.S. Experience with Copyright Formalities: A Love/Hate Relationship, Columbia Law School Working Paper (2010).

5. See Reports of the First Conference of the Berne Convention, September 8, 1894, remarks of Numa Droz, reproduced in 1886: Berne Convention Centenary 86 (WIPO 1986) (hereinafter "WIPO Centenary").

6. Stef van Gompel, Les formalités sont mortes, vive les formalités! (Copyright formalities and the reasons for their decline in nineteenth-century Europe), in Privilege and Property: Essays on the History of Copyright 157, 158 (R. Deazley, M. Kretschmer & L. Bently (editors, Open Book Publishers 2010). See also Stef van Gompel, Formalities in Copyright Law: An Analysis of their History, Rationales and Possible Future (2011, Kluwer Law International).

7. See Daniel Gervais, The Purpose of Copyright in Canada, University of Ottawa Journal of Law & Technology 315 (2006).

8. A potential obstacle in the effectiveness of this proposal is found in Article 5(2) of the Berne Convention, which reads:

> The enjoyment and the exercise of these rights shall not be subject to any formality; such enjoyment and such exercise shall be independent of the existence of protection in the country of origin of the work. Consequently, apart from the provisions of this Convention, the extent of protection, as well as the means of redress afforded to the author to protect his rights, shall be governed exclusively by the laws of the country where protection is claimed.

Professor Stef van Gompel has argued that a work which enters the public domain in its country of origin for failure to comply with formalities in that country must still be protected in other countries. He concludes therefore that a revision to the treaty is required to permit the reintroduction of effective formalities. See Stef van Gompel, Formalities in Copyright Law: An Analysis of their History, Rationales and Possible Future 417 (2011, Kluwer Law International).

9. See, e.g., Stef van Gompel, Formalities in the digital era: an obstacle or opportunity?, in Global Copyright: Three Hundred

Years Since the Statute of Anne, from 1709 to Cyberspace (Lionel Bently et al., editors, Edward Elgar Publisher, 2010); Stef van Gompel, Les formalités sont mortes, vive les formalités! (Copyright formalities and the reasons for their decline in nineteenth century Europe), in Privilege and Property: Essays on the History of Copyright 157 (Ronan Deazley, Martin Kretschmer & Lionel Bently (editors, Open Book Publishers 2010); Christopher Sprigman, Re(form)alizing Copyright, 57 Stanford Law Review 484 (2004).

10. 17 United States Code Section 412.

Chapter 10

1. See my Moral Panics and the Copyright Wars (Oxford University Press, 2009).

2. See http://en.wikipedia.org/wiki/Reefer_Madness.

3. See David Hajdu, The Ten-Cent Plague: The Great Comic-Book Scare and How It Changed America (Picador, 2009).

4. See Kimberlee Weatherall, "Submissions in the Attorney-General's Fair Use/Fair Dealing Inquiry: I've been reading" Weatherall's Law: Blogspot, 10 August, 2005 <http://weatherall.blogspot.com/2005_08_01_weatherall_archive.html#112367201793051437.

5. See Section 40(2) of the Australian Copyright Act.

6. Pierre Leval, Toward a Fair Use Standard, 103 Harvard Law Review 1105, 1110 (1990). In Canada, Supreme Court Chief Justice Beverley McLachlin pointed out that creativity is furthered by both those who stake out a claim of copyright infringement and by those who use such copyrighted works to further societal goals, and helpfully refused to weigh one interest above another: "User rights are not just loopholes. Both owner rights and user rights should therefore be given the fair and balanced reading that befits remedial legislation, [2004] 1 S.C.R. 339, 2004 SCC 13, ¶ 48.

7. See http://twitter.com/#!/derekslater/status/27445125989.

8. See, e.g., Ty, Inc. v. Publications International, Ltd., 292 F.3d 512 (7th Cir. 2002).

9. See, e.g., Bill Graham Archives v. Dorling Kindersley, Ltd., 448 F.3d 605 (2d Cir. 2006).

10. For a more liberal approach to the three-step test, see the July 17, 2008 "A Balanced Interpretation of the Three-Step Test in Copyright Law," available at: http://www.ip.mpg.de/ww/de/pub/aktuelles/declaration_on_the_three_step_.cfm.

11. C/508, July 16, 2009 (ECJ) [2009] ECDR 16, ably discussed in Jonathan Griffiths, Unsticking the centre-piece—the liberation of European copyright law?, 1 (2010) JIPITEC 87, paragraph 1.

12. See Article 5 of the Directive.

13. The reference is to Hayek's Road to Serfdom.

14. The general distinction between an exemption and a privilege is that with an exemption if you fall into a class of people covered by the exemption you are entitled to its benefits. With privileges, there is no class-based entitlement; rather each person must, on an ad hoc basis, prove their entitlement. The distinction does not hold in all cases, though, and sometimes the terms are used interchangeably.

15. See generally William Patry, Patry on Fair Use, Sections 1:5 to 1:17 (2011 and annual updates, West Publishing).

16. See note 4.

17. The category is NAICS 512. See http://data.bls.gov/pdq/SurveyOutputServlet?series_id=CES5051200001&data_tool=XGtable.

18. I speak here of common law legal systems. Other systems handle the issue differently.

19. See, e.g., criteria in section 40(2) of the Copyright Act 1968.

20. Professor Ruth Okediji has argued that the indeterminacy and breadth of fair use are inconsistent with the Berne Convention and the TRIPS Agreement, Ruth Okediji, Toward an International Fair Use Doctrine (2000) 39 Columbia Journal of Transnational Law 75, 117 (2000), but I do not share this view nor does the great Berne scholar Professor Sam Ricketson.

21. This is an example H.L.A. Hart often used and was the subject of a debate between Hart and Lon Fuller. See Frederick Schauer, A Critical Guide to Vehicles in the Park, 83 New York University Law Review, 1109 (2008), available at: http://www.law.nyu.edu/ecm_dlv/groups/public/@nyu_law_website_journals_law_review/documents/web_copytext/ecm_pro_059778.pdf. Their debate was not of course about vehicles in parks, but rather about the meaning of meaning.

22. Irish Minister for Jobs, Enterprise and Innovation Richard Burton made similar comments in May 2011, in connection with a similar Irish inquiry.

23. Ian Hargreaves, Digital Opportunity: A Review of Intellectual Property and Growth 45 (May 2011).

24. This is pretty much the approach taken by Professor Ian Hargreaves in his report Digital Opportunity: A Review of Intellectual Property and Growth 45 (May 2011).

25. See http://en.wikipedia.org/wiki/A_Declaration_of_the_Independence_of_Cyberspace. Cf. Jack Goldsmith and Tim Wu, Who Controls the Internet?: Illusions of a Borderless World (2008, Oxford University Press. See also Johnny Ryan, A History of the Interent and the Digital Future (2010, Reaktion Books).

26. Francis Gurry, The Future of Copyright, address delivered in Sydney, Australia, February 25, 2011.

27. Joseph Schumpeter, Capitalism, Socialism and Democracy 83 (Harper & Brothers 3d ed. 1950, 2006 paperback) (1942).

28. Sam Ricketson, WIPO Study on Limitations and Exceptions of Copyright Related Rights in the Digital Environment at page 4, Standing Committee on Copyright and Related Rights, 9th Session, Geneva, June 23 to 27, 2003, SCCR/9/7 (April 5, 2003).

Chapter 11

1. Moral Panics and the Copyright Wars (2009, Oxford University Press). My title for this book was Metaphors, Moral Panics, and Folk Devils in the Copyright Wars.

2. See references in Moral Panics and the Copyright Wars at 44–45.

3. Colin Turbayne, The Myth of Metaphor 3 (1962, University of South Carolina Press).

4. These are different points: hard copy works can be scanned or made available for sale in hard copy form online.

5. The Future of Copyright in a Digital Environment (Bernt Hugenholtz, editor, Kluwer, 1996).

6. Renee Summer, The single digital market: A vision for Europe, available at: http://www.ericsson.com/res//thecompany/docs/publications/business-review/2011/issue1/the-single.pdf.

Chapter 12

1. See F.M. Scherer, Quarter Notes and Bank Notes: The Economics of Music Composition in The Eighteenth and Nineteenth Centuries, Chapter 7 (2004, Princeton University Press); Perspectives: J.S. Bach, the Breitkopfs, and Eighteenth-Century Music Trade (George Stauffer editor 1996); Brook, Piracy and Panacea in the Dissemination of Music in the Late Eighteenth Century, 102 Proceedings of the Royal Musical Association 13 (1975–1976); Roth, The Business of Music: Reflections of a Music Publisher 61–62 (1966); Pohlman, Die Frühgeschichte des musikalischen Urheberrechts (1962).

2. See http://en.wikipedia.org/wiki/Trans-Pacific_Strategic_Economic_ Partnership.

3. See Annette Kur and Henning Grosse Ruse-Khan, Enough is Enough: The Notion of Binding Ceilings in International Intellectual Property Protection, Max Planck Institute for Intellectual Property, Competition and Tax Law, Law Research Paper Series No. 09–01 at 13–14:

   [A]part from the possibly detrimental effects for individual countries from FTAs with TRIPS-plus effects, the sheer number of countries where the protection level is ratcheted up. . . . can critically affect domestic lawmaking in both industrialized and developing countries as well as multilateral negotiations on the future flexibilities in the area of IP law: It is easy to imagine that once a substantial portion of trading partners have agreed to observe the same standards as those enshrined in present U.S./EU legislation, there is no way back to a meaningful lessening of what appear as widely accepted rules . . . creating a spiral endlessly moving upwards."

4. November 5, 2008 cable, available at: http://www.guardian.co.uk/ world/us-embassy-cables-documents/176810.

5. Available at: http://www.guardian.co.uk/world/us-embassy-cables-documents/236363.

6. Available at: http://www.citizen.org/documents/NZleakedIPpaper-1.pdf.

7. Social Science Research Council, Media Piracy in Emerging Economies 223 (May 2011).

8. See Joseph Stiglitz, Making Globalization Work, Chapter 4 (2007, paperback edition, W.W. Norton).

9. Months after writing this section I read Jacob Haker & Paul Pearson's Winner-Take-All Politics (2010, Simon & Schuster), which uses the same rising tide yacht and dinghy metaphors, see page 20. I hadn't thought of the locks metaphor, though, and I thank them for it.

10. As Archbishop Silvano Tomasi, the permanent representative of the Vatican to United Nations, observed in September 2010, "developing countries could experience net welfare losses in the short run because many of the costs of [increased] protection could emerge earlier than the dynamic benefits." http://www.visaepatentes. com/2010/11/critical-statement-on-ip-by-holy-see.html.

11. The current Director General, Dr. Francis Gurry, takes a refreshingly different approach to these issues.

12. The advantages of adherence to the WIPO Copyright Treaty (WCT) and the WIPO Performances and Phonograms Treaty (WPPT) at page 4. As Ahmed Abdel Latif notes, "This assertion seems at odds with both the letter and spirit of the WIPO Development Agenda, which fundamentally questions the validity of a 'one-size fits all' approach to global IP norm setting activities." http://www.ip-watch. org/weblog/2010/11/12/global-copyright-reform-a-view-from-the-south-in-response-to-lessig/.

The Development Agenda is discussed below.

13. http://www.visaepatentes.com/2010/11/critical-statement-on-ip-by-holy-see.html.

14. Gowers Review of Intellectual Property at 59, paragraph 4.57 (December 2006).

15. See B. Zorina Khan, Copyright Piracy and Development: United States Evidence in the Nineteenth Century, 10 Revista de Economia Institucional, Number 18, First Semester 2008; B. Zorina Khan, Does Copyright Piracy Pay? The Effects of U.S. International Copyright Laws on the Market for Books, 1790–1920, NBER Working Paper No. 10271(February 2004).

16. The passage in question is in the Wealth of Nations, and reads: "It is the great multiplication of the productions of all the different arts, in consequence of the division of labor, which occasions, in

a well-governed society, that universal opulence which extends itself to the lowest ranks of the people." Smith's faith in the division of labor providing wealth to all classes was naïve. He assumed that if large jobs were broken down into small jobs, workers would become experts in their own area, and would be more productive. Being more productive, they would be paid more. That isn't what happened, at least at the industrial level, thanks to the efforts of Frederick Winslow Taylor, who took Smith's theory but used it to deprive workers of knowledge of anything but the small task in front of them, tasks which were made repeatable and monotonous, thereby diminishing their skills. In addition, Taylor's methods of using stop watches and other forms of quantification led to laborers producing more in less time for less pay. Some opulence.

17. See Tyler Cowen, Creative Destruction: How Globalization is Changing the World's Cultures 14–16 (Princeton University Press, 2002), for a discussion of the different ways the term diversity is used.

18. http://famouspoetsandpoems.com/poets/walt_whitman/quotes.

19. "If I had gone directly to the people, read my poems, faced the crowds, got into immediate touch with Tom, Dick, and Harry instead of waiting to be interpreted, I'd have had my audience at once," quoted in David Reynolds, Walt Whitman's America: A Cultural Biography 339 (1995, Vintage Books).

20. Tyler Cowen, Creative Destruction: How Globalization Is Changing the World's Cultures 3 (Princeton University Press, 2002). Professor Cowen's book is devoted to refuting de Tocqueville's and similar theories. See also his In Praise of Commercial Culture (2000, Harvard University Press).

21. Tyler Cowen, Creative Destruction: How Globalization Is Changing the World's Culture 103 (2002, Princeton University).

22. Id. at 129.

23. Peter Manuel, Cassette Culture: Popular Music and Technology in North India 64 (1993, University of Chicago Press).

24. See http://en.wikipedia.org/wiki/Jab_We_Met.

25. Media Piracy in Emerging Economies, India Chapter.

26. See Larry Rohter, Gilberto Gil and the politics of music. International Herald Tribune, March 12, 2007.

27. See Ian Hargeaves, Digital Opportunity: A Review of Intellectual Property and Growth, Chapter 8, paragraph 8.40 (May 2011).

28. Media Piracy in Emerging Economies, at 1.

29. Media Piracy in Emerging Economies at iii.

30. ACE Report at paragraph 13.

31. Quoted in Julian Dibbell, We Pledge Allegiance to the Penguin, Wired, November 2004, available at: http://www.wired.com/wired/archive/12.11/linux.html

32. Quoted in F.M. Scherer, Quarter Notes and Bank Notes: The Economics of Music Compositions in the Eighteenth and Nineteenth Century 179 (2003, Princeton University Press).

33. Media Piracy in Emerging Economies at 65.

34. Hargreaves Review, Chapter 8, paragraph 8, 21. See also Joel Waldfogel, Bye, Bye, Miss American Pie? The Supply of New Recorded Music since Napster, Wharton School, University of Pennsylvania, January 3, 2011, available for download via subscription at: http://papers.ssrn.com/sol3/papers.cfm?abstract_id=1789463.

35. Media Piracy in Emerging Economies at 57.

36. See http://paidcontent.org/article/419-warner-bros.-targets-new-consumer-segment-pirates/.

37. See Ruben Cuevas, et al., Is Content Publishing in BitTorrent Altruistic or Profit-Driven?, available at: conferences.sigcomm.org/co-next/2010/CoNEXT_papers/11-Cuevas.pdf.

Index

A
Aardman Animations 21
ACAP 242
ACTA 246–247
Adorno, Theodor 121
Advertisements (circus) 19
Alexander, Isabella 83
Amazon.com 9, 20, 28, 45, 159
Ancien regime 12
Aquinas, St. 100
Art for Art's Sake 26
Athens 30–31
Attaway, Fritz 213

B
Baldwin, Alec 186
Bass Clarinet Commission
    Collective 26
Bauer, Robert 261
Beethoven, Ludwig von 35,
    100, 245
Bentham, Jeremy 140

Betamax (VCR) 43
Bharat, Krishna 153
Bieber, Justin 18, 26, 88
Birrell, Augustine 139
Black, Rebecca 89
Blackstone, Sir William 177–178
Blind (visually disabled) 10
Blount, Roy Jr. 9
Bodice rippers 26
Boyle, James 56, 285 nn.
Brahms, Johannes 36, 37, 46, 100
Branco, Marcelo D'Elia 259
Brazil 13
Bronfman, Edgar, Jr. 113
Brooks, Tim 116–117
Brown, Gordon 59–60
Buffet R13 clarinets 95
Buggy whip manufacturers 3
Brumel, Antoine 99–100
Burnham, Andy 59–60
Bush, George W. 50, 109
Business Software Alliance 62

C
Canada 31–32
Carter, Jimmy 109
Carter, Troy 9
Cary v. Kearsley 91
Charles, Ray 97–98
Chuck D 93–94
Clarinet Commission
   Collective 28
Clark, Charles, Chapter 11
Clinton, Bill 110, 119
Clinton, George 92
Cohen, Lyor 112–113
Colbert Report 213
Comic book scare 211
Cook, Philip 81
Cowen, Tyler 278 n., 316 nn.
Crow, Sheryl 172
Cyrus, Miley 89

D
Daily Show with Jon Stewart 213
Danger Mouse 101, 278
Defoe, Daniel 86
DeFranco, Buddy 97
Demsetz, Harold 126
Digital Economy Act
   (UK) 32–34
Dole, Bob 138
Donaldson v. Beckett 85. 86, 107
Douglas, Michael 186

E
Eisenhower, Dwight David 63
Elliot, T.S. 91
Ellenborough, Lord 91

Elkin-Koren, Niva 296 n.
Epstein, Edward Jay 22
E.T. (phone home) 25

F
Feist Publications, Inc. v. Rural
   Telephone Service 71–72, 134
Finkelstein, Herman 198
Frank, Robert 81
Frazier, Greg 13
Frey, Northrop 97
Funkadelics 92

G
Gadamer, Hans-Georg 91
Gaiman, Neil 157
Galloway, Susan 143
Geiger, Christophe, 295 n.
Gekko, Gordon 186
Germany 27–28
Gervais, Daniel 301 n.
"Get Off Your Ass and Jam" 93
Gil, Gilberto 255–256, 283 n.
Gillis, Greg 101
Ginsburg, Jane 301 n.
God (HaShem) 163
Goldacre, Dr. Ben 64–66
Gompel, Stef von 288n.,
   296–297 nn., 305 n., 309 n,
   301 nn.
Goths and Vandals (second
   irruption of) 85
Gowers report 51, 58–59
Goya, Francisco 19, 245
Gross, Terry 102
Gurry, Francis 40, 144, 225, 260

H
Hargreaves report 4–5, 40–41, 51,
   52, 63, 67, 141, 173, 192
Harris, Mark 24
Hart, H.L.A., 312 n.
Haydn (Papa) 245
Hayek, Frederick 264 n.
Heald, Paul 309 n.
Help! (Beatles song) 16
Holmes, Oliver Wendell Jr. 19, 20
Hootie and the Blowfish 138
Hoover, Herbert 109
Horkheimer, Max 121

I
Infopaq International A/S v.
   Danske Dagblades 213
iTunes 8

J
Jagger. Mick 31
Jay-Z 98, 101–102, 178
Johnson, Mark 135
Johnson, Samuel 15
Jones, Alex 148
Justifications for copyright 8

K
Kames, Lord 85
Karakunnel, Ben 261
Karp, Irwin 30
Kaspar clarinet mouthpieces 95
Keynes, John Maynard 90
Khan, Zorna 315 n.
Kickstarter program 28
Kindle 9

Kretschmer, Martin 302 nn., 303
Kur, Annette 314 n.
Kutiel, Ophir ("Kutiman") 101

L
Lady Gaga 9
Landes, William 103, 105
Lara Croft, Tomb Raider 22
Lennon, John 16, 95–96
Leval, Pierre 168, 196, 212
Litman, Jessica 299 nn.
Little Nicky (terrible movie) 28
Lobbynomics 6
Lula da Silva 259

M
Macaulay, Lord Thomas 70
Madison, James 131–132
Mallet, Sir Louis 85
Mamet, David 186
Manacles 91
Manet, Édouard 19
Marcellus, Robert 95
Marley, Bob 172
McCartney, Paul 16
Melos 30–31
Military bands 28
Mises, Ludwig von 39–40, 49
M&Ms 25
Model T cars 3
Monty Python 158
Moore, Joyce 8
Moore, Sam 8
Moses (Moshe Rabbeinu) 163
Mozart, Amadeus 15, 95, 100, 245
Mt. Sinai 163

O
O'Connor, Sandra Day 134
Orwell, George 45, 98–99

P
Palestrina, Giovonne Pierluigi 99
Pandora (music service) 20
Pantaleoni, Mario 138
Pareles, Jon 81
Patry-Martin, Margalit v
Patry-Martin, Yonah v
Peloponnesian Wars 30
Pigs (flying) 172
Png, Ivan 57
Pollock, Rufus 185, 305 n.
Posner, Richard 103, 105
Presley, Elvis 95
Prez, Josquin de 99
Promise Land 221
Punjabi truck drivers 255
Public Enemy 93–94

R
Radiohead 264 n.
Raven, James 279–280 nn.
Reagan, Nancy 143
Reagan, Ronald 50, 109, 110
Reefer Madness 211
Reese's Peanut Butter
    Cups 25
Richards, Keith 96
Rolling Stones 31
Rogers, Will 109
Rosen, Hilary 21
Rousseau, Henri 96
RZA 102

S
Salieri, Antonio 100
Salinger, J.D. 168
Sam & Dave (musical group) 8
Sandler, Adam 26
Sarbanes-Oxley law 32
Scherer, Frederick 36–37
Schoenberg, Arnold 91
Schocklee, Hank 93–94
Schultz, Jason 201
Schumann, Clara 36
Schumpeter, Joseph 137
Sell, Susan 297 n.
Shapiro, Carl 278 n.
Sharot, Tali 278 n.
Shaun the Sheep 21
Sherman, Cary 205–206
Sibley, Jessica 126
Simon, Herbert 138
Smith, Adam 88, 253
Smith, Frank 14
Smith, Michael D. 158
Socrates 1
Social Sciences Research
    Council 62, 67, 175, 256–260
South Africa 62
Sparta 30
Spielberg, Steven 25
St Clair, William 84
Steele, Danielle, 26
Summer, Renee 244
Swimming pool 16

T
Taruskin, Richard
    98

Tea Party (and the Know-Nothing Movement) 211
Third shift 32
Throsby, David 120
Tomasi, Archbishop 251
Toqueville, Alexis de 254
Towse, Ruth 113, 123
Trans Pacific Partnership 246–248
Turner, Big Joe 96
Tyler, Tom 165 ff.

V
Valenti, Jack 114–115, 192
Valkonen, Sami 270 n.
Varian, Hal 278 n.
Verdi, Giuseppe 36, 37, 260
Viacom 21, 113, 213

W
Wager, Hannu 277 n.
Wallace & Gromit 21
Wang, Qiu-hong 57
Warhol, Andy 16
Waters, Muddy 96
Weatherall, Kimberley 311 n.
Weber, Max 166
White Album (Beatles) 101, 178
Whitman, Walt 253–254
Winter, Johnny 96
Wu-Tang Clan 102

Y
YouTube 18, 89, 158, 254, 256

Z
Ziskin, Laura 24